Contract Law

YOU'VE GOT IT CRACKED

Nutshells – your essential revision and starter guides

- Presents you with the essentials of law in clear and straightforward language, explaining the basic principles

- Incorporates colour to help distinguish cases and legislation and aid ease of use

- Breaks the text down into bite-size chunks and includes bullets where appropriate to aid navigation, assimilation and retention of information

- Opens each chapter with a short introduction to outline the key concepts covered and condense complex and important information

- Closes each chapter with a checklist to enable you to check that all your learning needs have been met

- Provides a model question with answer plan at the end of each chapter to enable you to fully prepare for both exam and essay questions

- Includes diagrams throughout to illustrate difficult concepts

- Places important key definitions and statutory provisions in boxes to help highlight the key points to remember

- Contains a host of useful tools including tables of cases and statutes, a list of examination tips, and a list of useful web resources

Available from all good booksellers

NUTCASES

Contract Law

SIXTH EDITION

by
ANNE RUFF
LLB, LLM, Barrister
Visiting Senior Lecturer in Law, Middlesex University

SWEET & MAXWELL THOMSON REUTERS

First Edition – 1996
Reprinted – 1998, 1999, 2000
Second Edition – 1999
Reprinted – 2001
Third Edition – 2002
Fourth Edition – 2005
Fifth Edition – 2008
Sixth Edition – 2011

Published in 2009 by Thomson Reuters (Legal) Limited (Registered in England & Wales, Company No 1679046. Registered Office and address for service: 100 Avenue Road, London NW3 3PF) trading as Sweet & Maxwell

For further information on our products and services, visit www.sweetandmaxwell.co.uk

Typeset by YHT Limited, London
Printed in the Netherlands by Ten Brink, Meppel

*No natural forests were destroyed to make this product;
only farmed timber was used and re-planted.*

A CIP catalogue record for this book is available from the British Library.

ISBN 978-0-414-04601-6

Contents

Using this Book

Welcome to our new look NUTCASE revision series. We have revamped and improved the existing design and layout and added new features, according to student feedback.

NEW DETAILED TABLE OF CONTENTS
for easy navigation.

REDESIGNED TABLES OF CASES AND LEGISLATION for easy reference.

NEW CHAPTER INTRODUCTIONS to outline
the key concepts covered and condense
complex and important information.

 10

Protection of
in Land

....

INTRODUCTION

The estates and interests cap
Law of Property Act 1925. W'
law depends on its requi
on the Formal and In^
Upon th

NEW BOXED "THINK POINT"
at the end of each chapter with
further case analysis and questions
to encourage critical thinking.

.al tests for whethe,
.ie two tests set out in *Hollanu*
.ords in *Elitestone Ltd v Morris* [1997]
ecided that a bungalow erected on pillar:
   These cases were also approved in *Ch*
(2000) 22 E.G. 147, where it was held that a ho
ropes and connected to utilities was a chatte
nature of the tenancy of a houseboat was
annexation. In *Cinderella Rockerfellas Ltd v Ruu*
decided that a vessel which was moored per
of the land for the purpose of assessing its '
   at it was nonetheless a chattel rather th
      for rating purposes.
      ssex Reserve Forces & Cade

NEW COLOUR CODING throughout
to help distinguish cases and
legislation from the narrative.
At the first mention, cases are
highlighted in colour and italicised
and legislation is highlighted in
colour and emboldened.

Table of Cases

Table of Statutes

Introduction

The Key Characteristics of a Contract

INTRODUCTION

Contract law is the legal mechanism underpinning the operation of the free market. It provides the rules and sanctions for the sale and transfer of goods, services and property. Unlike many areas of law, contract law has a planning role and can be used by the parties to allocate risk and agree how future disputes should be resolved. It is not just used to resolve disputes once they have arisen. However, for a variety of reasons, including expense and delay, some businesses prefer to concentrate on the commercial realities and to avoid using lawyers. Contract law is not just concerned with commercial contracts. Even buying a cup of coffee is a contract subject to the rules of contract law!

The principles of contract law are primarily found in case law and in the main were agreed by the end of the nineteenth century. Refinements on these principles continue to emerge through new cases. Legislation and EU law have also contributed to a limited extent to the development of contract law. Freedom of contract remains an important principle and so, with some exceptions, the courts will leave the parties free to agree whatever terms they want.

The general principles of contract law apply to all types of contract, but certain specialised contracts also have additional rules which are only applicable to them. Examples of such contracts include sale of goods, construction, land, shipping, consumer credit, employment and insurance contracts.

The traditional view was that a contract was an agreement entered into after negotiation between two parties with equal bargaining power and that it reflected what the parties had agreed. It was based on *consensus ad idem*. Today the terms of many contracts are not freely negotiated by the parties but are imposed by one party on the other.

By entering into a contract the two parties' legal rights and obligations are determined as parties to a contract. If they think they have entered into a contract, but have not in fact done so, they have no rights under contract law. It does not mean that they have no legal rights in, for example, tort or equity.

The issues which are addressed by the law of contract include whether or not:

(1) The two parties have entered into a legally binding agreement.

(2) The contract can benefit or bind third parties.

(3) The contract must, for example, be in writing or contain particular terms.

(4) Both parties have the legal capacity to enter into the contract.

(5) The terms of the contract are or mean what one party claims.

(6) A clause has legally excluded or limited one party's liability for breach of contract.

(7) A contract is invalid because one party has misled the other, or put unlawful pressure on the other, or the contract has an illegal purpose.

(8) The contract has been terminated.

(9) One party is entitled to damages because of a breach by the other party.

In practice a case will usually be about more than one of these issues. For example, if there is dispute about the terms of the contract this may raise issues of certainty, interpretation of the terms and mistake. On the other hand if the court decides that no contract has been entered into that will be the end of the matter from a contractual perspective.

Finally, probably only a small percentage of contracts lead to a dispute that has to be resolved with the assistance of lawyers or other professionals. Of these some will be resolved informally and some by mediation or arbitration. Of those where legal proceedings are commenced only a tiny percentage will result in a court hearing. The effective contract lawyer will avoid litigation wherever possible by appropriate contract planning and by the use of alternative dispute resolution.

AGREEMENT

Key Principle

Whether there is a binding contract between the parties depends upon what they have objectively agreed, as indicated by their words and conduct.

RTS FLEXIBLE SYSTEMS LTD V MOLKEREI ALOIS MÜLLER GMBH & CO KG (UK) PRODUCTION 2010

The claimant (RTS) made a written offer to install two food packaging production lines for the defendant (M), which produced dairy products for sale in shops and supermarkets. The new production lines were scheduled to be in use by September 30, 2005. On February 21, 2005 M wrote to RTS indicating their willingness to proceed with the project, subject to an agreement being signed within four weeks which contained the full contractual terms. On February 23, 2005 RTS started work on the project. Detailed negotiations continued. Agreement was reached on almost all the terms of the contract by July 5, but no formal agreement was signed. Delays occurred between June and August. The delivery plans were varied on August 25. The first production line started operation on October 10; the second in late December 2005 or early January 2006. By the end of January 2006 Muller had paid RTS 70 per cent of the contract price, but had not paid the 20 per cent due on delivery. The Court of Appeal held that no legally binding agreement had been entered into by RTS and M.

Held

❖ (SC) There was a valid contract. The essential terms were agreed. By August 25 the parties' communications and actions led to the conclusion that there was a contract based on the terms agreed between them as at July 5, which included a draft version of the amended standard form contract, as varied on August 25. [2010] 1 W.L.R. 753.

Commentary

(1) Lord Clarke of Stone-cum-Ebony observed that:
  (a) This [case] demonstrates "the perils of beginning work without agreeing the precise basis upon which it is to be done. The moral of the story is to agree first and to start work later" (para.1). Businesses generally prefer to avoid the delay that this approach is likely to produce.
  (b) The court should not impose binding contracts on the parties which they have not reached (para.47).
  (c) "The striking feature of this case is that essentially all the terms were agreed between the parties and that substantial works were then carried out and the agreement was subsequently varied in important respects" (para.61).

(2) See also Ch.2 on "subject to contract".

Key Principle

The governing criterion is the reasonable expectations of honest men

G. Percy Trentham Ltd v Archital Luxfer Ltd 1993

The plaintiffs T obtained quotations from the defendants A for the design, supply and installation of windows. The parties continued to negotiate both orally and in writing over the contract terms. The defendants undertook the required work and the plaintiffs paid them for it. There were defects in the windows and the plaintiffs claimed that the defendants were in breach of contract. The defendants denied that any contract had come into existence.

Held

❖ (CA) Where the transaction was fully performed a contract could be concluded by conduct, or come into existence during performance. There was therefore a legally binding contract. The parties plainly intended to enter into such a contract. [1993] 1 Lloyd's Rep. 25.

Commentary

(1) Steyn L.J. stated that English law generally adopts an objective rather than a subjective theory of contract formation. (See also Ch.2 and compare *BSC v Cleveland Bridge and Engineering Co Ltd* (1984) (see below)).

(2) In *RTS Flexible Systems Ltd v Molkerei Alois Müller Gmbh & Co KG (UK) Production 2010* Lord Clarke referred to the perception of "the reasonable honest businessman" in the position of RTS and M.

(3) The traditional approach of the courts to the law of contract is that it is a tool for commerce. To this end the law should be certain (but see Ch.15 *Golden Strait Corporation v Nippon Yusen Kubishka Kaisha* [2007] UKHL 12; [2007] 2 W.L.R. 691), it should reflect the needs of business (see e.g. at Ch.7 *Sirius International Insurance Co v FAI General Insurance Ltd and others* [2004] UKHL 54), and that contract terms should be upheld wherever possible (see e.g. Ch.15 *Murray v Leisureplay plc* [2005] EWCA Civ 963; [2005] IRLR 946).

Key Principle

A promise is usually the basis of a contractual obligation. It is normally a statement as to future conduct rather than a statement of present fact.

KLEINWORT BENSON LTD V MALAYSIA MINING CORPORATION BERHAD 1989

The defendants formed a subsidiary company M. The plaintiff bankers lent a total of £10 million to the subsidiary company having relied on a "comfort letter" provided by the defendants to the plaintiffs. In the letter the defendants stated that: "It is our policy to ensure that the business of [M] is at all times in a position to meet its liabilities to you." M ceased trading and did not pay its debts. The plaintiffs asked the defendants to ensure that they were repaid the money owed to them by M. The defendants refused to do so and claimed that the defendant's statement did not impose a legally binding obligation upon them to pay off their subsidiary's debts.

Held

❖ (CA) The statement in the comfort letter was not a contractually binding promise. It was a statement of present fact, not a statement that the policy would be continued in the future. Therefore the plaintiffs were unable to recover any of the money lent to M. [1989] 1 W.L.R. 379.

Commentary

(1) The Court of Appeal commented that the consequences of the decision by the defendants to repudiate their moral responsibility, to ensure that the plaintiffs were repaid, were not matters that the court should consider.

(2) A comfort letter is a letter written usually by a parent company, but it could be by a government, to the lender of money, giving comfort to the lender about a loan made to a subsidiary company or a public entity. It is commonly used where the "guarantor" is not willing to accept a legally binding commitment.

(3) Whether a letter of comfort is intended to be legally binding is a question of fact.

Key Principle

Contracts are agreements which are voluntarily entered into by both parties.

NORWEB PLC V DIXON 1995

The appellants N were under a statutory duty to supply electricity upon being required to do so by the owner or occupier of any premises. The respondent D made such a request. One of the issues that arose was whether such an arrangement amounted to a contract.

Held

❖ (QBD) The legal compulsion as to both the creation of the relationship between a public electricity supplier and a tariff customer, and the fixing of its terms, is inconsistent with the existence of a contract. The supply of electricity in these circumstances is governed by statute not by contract. [1995] 1 W.L.R 636.

Commentary

Compare *Dwr Cymru Cyfyngedig (Welsh Water) v Corus Ltd* [2007] EWCA Civ 285 where the CA held that an agreement between two parties, for the supply of water to the claimant's steel works, in accordance with the Water Industry Act 1991, had contractual effect.

CONTRACT TORT RESTITUTION

Key Principle

The same set of facts may give rise to liability in the tort of negligence as well as in contract.

> MUIRHEAD V INDUSTRIAL TANK SPECIALITIES LTD AND OTHERS 1986
> The plaintiff was a wholesale fish merchant. The first defendants I.T.S. entered into a contract with the plaintiff for the supply and installation of a tank and pumps for the storage of live lobsters. The manufacturers of the pumps, Leroy Somer Electric Motors Ltd, were the third defendants. The pumps were defective and the whole stock of lobsters died. The plaintiff claimed compensation for the lobsters, the loss of profit on the intended sales, and other consequential financial losses. The plaintiff was successful in his claim against I.T.S., but the company went into liquidation and no money was forthcoming. The plaintiff continued with his claim against the third defendants. Since there was no contract between the plaintiff and the third defendants this claim was brought in the tort of negligence.

Held

❖ (CA) The plaintiff could recover damages in tort from the third defendants because it was reasonably foreseeable that if the pumps failed to work then the lobsters would suffer physical harm. The plaintiff could also recover any financial loss caused by the death of the lobsters. [1986] Q.B. 507.

Commentary

However, the Court of Appeal further stated that the plaintiff could not recover damages for pure economic loss from the third defendants. The loss of profit on the intended sales appears to have been regarded as pure economic loss. The court considered that such loss was only recoverable from I.T.S., the other party to the contract. However, loss of intended future profits is not always recoverable in a contract claim (*see Parsons v Uttley Ingham* (1978) (see Ch.15)).

Key Principle

If the parties to a contract intend their relationship to be governed solely by the contract then a court will not impose a concurrent liability in tort.

> GREATER NOTTINGHAM CO-OPERATIVE SOCIETY LTD V CEMENTATION
> PILING AND FOUNDATIONS LTD 1989
> The plaintiffs were owners of a building. They entered into a building contract with the main contractor. The defendant sub-contractors also entered into a contract with the main contractor. In addition the plaintiffs entered into a collateral contract with the defendants, but the contract did not impose liability on the defendants for negligent performance of the contract. The defendants negligently operated drilling equipment which caused physical damage and financial loss. The plaintiffs sued the defendants in the tort of negligence.

Held

❖ (CA) The plaintiffs could not recover for the financial loss. Entering into a collateral contract was inconsistent with the existence of liability in the tort of negligence. [1989] Q.B. 71.

Commentary

(1) In *Riyad Bank & ors v Ahli United Bank (UK) Plc (formerly the United Bank of Kuwait Plc)* [2006] EWCA Civ 780 the CA considered that tort liability is less likely to exist where there is a formal construction contract with a contractual chain. In this case, the claimant banks and D bank entered into an agreement to establish a "sharia-compliant" fund. The Fund suffered losses resulting from D's negligent advice. D unsuccessfully argued that no duty of care could arise in tort because the contractual structure was inconsistent with any such duty. Neuberger L.J. considered that the question to be asked was whether the nature, terms and circumstances of the contract lead to the conclusion that the parties have agreed that there will be no tortious duty.

(2) See also *Robinson v PE Jones (Contractors) Ltd* [2011] EWCA Civ 9.

Key Principle

Restitution may provide a remedy to a party who has rendered performance or paid money where in fact there is no valid contract.

BRITISH STEEL CORPORATION V CLEVELAND BRIDGE AND ENGINEERING CO LTD 1984

The plaintiffs were asked by the defendants to produce cast-steel nodes. The plaintiffs produced an initial estimate, but discussions continued about the precise specifications of the nodes. The defendants then sent a "letter of intent" to the plaintiffs which, inter alia, asked them to start work immediately, which they did. Negotiations continued about the specifications, the payment and liability for loss for late delivery. All the nodes were delivered apart from one which was delayed because of an industrial dispute at the plaintiff's plant. The plaintiffs claimed a reasonable price (quantum meruit) for the nodes, arguing that no agreement had been reached by the parties. The defendants refused to pay for the nodes and counterclaimed for damages for breach of contract because of, inter alia, the late delivery of one node.

Held

❖ (QBD) Since the parties had not reached agreement on the price and other essential terms, such as liability for late delivery, no contract had been entered into by them for the manufacture of the nodes. However, the defendants were bound to pay a reasonable sum for the manufacture of the nodes as it was done at their request. [1984] 1 All E.R. 504.

Commentary

(1) A quantum meruit claim is an example of an action based on the equitable principle of restitution. Such a claim is sometimes classified as "quasi-contract". In *Lipkin Gorman v Karpnale Ltd* [1991] 2 A.C. 548 the House of Lords recognised for the first time the existence of a principle of restitution based upon unjust enrichment. Restitution, like tort and contract, comes under the umbrella of the law of obligations.

(2) Such a claim, as opposed to a claim for breach of contract, is unlikely to enable recovery of any future losses.

(3) See *Yeoman's Row Management Limited v Cobbe* [2008] UKHL 55 where their Lordships found that, although the parties had not entered into a contract, the owner of property had acted unconscionably by reneging on an arrangement made with a property developer once the developer obtained planning permission for the property. The arrangement had been that when the property developer obtained planning permission for the property they would then enter into a contract which would enable both of them to benefit from the proposed development. As a consequence the owner was unjustly enriched because she obtained the value of the developer's services without

having to pay for them. The owner was not required to pay the difference in the market value of the property with and without the planning permission but she was required to make a reasonable payment for the developer's services.

Key Principle

Costs incurred by way of accelerated performance of an anticipated contract which does not materialise are recoverable under the law of restitution.

REGALIAN PROPERTIES PLC V LONDON DOCKLANDS DEVELOPMENT CORPORATION 1995

In 1986 the plaintiffs and defendants began negotiations for the development of land for housing in Wapping. The plaintiffs offered £18.5 million for a licence to build, which the defendants accepted "subject to contract". Various delays meant that the building work did not start, and in 1988 the market value of residential land fell so much that it was not worth proceeding. The plaintiffs claimed £3 million from the defendants as reimbursement for the costs they incurred in preparing for the proposed contract.

Held

❖ (ChD) The plaintiffs were unsuccessful because they incurred the costs for the purpose of putting themselves in a position to obtain and then perform the contract, rather than by way of accelerated performance. [1995] 1 W.L.R. 212.

Commentary

BSC v Cleveland Bridge and Engineering Co Ltd (1984) (see above) was distinguished.

Key principle

Prudent parties to a contractual dispute usually try to avoid litigation where possible because of its uncertainty and expense

SUPERSHIELD LIMITED V SIEMENS BUILDING TECHNOLOGIES FE LIMITED 2010

The respondent settled the claim against it and sought to recover 20 per cent of the settlement costs from the appellant. The appellant argued that the sum for which the respondent settled was not reasonable bearing in mind the strength of the defences available to it (see Ch.15).

Held

❖ (CA) The respondent had shown that it was reasonable for it to settle the claim as it did. It would have been a rash lawyer who would have advised the respondent that it was likely to succeed on the causation point let alone that it could be confident of doing so. [2010] EWCA Civ 7.

Commentary

Toulson L.J. quoted Megarry J. who "once described the law reports as the wrecks of unsinkable cases".

THINK POINT

Identify all those contracts that you have entered into today.

Would a claimant normally be awarded more compensation by claiming restitution or by claiming damages for breach of contract?

The Agreement

The Formation of an Agreement

INTRODUCTION

A contract is an agreement which can be enforced through the courts. In most cases there is no need for the contract to be in writing. A contract can be an exchange of promises, or conduct in exchange for a promise. Generally the courts take an objective rather than a subjective view as to whether or not an agreement has been reached.

There must be an "offer" by one party which has been "accepted" by the other party. An offer is normally made by A to B. This is known as a bilateral contract. It is also possible for A to make an offer "to the world", for example to offer a reward to someone who finds and returns A's diamond bracelet. This is known as a unilateral contract.

An acceptance of an offer must normally be received to be effective, although there are important exceptions, in particular where the post is used. The rules on communication of acceptance have been extended to apply to electronic communication.

Where the terms of the offer and acceptance are not clear or are incomplete the courts may decide that there is no agreement. The courts are not generally prepared to insert words into the contract to make it certain.

Key Principle

Offer and acceptance will, in the vast majority of cases, represent the mechanism of contract formation.

> G PERCY TRENTHAM LTD V ARCHITAL LUXFER LTD 1993
> The facts and the decision are set out at Ch.1.

Held

❖ (CA) Steyn L.J. considered, obiter, that there are four matters of importance in contract formation.
  (1) English law generally adopts an objective theory of contract formation.
  (2) The coincidence of offer and acceptance will in the vast majority of cases represent the mechanism of contract formation.

(3) Where a transaction has been performed by both parties the court is more likely to find that there is a binding contract.

(4) Where a contract only comes into existence during and as a result of performance the court is likely to hold that the contract impliedly and retrospectively covers pre-contractual performance.

Commentary

On-line contract formation is also subject to the Electronic Commerce (EC Directive) Regulations 2002 (SI 2002/2013).

OFFER

Key Principle

An offer is a statement which objectively indicates that the offeror is prepared to contract on specified terms.

GIBSON V MANCHESTER CITY COUNCIL 1979

The plaintiff wanted to buy his council house from the defendant Council. The Council wrote to him stating that it "may be prepared to sell the house" and inviting him to make a "formal application to buy" on the enclosed application form. He did so using the Council's printed form which stated "I . . . now wish to purchase my council house." Four months later the Council informed the plaintiff that it was not prepared to sell him the house. The plaintiff claimed that the Council's first letter was an offer which he had accepted when he submitted the application form, and so there was a binding contract.

Held

❖ (HL) There was no binding contract. The words used made it quite impossible to construe the Council's letter to the plaintiff as a contractual offer capable of being converted into a legally enforceable contract by the plaintiff's written acceptance. The letter was just a step in the negotiations. [1979] 1 W.L.R. 294.

Commentary

(1) Lord Diplock favoured the conventional approach of looking to see whether, on the true construction of the documents, there is an offer and an acceptance. He disagreed with Lord Denning's view in the Court of Appeal that the court should look at the correspondence as a whole and the conduct of the parties to see whether they have reached agreement.

(2) Compare *Storer v Manchester City Council* [1974] 1 W.L.R. 1403 where the Court of Appeal held that the council house tenant had accepted the Council's offer to sell when he signed and returned an Agreement for Sale to the Council.

Key Principle
An offer can be made to the world at large and it can be accepted by anybody who performs the necessary actions.

> CARLILL V CARBOLIC SMOKE BALL CO 1893
> In a newspaper advertisement the Carbolic Smoke Ball Co stated that it would pay £100 to any person who became ill with flu after using the smoke ball as directed and that to show its sincerity it had deposited £1,000 in a bank account. Mrs Carlill used the smoke ball, but nevertheless caught flu.

Held
❖ (CA) The advertisement was an offer to the world which was accepted by Mrs Carlill when she used the smoke ball as directed. She was entitled to the £100. [1893] 1 Q.B. 256.

Commentary
(1) Newspaper advertisements are usually considered to be invitations to treat. See, e.g. *Partridge v Crittenden* (1968) (see below).

(2) This is an example of a unilateral offer and acceptance (see below). If such an offer is revoked, the revocation does not have to be communicated to every single offeree.

(3) The consideration for the Company's promise to pay was the inconvenience suffered by Mrs Carlill when using the smoke ball and the likely increase in sales for the Company.

(4) In *Bowerman v Association of British Travel Agents Ltd* 1995, (The Times, November 24, 1995) the CA held that a notice displayed prominently in a tour operator's office was an offer to the world.

Key Principle
An offer must contain an express or implied promise.

HARVEY V FACEY 1893

The appellant sent a telegram to the respondent asking "Will you sell us Bumper Hall Pen? Telegraph lowest cash price." The respondent replied, "Lowest cash price for Bumper Hall Pen £900." The appellant agreed to buy the property for £900.

Held

❖ (JCPC) The respondent's reply was not an offer containing a promise; it was merely a response to the second question in the appellant's telegram. [1893] A.C. 552.

Key Principle

An offer is a proposal made by one party (X) which is capable of being accepted by the other party (Y) and by which Y, acting reasonably, would understand that X intended to be bound in the event of an unequivocal acceptance by Y.

CREST NICHOLSON (LONDINIUM) LTD V AKARIA INVESTMENTS LTD 2010

In February 2004 C entered into an agreement with A for the development of land in Hemel Hempstead owned by A. C agreed to seek tenants who would pay the "open market rent" and to use reasonable endeavours to obtain the higher "Target Rent". The agreement contained a profit sharing provision which set out that where any unit remained un-let two years after the completion of the project A would pay an agreed profit payment to C based on the "open market rent". The project was completed in March 2006. On June 21, 2007 C sent a letter to A which referred to the profit sharing provision and to the Target Rent schedule showing the "open market rents" for the remaining un-let units. A replied by e-mail accepting C's proposals. C replied by e-mail thanking A for their confirmation on these issues.

Held

❖ (CA) C's letter of June 21 did not contain an "offer" capable of acceptance in relation to the treatment of "Target Rents" as "open market rents". The properly informed reader would have appreciated that the statement in the letter that the Target Rent schedule showed the "open market rents" for the remaining un-let units was incorrect because it did not reflect the terms of the original agreement and the terms were not interchangeable. The correct analysis was that A's e-mail contained an unequivocal acceptance of the other proposals in C's letter dated June 21. [2010] EWCA Civ 1331.

Commentary

(1) The CA stated that the judge had adopted the wrong approach when deciding whether the C's letter of June 21 could be treated as an offer capable of acceptance. This was because he used the approach used for interpreting the meaning of express terms, that is what did the parties intend by the words used in the agreement which they made (see Ch. 7, *Chartbrook Ltd v Persimmon Homes Ltd* 2009). The two approaches are distinct.

(2) The correct approach is based on the decision in *Harvey v Facey* 1893.

INVITATIONS TO TREAT DISTINGUISHED FROM OFFERS

Key Principle

Advertisements are normally invitations to treat because it is clear that the advertiser does not intend to be bound.

> **PARTRIDGE V CRITTENDEN 1968**
> The defendant placed an advertisement in a magazine stating "Bramblefinch cocks and hens, 25s".

Held

❖ (DC) The advertisement did not amount to an offer to sell. [1968] 1 W.L.R. 1204.

Key Principle

An advertisement for an auction is normally an invitation to treat, and the bid is the offer which can be accepted by the auctioneer.

> **HARRIS V NICKERSON 1873**
> The defendant auctioneer advertised that certain items including "office furniture" were to be sold at an auction sale. The plaintiff attended the sale to buy the office furniture, but it was withdrawn from the sale. The plaintiff claimed that the advertisement amounted to an offer to sell the furniture which he accepted by attending the auction.

Held

❖ (Q.B.) The advertisement did not amount to a promise to sell the furniture. (1873) L.R. 8 Q.B. 286.

Key Principle

At an auction without reserve, the auctioneer is bound to sell to the highest bidder.

BARRY V DAVIES (T/A HEATHCOTE BALL & CO) 2000

The auctioneer withdrew two engine analysers from an auction without reserve because he considered that the bids were too low.

Held

❖ (CA) There was a collateral agreement that the auctioneer would sell to the highest bidder. The auctioneer was liable to pay damages to the highest bidder, amounting to the difference between the highest bid (£400) and the market price of the machines (£28,000). [2001] 1 All E.R. 944.

Commentary

Note that in this case, unlike *Harris v Nickerson* (above), the auctioneer only withdrew the goods after the bidding had started.

Key Principle

A circular inviting the submission of tenders is normally an invitation to treat and the submission of the tender is the offer.

SPENCER V HARDING 1870

The defendant sent out a circular inviting tenders for the purchase of stock. The plaintiffs submitted the highest tender, but the defendant refused to sell the stock to them.

Held

The circular was not an offer to sell to the highest bidder, it was merely inviting offers to buy. (1870) L.R. 5 C.P. 561.

Commentary

Note that different principles apply to the acceptance of tenders which are standing offers. See *Great Northern Railway v Witham* (1873) (see below).

Key Principle

An invitation to submit tenders is an offer to open and consider all conforming tenders together.

The defendant local authority invited tenders for a concession to operate pleasure flights from the local airport. The letter stated that "No tender which is received after the last date and time specified" would be considered. The plaintiff's tender was posted by hand in the defendant's letter box before the deadline expired, but the defendant's staff did not empty the box and the plaintiff's tender was not considered.

Held

❖ (CA) It was implied that all tenders submitted which complied with the tendering procedure would be opened and considered together with other conforming tenders. The invitation to tender was a unilateral offer which was accepted by the submission of a tender. [1990] 1 W.L.R. 1195.

Commentary

English and EC legislation regulates invitations to tender issued by local authorities for public works and public service contracts.

Key Principle

An invitation to submit tenders may amount to an offer where it is clear that the seller intends to sell to the highest bidder.

HARVELA INVESTMENTS LTD v ROYAL TRUST CO. OF CANADA 1985
The defendant invited the plaintiff and a third party to make an offer for the purchase of shares and undertook to accept the highest offer. The plaintiff offered $2,175,000, while the third party offered $2,100,000 or $101,000 in excess of any other offer. The defendant accepted the third party's bid because they thought they were obliged to do so. The plaintiff sought an injunction.

Held

❖ (HL) The third party's bid was a referential bid and was not a valid offer. The defendant's invitation was an offer which was accepted by the submission of the highest valid bid. [1985] 3 W.L.R. 276.

Key Principle
The display of goods for sale on a supermarket shelf is an invitation to treat, and the offer to buy is made by the customer presenting the goods to the cashier.

PHARMACEUTICAL SOCIETY OF GREAT BRITAIN V BOOTS CASH CHEMISTS LTD 1953
The defendants, Boots, displayed medicines on their shelves which under statute must be sold under the supervision of a registered pharmacist. In this shop the pharmacist could refuse to allow the purchase at the cash desk.

Held
❖ (CA) The contract of sale occurred at the cash desk not when the customer took the medicines off the shelves and placed them in a basket, and so the statutory requirement was satisfied. [1953] 2 W.L.R. 427.

Commentary
(1) This principle also applies to a display of goods in a shop window: *Fisher v Bell* [1961] 1 Q.B. 394 display of flick knives. Note that a number of these cases have arisen because it is a criminal offence to "offer for sale" a particular item.

(2) It is not clear whether the offer is accepted when the seller asks for the price or when the buyer pays the money.

TERMINATION OF OFFER

Key Principle
If no time is fixed for an offer to lapse, then it lapses after the passage of a reasonable time.

RAMSGATE VICTORIA HOTEL CO LTD V MONTEFIORE 1866
In June the defendant offered to buy shares in the plaintiff's company and paid a deposit. The plaintiffs informed him at the end of November that he had been allocated shares and that the balance was now due.

The defendant was entitled to refuse to take up the shares. His offer had lapsed because an excessive amount of time had passed. (1866) L.R. 1 Ex. 109.

Commentary

What is reasonable is a question of fact and will depend upon the subject-matter and the context of the contract.

Key Principle

An offer can be revoked by the offeror at any time before acceptance, but the revocation is only effective once it is communicated to the offeree.

> BYRNE V VAN TIENHOVEN 1880
>
> On October 1, the defendants posted a letter in Cardiff to the plaintiffs in New York offering to sell them tin plates. On October 8, the defendants revoked their offer by post. On October 11, the plaintiffs accepted the offer by telegraph, and confirmed their acceptance by a letter dated October 15. On October 20, the plaintiffs received the defendants' letter of revocation.

Held

The revocation of the offer was not effective because it was only communicated on October 20, which was after the acceptance of the offer on October 11. (1880) 5 C.P.D. 344.

Commentary

(1) The communication can be made through a third party: *Dickinson v Dodds* [1876] 2 Ch.D. 463. Treitel has criticised this decision because it leads to uncertainty.

(2) See *Grant v Bragg* [2009] EWCA Civ 1228 for the application of this principle by the Court of Appeal to e-mail communications.

Key Principle

A later offer may revoke an earlier offer where the making of the second offer clearly indicates an intention on the part of the offeror to withdraw the first offer.

PICKFORDS LIMITED V CELESTICA LIMITED 2003

In 2001 C wanted to move workshop and office equipment from Staffordshire to Shropshire. On September 13 P offered to carry out the work, specifying its charges, and stated that the cost would not exceed £100,000. On September 27 P provided more details and offered to carry out the work at a fixed price of £98,760.00. On October 15 C purported to accept the offer made on September 13.

Held

❖ (CA) The second offer on September 27 superseded and revoked the first offer. The "acceptance" by C on 15 October of the first offer amounted to a counter-offer which was accepted by conduct when P carried out the work.

Commentary

(1) Dyson L.J. noted that there was a substantial difference between the two offers.

(2) He also commented that it was as if the facts of this case had been devised for an examination question on the law of contract for first year law students.

Key Principle

Actual communication of the revocation to a particular individual is not necessary where the offer has been made to a company.

THE BRIMNES 1975

The defendants hired a ship from the plaintiffs, but did not pay the hire due by a particular date, so the plaintiffs sent a telex message withdrawing the use of the ship from the defendants.

Held

❖ (CA) The withdrawal was effective when the telex arrived at the defendants' office during ordinary business hours. [1975] Q.B. 929.

Commentary

(1) Although this case concerned the termination of a contract rather than the withdrawal of an offer, it is likely that the principle as to communication is the same.

(2) Where the communication arrives outside business hours it is likely that it is only effective at the start of the next business day: *Scheldte Delta Shipping BV v Astarte Shipping Ltd* [1995] 2 Lloyd's Rep 249.

(3) Actual communication of the revocation is not necessary where a unilateral offer (see *Carlill v Carbolic Smoke Ball Co* (1893)) is revoked. The offeror is required to take reasonable steps to bring notice of the revocation to anyone who was likely to be aware of the original offer.

Key Principle

An attempt to accept an offer on new terms, not contained in the offer, is a rejection of the offer accompanied by a counter-offer.

> HYDE V WRENCH 1840
>
> The defendant offered to sell his farm to the plaintiff for £1,000. The plaintiff responded by offering to buy it for £950. The defendant refused to sell it for that amount. The plaintiff then tried to accept the defendant's original offer to sell for £1,000.

Held

There was no contract. Having rejected the defendant's offer to sell by his offer of £950, the plaintiff could not then revive and accept the defendant's offer. (1840) 49 All E.R. Rep.132.

Commentary

In *Society of Lloyd's v Twinn*, *The Times*, April 4, 2000, the Vice-Chancellor stated that there was no reason why an offeree should not accept an offer unconditionally and, at the same time, make a collateral offer to the original offer. Whether a particular statement amounts to a counter offer or a collateral offer is a question of fact.

Key Principle

A request for information in response to an offer is not a rejection and counter offer.

> STEVENSON, JACQUES & CO. V MCLEAN 1880
>
> The plaintiffs and the defendants were negotiating about the sale of iron. The defendant wrote offering to sell the iron for cash. The plaintiff telegraphed asking whether the iron could be delivered over a two-month period.

Held

The plaintiff's telegraph was not a rejection of the defendant's offer it was merely an inquiry, and so the plaintiff could subsequently accept the defendant's offer. (1880) 5 Q.B.D. 346.

ACCEPTANCE

Key Principle

An acceptance must amount to a final and unqualified assent to the terms of the offer.

> BUTLER MACHINE TOOL CO V EX-CELL-O CORPORATION LTD 1979
> The plaintiffs offered to sell a machine tool to the defendants for £75,535, delivery to be in 10 months' time. The plaintiffs' offer included a price variation clause, and stated that their terms and conditions would prevail over any terms and conditions in the defendants' order. The defendants placed an order on their own terms and conditions, which did not include a price variation clause. At the bottom of the defendants' order was a tear-off acknowledgment slip for completion by the plaintiffs, which stated: "We accept your order on the terms and conditions stated thereon". The plaintiffs completed, signed and returned the slip with a letter stating that the order had been entered in accordance with their original offer. The plaintiffs delivered the machine and relied on their price variation clause to increase the price by £2,892. The defendants refused to pay.

Held

❖ (CA) The defendants' terms prevailed and so the price variation clause was not a term of the contract. The defendants' order was not an acceptance because it contained additional requirements. It was a rejection and counter-offer, which was accepted when the plaintiffs returned the acknowledgment slip. [1979] 1 W.L.R. 401.

Commentary

(1) This is an example of "battle of the forms" where both parties use standard forms in their business, which they do not appear to have read!

(2) See also *Hyde v Wrench* (1840) (above).

(3) In *Texdata Interconnections Ltd v Amphenol Ltd* [2009] EWCA Civ 1209 the Court of Appeal held that in a "battle of the forms" case the traditional offer and acceptance analysis must be adopted unless the documents passing between the parties and their conduct show that their common intention was that some other terms were intended to prevail. This did not mean that the context of a long term relationship and the conduct of the parties can never be so strong as to displace the result which a traditional offer and acceptance analysis would dictate.

(4) see e.g. *Allianz Insurance Co—Egypt v Aigaion Insurance Co SA* [2008] EWCA Civ 1455 for the application of this principle to e-mail communications. A reinsurance contract had been transacted entirely in a series of e-mails. The Court of Appeal held that the defendant had inadvertently accepted the claimant's terms by their e-mail response which because of its expression of finality amounted to an acceptance rather than a counter-offer. As a consequence the defendant was obliged to pay out under the insurance policy for the loss of the claimant's tug.

Key Principle

Acceptance can be by words or by conduct.

> BROGDEN V METROPOLITAN RAILWAY CO. 1877
>
> After supplying coal to the railway company for some years, Brogden agreed to a draft contract proposed by the company. The company inadvertently never formally accepted the contract. Nevertheless the company ordered and Brogden supplied coal in accordance with its terms. A dispute arose and Brogden claimed that no binding contract existed.

Held

❖ (HL) There was a binding agreement because both parties acted upon the draft and treated it as binding. The company ordered the coal and Brogden supplied it, which showed that the offer was accepted. [1877] 2 App. Cas. 666.

Commentary

See also *G. Percy Trentham Ltd v Archital Luxfer Ltd* (1993) (see p.1).

Key Principle
Acceptance of a standing offer occurs when an order is placed.

> GREAT NORTHERN RAILWAY V WITHAM 1873
> The plaintiff advertised for tenders for the supply of railway stores. The defendant submitted a tender offering to provide the required articles for 12 months. The plaintiff placed orders, all of which were carried out except for the last one. The defendant argued that he was not legally obliged to supply the goods, and so was not in breach of contract.

Held
The agreement to supply for a year was a standing offer which was accepted each time an order was placed. [1873] L.R. 9 C.P. 16.

Commentary
(1) A standing offer arises where the offeror agrees to supply goods or services as and when required over a specific period.

(2) A standing offer can be revoked at any time before acceptance.

(3) Placing the order is also consideration for the offeror's promise to supply goods over a period of time.

Key Principle
Where there is a unilateral offer acceptance occurs when the offeree fully performs the required act.

> CARLILL V CARBOLIC SMOKE BALL CO. 1893
> (see facts above).

Held
❖ (CA) The advertisement was an offer to the world which was accepted by Mrs Carlill when she used the smoke ball as directed. She was entitled to the £100. [1893] 1 Q.B. 256.

Commentary
(1) There is no need for the offeree to give advance notice of acceptance to the offeror.

(2) It has not been settled when acceptance of a unilateral offer takes place. Is it when the offeree starts to perform the condition or when performance is complete? In *Daulia Ltd v Four Millbank Nominees Ltd* [1978] 2 All E.R. 557 the Court of Appeal considered that a unilateral offer could not be withdrawn once performance had started.

COMMUNICATION OF ACCEPTANCE

Key Principle
Acceptance of an offer must be communicated to the offeror.

> HOLWELL SECURITIES LTD V HUGHES 1974
> The plaintiff had an option to purchase property from the defendant. Clause 2 of the option agreement stated: "The said option shall be exercisable by notice in writing to the Defendant at any time within 6 months from the date hereof". The plaintiff's solicitors wrote a letter to the defendant giving notice of the exercise of the option. The letter was posted, properly addressed and stamped but was never actually delivered to the defendant. Was there an effective communication of the plaintiff's acceptance? [1974] 1 W.L.R. 155.

Held
❖ (CA) The words "notice ... to" in the option agreement required actual communication of the acceptance, and so no contract came into force.

Commentary
The plaintiff unsuccessfully argued that the postal rule (see below) applied and that there was a valid contract.

Key Principle
An acceptance by telex has no effect until it is received by the offeror.

> ENTORES V MILES FAR EAST CORPORATION 1955
> The plaintiffs in London made an offer to the defendants in Amsterdam. The defendants accepted by telex. Was the contract entered into in Amsterdam where the telex was sent or in London where it was received?

Held

❖ (CA) The contract was only complete when the acceptance was received by the plaintiffs in London. [1955] 3 W.L.R. 48.

Commentary

This principle is applicable to other forms of instantaneous communications such as telephone, and presumably also to fax and email.

Key Principle

No universal rule can cover the many variations in telex communications.

> BRINKIBON LTD V STAHAG STAHL, ETC., 1983
>
> The plaintiffs in London accepted by telex an offer made by the defendants in Vienna. Where was the contract made?

Held

❖ (HL) The contract was made in Vienna since in the case of instantaneous communications that was where the acceptance was received. [1983] 2 A.C. 34.

Commentary

(1) However, Lord Wilberforce stated that in deciding whether the normal rule should apply the courts should take into account: the intentions of the parties; sound business practice; and sometimes decide where the risks should lie.

(2) See also *The Brimnes* (1975) (see above) on termination of an offer by telex.

Key Principle

Where the post is used an acceptance is effectively communicated on posting.

> HOUSEHOLD FIRE INSURANCE V GRANT 1879
>
> The defendant offered to buy shares in the plaintiff company. The company posted a letter accepting the offer. The letter never arrived but the defendant's name was entered as a shareholder. Was the defendant bound to pay the balance due on the shares?

Held

❖ (CA) As soon as the letter of acceptance is posted there is a binding contract, even if the letter is lost or delayed. The post office acts as the agent for both parties. (1879) 4 Ex. D. 216.

Commentary

The postal rule can be excluded by the terms of the offer (e.g. *Holwell Securities v Hughes* (1974) (see above)). A postal acceptance can prevail over a revocation of an offer posted earlier (*Byrne v Van Tienhoven* (1880) (see above)).

Key Principle

For the postal rule to apply it must be reasonable to use the post to accept the offer.

QUENERDUAINE V COLE 1883

D made an offer by telegram, P purported to accept by letter.

Held

It was not reasonable to use the post to reply to a telegram, and so the acceptance was only effectively communicated when it was received. (1883) 32 W.R. 185.

Commentary

The decision is also applicable to offers made by instantaneous means of communication.

PRESCRIBED MODE OF ACCEPTANCE

Key Principle

Silence cannot normally be prescribed as a mode of acceptance.

FELTHOUSE V BINDLEY 1862

The plaintiff offered to buy his nephew's horse and wrote: "If I hear no more ... I consider the horse is mine." The nephew did not respond although there was evidence that the nephew intended to accept his uncle's offer. Was there a binding contract?

Held

The nephew had not communicated his intention and had not done anything to bind himself, so there was no valid acceptance. (1862) 6 L.T. 157.

Key Principle

Where there is a prescribed method of acceptance it is possible to use another method so long as it is not less advantageous.

> YATES BUILDING CO LTD V PULLEYN LTD 1975
> The plaintiff had the option of purchasing land from the defendants. It was a term of the agreement that the option was exercisable by notice in writing, and that such notice was to be sent "by registered or recorded delivery post". The plaintiffs exercised their option by sending a letter using the ordinary post. Was the letter a valid acceptance? (1975) 119 Sol. J. 370.

Held

❖ (CA) In this case the use of registered or recorded delivery was not compulsory. Its use was more advantageous to the plaintiff than to the defendant. What mattered was that the substance of the requirement was fulfilled. Therefore, a binding contract had been concluded.

CERTAINTY

Key Principle

Where a term is so vague that further agreement is necessary then no contract has been concluded.

> SCAMMELL V OUSTON 1941
> The plaintiff ordered a van from the defendant. The balance of the purchase price was to be paid on "hire-purchase terms" over two years. The defendant then refused to supply the van.

Held

❖ (HL) There was no contract because the language was not capable of any definite meaning as there were many kinds of hire purchase agreement, and so the agreement was incomplete. [1941] 1 All E.R. 14.

Commentary

(1) Note that the courts will try to find a valid contract where possible and will use various devices such as custom and reasonableness to make sense of a vague term.

(2) In *Baird Textile Holdings Ltd v Marks & Spencer Plc* [2001] EWCA 274 (see also Ch.3 and Ch.4), the Court of Appeal considered that any obligations imposed on D were insufficiently certain to be terms of a contract because there were no objective criteria by which the court could assess what would be reasonable either as to quantity or price. P had been a principal supplier of garments to D for 30 years when without warning in October 1999, D terminated the arrangement from the end of the current production season. It was accepted that there was no express legally binding contract between P and D. P argued unsuccessfully that either there was an implied contract or that D were estopped from terminating the arrangement without giving reasonable notice.

Key Principle

A bare agreement to negotiate lacks certainty and is unenforceable.

> ### WALFORD V MILES 1992
>
> The plaintiffs were interested in purchasing the defendants' business. The defendants agreed to terminate negotiations with any third party (a lock-out agreement), and to negotiate only with the plaintiffs. Subsequently they sold the business to a third party. [1992] 2 W.L.R. 174.

Held

❖ (HL) The agreement to negotiate was, like an agreement to agree, unenforceable because it lacked certainty. In particular there was no time limit on the negotiations, nor was there any provision for either party to withdraw from them. English law does not recognise a duty to negotiate in good faith.

Commentary

Willis Management (Isle of Man) Ltd and Willis UK Ltd v Cable and Wireless Plc and Pender Insurance Ltd [2005] 2 Lloyd's Rep. 597 is an example of an agreement to agree which was held not to create a binding contract by the Court of Appeal. W agreed to pay a fair share of losses suffered by C & W as a consequence of fraud allegedly perpetrated by one of W's employees, but W withdrew from the arrangement before the parties had discussed and agreed how such a share was to be determined. Tuckey L.J. stated that 'the court cannot make for the parties the agreement which they have not made for themselves'.

Key Principle

The use of the words "subject to contract" means that there is no legally binding contract.

REGALIAN PROPERTIES PLC V LONDON DOCKLANDS DEVELOPMENT CORPORATION 1995

The plaintiffs offered the defendants £18.5 million "subject to contract" for a licence to build on the defendants' land. The property market then collapsed and it was not financially worthwhile proceeding with the contract. The plaintiffs tried to recover from the defendants the £3 million which they had spent in preparation for the proposed contract.

Held

❖ (Ch D) The words "subject to contract" meant that the loss lay where it fell. The plaintiffs could not recover in restitution (see Ch.1) because the costs which the plaintiffs incurred did not amount to accelerated performance of the contract, and the decision not to enter into the contract was not made unilaterally by the defendant. [1995] 1 W.L.R. 212.

Key Principle

Parties may expressly or by inference waive a condition that their agreement is "subject to contract".

RTS FLEXIBLE SYSTEMS LTD V MOLKEREI ALOIS MÜLLER GMBH & CO KG (UK) PRODUCTION 2010

The claimant (RTS) made a written offer to install two food packaging production lines to the defendant (M), which produced dairy products for sale in shops and supermarkets. The new production lines were scheduled to be in use by September 30. On February 21, 2005 M sent a letter of intent to RTS indicating their willingness to proceed with the project, which was worth in total approximately £1.6m, subject to an agreement being "agreed and then signed", within four weeks. No such agreement was signed (see Ch. 1). Delays occurred between June and August. The delivery plans were varied on August 25. The first production line started operation on October 10; the second by January

2006. By January 2006 Muller had paid RTS 70 per cent of the contract price, but not paid the 20 per cent due on delivery.

Held

❖ (SC) There was a valid contract. The essential terms were agreed. The parties had waived the requirement that the contract must be signed. By August 25 the parties' communications and actions led to the conclusion that there was an a contract based on the terms agreed between them as at July 5, which included a draft version of the amended standard form contract, as varied on August 25. [2010] 1 W.L.R. 753.

Commentary

Lord Clarke of Stone-cum-Ebony stated that:

(a) waiving reliance on a "subject to contract" term or understanding will depend on all the circumstances of the case, and the courts will "not lightly so hold";

(b) the parties had agreed the price. The letter of intent had stated that the agreement would be based on Muller's amended version of the standard form contract. A significant amount of work had been carried out, agreement on essential terms had been reached by July 5, and a variation to those terms was agreed on August 25.

Key Principle

There is no hard and fast rule whether a letter of intent gives rise to a binding agreement.

BRITISH STEEL CORPORATION V CLEVELAND BRIDGE AND ENGINEERING CO LTD 1984
(see facts Ch.1).

Held

❖ (QBD) Since the parties had not reached agreement on the price and other essential terms, such as liability for late delivery, there was no binding contract. So the plaintiffs were not liable to pay damages for breach of contract because of the late delivery of one node. However, the defendants were bound to pay a reasonable sum (in restitution) for the manufacture of the nodes as it was done at their request. [1984] 1 All E.R. 504.

Commentary

In *RTS Flexible Systems Ltd v Molkerei Alois Müller Gmbh & Co KG (UK) Production* 2010 Lord Clarke of Stone-cum-Ebony distinguished the *British*

Steel Corporation case on the ground that in the BSC case the parties were still negotiating terms which they regarded as essential.

Key Principle

Where a subsidiary term of an agreement is left open and is capable of being ascertained then the contract will be upheld.

> SUDBROOK TRADING ESTATE LTD V EGGLETON 1982
>
> The plaintiff tenants gave notice to their landlords that they wanted to exercise an option in their lease to purchase the freehold. The price was to be fixed by two valuers, one nominated by the landlords and one by the tenants. The landlords refused to nominate a valuer.

Held

❖ (HL) There was a valid contract. The main purpose of the option agreement was the sale of the land at a fair and reasonable price. The price was capable of being ascertained, and the method of ascertaining it was not an essential part of the agreement. [1982] 3 W.L.R. 315.

Key Principle

The fact that a transaction has been performed on both sides will make it difficult to argue that the contract is void for vagueness or uncertainty.

> G PERCY TRENTHAM LTD V ARCHITAL LUXFER LTD 1993
> (see facts Ch.1).

Held

❖ (CA) Where the transaction was fully performed a contract could be concluded by conduct, or come into existence during performance. So there was a legally binding contract. The parties plainly intended to enter into such a contract. [1993] 1 Lloyd's Rep. 25.

Commentary

Cf. *BSC v Cleveland Bridge and Engineering Co Ltd* (1984).

What is the correct way of analysing whether or not there has been an offer and an acceptance? Are there any exceptions?

If the facts of *British Steel Corporation v Cleveland Bridge and Engineering Co Ltd* 1984 were to arise today, do you think that the outcome would be the same?

Consideration

INTRODUCTION

Consideration is the third crucial element of a legally enforceable agreement. Only where the contract is in the form of a deed is no consideration necessary. Consideration is the price for the promise.

For example, if A promises to give B £1 million B will not be able to enforce that promise unless B gives A something of economic value in return, or if A's promise is contained in a deed. If A promises to sell B her car for £3,000 and B agrees to buy it for £3,000, each of them has made a promise to the other. Each of them has received a benefit and suffered a detriment. Promising to hand over the car to B is a detriment to A, and a benefit to B. Promising to hand over the £3,000 to A is a detriment to B, and a benefit to A.

The party who is trying to enforce a promise must have suffered a detriment.

There are three types of consideration. These are:

(1) Executory consideration, which is an exchange of promises as in the car example above.

(2) Executed consideration, which is an act (or forbearing to act) in return for a promise. For example, B promises to pay A £3000 for her car and so A leaves her car in B's driveway for B.

(3) Past consideration. This arises where A carries out an act which benefits B and subsequently B promises to give money for the act. For example, A leaves her car in B's driveway so that B takes responsibility for it because she is unable to pay the road tax and care insurance. One month later B promises to pay A £3,000 for the car.

Past consideration is NOT good consideration, which means that there is no binding agreement.

The case of *Williams v Roffey* 1990 has alleviated the strictness of the doctrine of consideration by extending the definition of "benefit" and "detriment" at least in the context of where a person promises to do something which they are already legally bound to do.

One of the major exceptions to the requirement that consideration is required to make a contract enforceable was the creation, by Mr Justice Denning (as he then was), in the 1947 *High Trees* case of the principle of promissory estoppel. At the moment this principle can only be used as a defence.

Key Principle

For a promise to be enforceable as a contract some consideration must be given in exchange for the promise; that is the promisor must receive a benefit or the promisee must suffer a detriment.

> ### CURRIE V MISA 1875
> P sued D on a cheque given to pay off a pre-existing debt. D argued that P had not provided fresh consideration for the debt.

Held

P was entitled to the money. (1875) L.R. 10 Ex. 153.

Commentary

(1) This case is important because of the following definition of consideration given by the court of first instance. "A valuable consideration, in the sense of the law, may consist either in some right, interest, profit, or benefit accruing to one party or some forbearance, detriment, loss or responsibility, given suffered or undertaken by the other."

(2) Since *Williams v Roffey* (1991) (see below) a factual benefit or detriment is sufficient.

(3) Many of the cases in this chapter are concerned with an agreed variation or termination of an existing contract, which normally requires accord (agreement) and satisfaction (consideration) to be legally binding. See discharge by agreement (Ch.13).

(4) The decision on the precise facts has been replaced by s.27 of the Bills Of Exchange Act 1882.

Key Principle

Consideration must move from the promisee.

> ### TWEDDLE V ATKINSON 1861
> The father of the bride and the father of the bridegroom agreed with each other that they would both pay a sum of money to the bridegroom on account of the marriage. They further agreed that the bridegroom should be able to sue either of them if they failed to pay. The bride's

father died without paying the money and the bridegroom Tweddle sued his father-in-law's executor for the money.

Held

Tweddle, the promisee, had not provided consideration for his father-in-law's promise. Therefore, he could not enforce the promise. [1861–1873] All E.R. Rep. 369.

Commentary

The court further stated that natural love and affection is not valid consideration. The decision is also authority for the doctrine of privity of contract (see Ch.5).

PAST CONSIDERATION

Key Principle

Past consideration is not good consideration

> RE MCARDLE 1951
> Adult children were entitled to their mother's house after her death. One of the children and his wife lived in the house with his mother. The wife carried out certain improvements to the house. Subsequently all the children promised to pay her a sum of money when the house was eventually sold to recompense her for the money she had spent on the improvements.

Held

❖ (CA) The wife had not provided consideration in exchange for the children's promise, because the improvements had been completed before the promise was made. [1951] Ch. 669.

Commentary

(1) The children's promise was subsequent to and independent of the improvements being carried out.

(2) Executory and executed consideration are regarded as good consideration.

Key Principle

If the act was done or promise made at the request of the promisor, and it was understood that payment would be made, then the *subsequent* promise to pay is enforceable.

> PAO ON V LAU YIU LONG 1979
>
> As part of a larger agreement the plaintiffs promised not to sell 2.5 million of the 4.2 million shares they owned in a company controlled by the defendants. Subsequently the defendants agreed to buy back 2.5 million shares at a fixed price. The plaintiffs then realised that this was a bad bargain because the price was fixed at $2.50 even if the value of the shares rose. So the plaintiffs refused to proceed with the first agreement unless the defendants cancelled the second agreement and replaced it by an indemnity which guaranteed a minimum price of $2.50 per share. The defendants provided the indemnity which also referred to the plaintiffs promise in the first agreement not to sell the shares. The value of the shares fell and the plaintiffs claimed the money due under the indemnity.

Held

❖ (JCPC) It was understood at the time of the first agreement that the plaintiff's promise not to sell the shares would be compensated for by the defendants promising to indemnify the plaintiffs against any fall in the price of the shares. Therefore, the subsequent indemnity was not independent of the original promise, and the consideration for the defendants' promise was good. [1980] A.C. 614.

Commentary

This case is also concerned with sufficiency of consideration (see below) and economic duress (see Ch.11).

ADEQUACY OF CONSIDERATION

Key Principle

Consideration need not be adequate.

> CHAPPELL & CO LTD V NESTLÉ CO LTD 1960
>
> The defendant chocolate manufacturers sold a record to the public in return for money and three chocolate bar wrappers. The plaintiffs owned the copyright of the record. They were entitled to a royalty calculated by reference to the "ordinary retail selling price", which the

defendants claimed was the money payment alone, and did not include the wrappers.

Held

❖ (HL) The chocolate wrappers formed part of the consideration. They had some economic value because they induced people to buy chocolate which they might otherwise not have bought. [1959] 3 W.L.R. 168.

Commentary

Adequate in this context means reasonable or proportionate.

SUFFICIENCY OF CONSIDERATION

Key Principle

Consideration must be of some economic value.

> WHITE V BLUETT 1853
> A son promised not to bore his father with his complaints if his father did not sue him on a promissory note.

Held

The son's promise had no economic value and so the son had provided no consideration for his father's promise. (1853) 23 L.J. Ex. 36.

Commentary

Sufficiency of consideration means that the consideration must have some economic value. This issue arises firstly in relation to the performance of an existing duty and secondly in relation to a creditor accepting a smaller amount of money than that due under the contract.

PERFORMANCE OF AN EXISTING DUTY

Key Principle

A promise to do something which you are already bound to do under the general law is not good consideration.

> COLLINS V GODEFROY 1831
> Godefroy was the plaintiff in a case in which Godefroy promised to pay the witness, Collins, six guineas as an attendance fee. Collins had been ordered by the court to give evidence.

Held

Collins had not provided consideration for Godefroy's promise. (1831) 1 B. & Ad. 950.

Key Principle

A promise to do more than you are already bound to do under the general law is good consideration.

> GLASBROOK BROS V GLAMORGAN COUNTY COUNCIL 1925
> The police, at the request of a colliery owner, stationed police continuously at his mine during industrial action by the miners.

Held

❖ (HL) The police went beyond the duty imposed upon them by the general law to provide protection, and so provided consideration for the colliery owner's promise to pay them. [1925] A.C. 270.

Commentary

(1) If there is any suggestion that the promise to pay has been induced by, for example, extortion or corruption then the court is unlikely to find that consideration has been provided.

(2) *Reading Festival Limited v West Yorkshire Police Authority* [2006] 1 W.L.R. 2005 is a recent example of the application of this principle, now found in s.25(1) Police Act 1996 which provides that the police are entitled to charge for "special police services". The appeal concerned a music festival in Leeds and has implications for major sporting events and similar large gatherings. The Court of Appeal held that there was no contract because there was no agreement between the parties as to how the police services were to be deployed and how they were to be paid. Therefore, the police were not entitled to recover the cost of additional policing outside the private premises where the festival was held because the promoter did not request the police to provide such policing and the police were merely performing their public duty of keeping law and order in a public place rather than providing a special service to the appellants.

Key Principle

A promise to do something that you are already bound to do under an existing contract with the promisee is not good consideration.

STILK V MYRICK 1809

Stilk, a seaman, signed up for a voyage from London to the Baltic and back. During the voyage two seamen deserted. The master of the ship agreed to divide their pay between the remaining members of the crew if they would work the ship back to London without the two deserters being replaced. On their return the master refused to pay Stilk and the other seamen.

Held

Stilk and the other seamen had not provided any consideration for the master's promise. They merely agreed to do what they were already bound to do. (1809) 170 All E.R. Rep. 851.

Commentary

(1) The court was also concerned that seamen would be able to hold their masters to ransom if the master's promise was enforceable. The principle of economic duress would now provide an alternative ground for holding a promise invalid in such circumstances.

(2) This decision can now be distinguished in most cases so that the principle is of little practical importance (see the next three cases).

Key Principle

A promise to do more than you are already bound to do under the original contract is good consideration.

PINNEL'S CASE 1602

Cole owed Pinnel £8.50 which was due to be paid on November 11, 1600. At Pinnel's request Cole paid £5.11 on October 1, 1600, in full satisfaction of the debt.

Held

In principle, payment of a lesser sum before the date due is good consideration. However, because of a defect in the defendant's pleadings Pinnel was able to recover the balance. (1602) 5 Co. Rep.117a.

Commentary

(1) The court stated that payment of a lesser sum in satisfaction of a greater sum is generally not good consideration (see *Foakes v Beer 1884*, et seq., below).

(2) The court also considered that payment at a different place than that originally agreed, or payment in kind such as "the gift of a horse, hawk, robe," would be good consideration.

Key Principle

Where you are legally entitled to refuse to perform the original contract, then a promise to do something that you were bound to do under that contract is good consideration.

> HARTLEY V PONSONBY 1857
>
> The plaintiff, an able seaman, signed up with the master of a ship for a voyage from London to Australia and back. There was a crew of 36, but 17 of them deserted on arrival in Australia. The master agreed to pay the plaintiff £40 if he helped to sail the ship to Bombay with the remaining crew.

Held

The plaintiff's original contract was terminated because it was dangerous to sail the ship with a crew of 19 men. The plaintiff had entered into a new contract and had provided good consideration for the master's promise. (1857) 7 El. & Bl. 872.

Commentary

(1) £40 was not regarded an exorbitant sum in the circumstances.

(2) In *Compagnie Noga d'Importation et D'Exportation SA v Abacha (No.2)* [2003] 2 All E.R. (Comm.) 915 the Court of Appeal distinguished the principle in *Stilk v Myrick* and confirmed that it only applied where the earlier contract was varied. It does not apply where it has been terminated by agreement and replaced by a new agreement. Consideration for both the termination and the new agreement may be provided by each party releasing the other party from their original contractual obligations

Key Principle

If the promisee obtains a benefit or avoids a detriment from the performance of a promise, that is good consideration, even if the promisor was already bound to perform the promise under an existing contract with the promisee.

WILLIAMS V ROFFEY BROS & NICHOLLS (CONTRACTORS) LTD 1990
The defendant building contractors were refurbishing a block of flats for
the owners. They sub-contracted the carpentry work to the plaintiff. The
plaintiff started the work but ran into financial difficulties and there
was a risk that they would not complete the job. Under the main
contract the defendants were liable to pay a financial penalty if the
refurbishment was not completed on time. The defendants agreed to
pay an additional sum of money per flat to the plaintiff if they completed the work on time.

Held

❖ (CA) The plaintiff could recover the additional sum. The defendants
received a practical benefit because the work was completed on time, and
they did not have to engage another sub-contractor. [1991] 1 Q.B. 1.

Commentary

(1) The plaintiff did not incur a "legal" detriment nor did the defendants
receive a "legal" benefit because the plaintiff did not carry out any work in
addition to that agreed under the original contract. Factual detriment and
benefit would now appear to be good consideration. In most cases a party to
a contract would receive a factual benefit if the other party promises to keep
their side of the bargain rather than breaching the contract.

(2) There is a narrow line between this case and economic duress (see Ch.11).
In this case both parties accepted that the price the plaintiff quoted for the
work was too low, but the promisor volunteered to pay the additional sum of
money to the plaintiff.

Key Principle

A promise to perform or the performance of a pre-existing contractual obligation to a third party is good consideration.

PAO ON V LAU YIU LONG 1979
(For full facts see above). The plaintiffs refused to proceed with an
agreement made with a third party (a company controlled by the
defendants) unless the defendants cancelled the subsidiary agreement
and replaced it by an indemnity which guaranteed a minimum price of
$2.50 per share.

Held

(JCPC) The promise to perform the first agreement was good consideration for the defendants' promise to indemnify the plaintiffs. [1980] A.C. 614.

PAYMENT OF A LESSER SUM

Key Principle

Payment of a lesser sum by the debtor is not satisfaction for a greater sum.

> FOAKES V BEER 1884
>
> The plaintiff had obtained judgment against the defendant for £2,090. However, she agreed to allow the defendant to pay her by instalments and not to take any proceedings to enforce the judgment. A judgment debt attracts interest from the date of the judgment. The defendant paid the debt, and the plaintiff claimed the interest.

Held

❖ (HL) The plaintiff was entitled to recover the interest. Even if the plaintiff had agreed to forgo the interest the defendant had not provided any consideration for such a promise. [1881–1885] All E.R. Rep. 106.

Commentary

(1) The court applied *Pinnel's Case* (1602) (see above).

(2) "Satisfaction" means "consideration" in this context.

Key Principle

Even where it is beneficial to the creditor to be paid a lesser sum this will still not be satisfaction for the greater sum.

> RE SELECTMOVE LTD 1995
>
> A company owed money to the Inland Revenue. The company promised to pay off its existing and future debts by instalments. The Inland Revenue sought to have the company wound up and to recover the debt due.

Held

❖ (CA) The company's promise did not constitute good consideration, even if there was a practical advantage to the Inland Revenue in that they were more likely to recover the money by accepting payment by instalments. [1995] 1 W.L.R 474.

Commentary

(1) *Foakes v Beer* (1884) applied, with some regret.

(2) *Williams v Roffey* (1991) distinguished. The principle in *Williams v Roffey & Nicholls* (see above) applied to a contract for the supply of goods and services, but should not be extended to an obligation to pay money such as that arising in *Foakes v Beer*. Is this logical?

(3) The court decided that on the facts the company could not successfully raise the defence of promissory estoppel (see below).

Key Principle

Payment of a lesser sum by a third party is treated as satisfaction for a greater sum.

> HIRACHAND PUNAMCHAND V TEMPLE 1911
> A father wrote offering to pay a proportion of his son's debt in full settlement of the whole debt. The plaintiff creditor cashed the banker's draft enclosed with the father's letter.

Held

❖ (CA) The plaintiff could not recover the balance from the son. [1911] 2 K.B. 330.

Commentary

(1) The main reason for the decision is that it would be a fraud upon a third party to the original contract if the creditor was allowed to recover the balance from the debtor. No consideration is given by the debtor for the creditor's promise.

(2) Fraud (on the other creditors) is also the reason why compositions with creditors are upheld, even though the debtor has not provided any consideration for his creditors agreeing between themselves to accept, e.g. 10 per cent of what the debtor owes each of them.

PROMISSORY ESTOPPEL

Where A makes a promise to B which is intended to be binding and to be acted upon, and is in fact acted upon, then A is bound by the promise even where B has provided no consideration for it.

> CENTRAL LONDON PROPERTY TRUST LTD V HIGH TREES HOUSE LTD 1947
> In 1937 the plaintiff granted the defendant a 99–year lease of a block of flats at a rent of £2,500 a year. When the Second World War broke out in September 1939 the defendant had not fully sub-let all the flats, and so was unable to pay the annual rent. The plaintiff agreed that the rent should be halved as from the beginning of the lease. By the beginning of 1945 the flats were fully let. The plaintiff initially claimed all the arrears, but the case was heard on the basis that the full rent should be paid from July 1945.

Held
❖ (KBD) The plaintiff was entitled to the full rent as from July 1945. By then the conditions prevailing when the promise was made had completely passed away. If the plaintiff had claimed the balance of the rent for the war years, Denning J. stated that they would not have succeeded. [1947] K.B. 130.

Commentary
(1) Denning J. established the equitable principle of promissory estoppel by fusing two existing equitable principles: estoppel by representation; and equitable waiver (see *Hughes v Metropolitan Railway* (1877)). This enabled him to avoid having to follow the principle of *Foakes v Beer* (see above).

(2) There must be a clear and unambiguous promise for the principle to apply.

(3) This decision is a major landmark in the law of contract because a promise was enforced even though no consideration was given for it. However, its importance may be reduced because of the wider definition of consideration accepted in *Williams v Roffey* (see above).

(4) For a recent discussion on the law of promissory estoppel by the CA, see *Collier v P & MJ Wright (Holdings) Ltd* [2007] EWCA Civ 1329.

Promissory estoppel can only be used as a defence, not as a cause of action.

COMBE V COMBE 1951

A wife obtained a divorce (decree nisi) from her husband, who then promised to pay her £100 a year as a maintenance payment. So the wife did not apply to the court for maintenance payments. The divorce was finalised (decree absolute). The husband never paid the wife any maintenance and she sued him on his promise.

Held

❖ (CA) The wife could not enforce the promise. She had provided no consideration and promissory estoppel merely prevented a party from insisting upon their strict legal rights, when it would be unjust to allow them to do so. Promissory estoppel should be used as "a shield not as a sword". [1951] 1 All E.R. 767.

Commentary

(1) In *Baird Textile Holdings Ltd v Marks & Spencer plc* [2001] EWCA 274 (see Ch.2) the Court of Appeal confirmed that promissory estoppel and estoppel by convention merely provide defences to a claim. They do not establish enforceable obligations, although Judge L.J. considered that the House of Lords might review this limitation in the future.

(2) Compare with proprietary estoppel which may be used as a "sword". In *Gillett v Holt* [2000] 3 W.L.R. 815; [2000] 2 All E.R. 289, the Court of Appeal held that detrimental reliance on a promise to leave a farming business to the appellant on the respondent's death made the promise irrevocable and enforceable by the appellant.

(3) Note that proprietary as opposed to promissory estoppel normally arises where a promise is made as to future rights over land. The promisor is estopped from going back on the promise where the promisee has relied on the promise to his detriment.

(4) In *Cobbe v Yeoman's Row Management Ltd* [2008]1 W.L.R. 752, Lord Scott of Foscote stated obiter that propriety estoppel is a sub-species of promissory estoppel and in principle is equally available in relation to personal property such as goods.

Key Principle

A promise to suspend payments operates until the creditor gives reasonable notice of their intention to resume their strict legal rights.

Tool Metal Manufacturing Co Ltd v Tungsten Electric Co Ltd 1955

In 1937 the appellants (TMMC) licensed the respondents to trade in hard metal alloys. The appellants were entitled to be paid compensation if, for example, the respondents used more than a certain amount of alloys in any month. The respondents paid the compensation until the outbreak of war in 1939, when the appellants agreed to suspend the payments on the understanding that a new agreement would be negotiated to come into effect at the end of the war. Negotiations broke down in 1944, and in March 1945 the appellants claimed compensation under the original agreement as from June 1, 1945. The case reached the Court of Appeal which held that although the agreement in 1939 was to suspend not to end the payments, the appellants had not given reasonable notice to the respondents of their intention that the compensation payments be resumed. The appellants then started another action claiming compensation as from January 1, 1947, reasonable notice of their claim having been given in March 1945.

Held

❖ (HL) Reasonable notice had now been given and the appellants were entitled to the payments agreed under the 1937 licence agreement. [1955] 1 W.L.R. 761.

Commentary

The principle of equitable waiver (*Hughes v Metropolitan Railway* (1877)) was the basis of the decision, but the key principle also applies to promissory estoppel.

Key Principle

The promise only becomes final and irrevocable if the promisee cannot resume their position.

Ajayi v Briscoe 1964

The plaintiff sued the defendant to recover instalments due under an agreement to hire purchase 11 lorries. The defendant pleaded promissory estoppel on the ground that the plaintiff had agreed to accept the suspension of the payments until certain conditions were fulfilled.

Held

❖ (JCPC) The defendant was not successful because he was unable to prove that the conditions had not been fulfilled. [1964] 1 W.L.R. 1326.

Commentary

Lord Hodson stated that the doctrine of promissory estoppel is subject to three qualifications:

(1) the promisee should have altered their position in reliance on the promise;

(2) the promisor can go back on their promise on the giving of reasonable notice (see above); and

(3) the promise only becomes final and irrevocable if the promisee cannot resume their position.

Key Principle

The promisee need not have relied on the promise to their detriment; the question is whether it would be inequitable to allow the promisor to enforce their rights.

THE POST CHASER 1982

The buyers of palm oil re-asserted their contractual right to reject the oil two days after promising not to do so. The sellers subsequently sold the oil at a loss.

Held

It was not inequitable to allow the buyers to assert their strict contractual rights. [1982] 1 All E.R. 19.

Commentary

Robert Goff J. also found that the promisee had not suffered any prejudice or detriment. Would it have made a difference if they had?

Key Principle

The promise must have been given with full consent, not extracted by threats from the promisee.

D & C BUILDERS v REES 1966

The plaintiffs were a small firm of builders. They were owed £482 for some work which they had done for the defendant. After making several requests to be paid the plaintiffs were offered £300 in full satisfaction of the debt. The defendant stated that it was £300 or nothing. The plaintiffs reluctantly accepted £300 because they were close to bankruptcy. Subsequently, the plaintiffs sued for the balance.

Held

❖ (CA) The plaintiffs were not estopped from claiming the balance because they did not voluntarily accept the lesser sum. [1966] 2 W.L.R. 288.

Commentary

The defendant paid by cheque rather than by cash. The court rejected the defendant's argument that payment by cheque introduced a new element and amounted to consideration for the plaintiff's promise.

THINK POINT

In the *High Trees* case could the plaintiff have successfully claimed the full rent from 1941 onwards?

Could the doctrine of promissory estoppel have been applied in *Williams v Roffey*?

Intention to Create Legal Relations

The law recognises that flippant or boastful statements may be just hot air or "puffs" and are not intended to and should not give rise to legal liability. However, there is a narrow line between a cosmetic advertisement for a cream promising eternal youth and one stating that a particular ingredient of the cream will make brown age spots disappear if used for a month. A buyer may be able to sue if the cream does not do the latter, but is unlikely to be successful if the cream fails to deliver eternal youth.

Assuming that there is a valid agreement there is a rebuttable presumption that where parties enter into a commercial arrangement or agreement they intend it to be legally binding.

On the contrary in respect of domestic and social arrangement there is a rebuttable presumption that the parties do not intend the arrangement or agreement to be legally binding. The second presumption is now easier to rebut in an increasingly rights based and litigious environment than perhaps it was 50 years ago.

MERE PUFFS

Key Principle
Mere puffs are statements which are not intended to be taken seriously and which have no legal effect.

> LAMBERT V LEWIS 1981
> A manufacturer stated in promotional literature their product, a towing hitch, was "foolproof" and that it "required no maintenance".

Held
These statements were not promises which could give rise to a contract between the manufacturer and a dealer, because they were not intended to be terms of a contract. [1981] 1 All E.R. 1185.

In *Carlill v Carbolic Smoke Ball Co* (see Ch.2) D claimed unsuccessfully that
the advertisement was a mere puff.

PRESUMPTIONS

Commercial Agreements

Key Principle

The presumption that parties to a commercial agreement intend to create
legal relations can be rebutted by an "honour clause".

> ROSE AND FRANK CO V J R CROMPTON 1923
> In 1913 P & D agreed in writing that D would supply paper tissues to P.
> Prices were quoted for six-month periods. However a clause provided:
> "This arrangement is not entered into, nor is this memorandum written,
> as a formal or legal agreement, and shall not be subject to legal jur-
> isdiction in the law courts ... ". In 1919 D terminated the arrangement.
> P sued for breach of contract and non-delivery of goods.

Held

❖ (HL) The arrangement of 1913 was not a binding contract. Nevertheless,
each order accepted was a binding contract. There was no reason why even in
business matters, the parties should not intend to rely on an honourable
understanding, however they should express themselves so precisely that
outsiders have no difficulty in understanding what they mean. [1925] 2 A.C.
445.

Commentary

(1) HL adopted the reasoning of Atkin L.J. in CA.

(2) Similar provisions are found in football pool coupons (e.g. *Jones v Ver-
non's Pools* (1938)).

(3) In *Baird Textile Holdings v Marks & Spencer Plc* (see Ch.2) the Court of
Appeal considered that the lack of certainty as to the parties' obligations
confirmed the absence of any clear evidence of an intention to create legal
relations.

Key Principle

The onus of rebutting the presumption rests on the party claiming that it does not apply.

EDWARDS V SKYWAYS LTD 1964

D airline agreed with British Airline Pilots Association to pay "ex gratia" payments "approximating to" an easily calculated sum to pilots made redundant. P, a pilot, sued for such a payment under the agreement. D claimed that there was no intention to create legal relations and that the promise was too vague.

Held

❖ (QBD) It was a commercial agreement. Therefore the presumption was that there was an intention to create legal relations. The onus was on D to rebut the presumption which they had not done. The use of words "ex gratia" merely meant that D did not admit any pre-existing liability, rather than there was no legally binding agreement. [1964] 1 W.L.R. 349.

Key Principle

If there is any doubt about whether the presumption should apply then the court should use an objective test to decide the issue.

ESSO PETROLEUM LTD V COMMISSIONERS OF CUSTOMS AND EXCISE 1976

In 1970 garage owners selling Esso petrol offered a "free" World Cup coin with every four gallons of petrol bought. The coins were of little intrinsic value. P claimed that the coins were chargeable to tax because they were "produced in quantity for general sale."

Held

❖ (HL) There was no "sale" of the coins. On the question of whether the coins were the subject-matter of a contract between the garage owner and a motorist, three judges held that there was an intention to create legal relations because:
(1) Esso's advertising literature was produced for commercial advantage;
(2) it was generally undesirable to allow commercial promoters to claim that statements were mere puffs; and
(3) precedent supported this view. [1976] 1 W.L.R. 1.

Commentary

Two judges held that there was no intention to create legal relations because:

(1) it was not necessary for the success of the scheme for garage owners to subject themselves to contractual liability;

(2) the coins were trivial and of little value; and

(3) garage owners were unlikely to renege, because it was not in their interest to do so.

Key Principle

The court should look at the totality of the evidence in deciding whether the presumption is rebutted.

> J EVANS, ETC. V ANDREA MERZARIO LTD 1976
>
> D proposed that in future D would ship P's goods in containers. D's representative gave an oral assurance that the containers would be shipped below deck not on deck and on this basis P agreed to D's proposal. Subsequently, a container was placed on deck by mistake, and was not properly fastened down. The container fell overboard and was lost.

Held

❖ (CA) D's oral assurance even though it was made during a courtesy call was intended to be legally binding. It was clear from all the evidence that P only agreed to the use of containers because of D's promise that they would be carried below deck. [1976] 1 W.L.R. 1078.

DOMESTIC AND SOCIAL ARRANGEMENTS

Key Principle

There is a presumption that in arrangements between husband and wife the parties do not intend to create legal relations.

> BALFOUR V BALFOUR 1919
>
> D, the husband, worked in Ceylon. P, his wife, had to stay in England for medical reasons. D agreed to pay P £30 a month. P and D subsequently separated. P sued D for money owing under their agreement.

Held

❖ (CA) P could not recover the money because such arrangements are not usually intended to be legally binding. If they were it would result in a flood of litigation. Domestic affairs should be dealt with privately. [1919] 2 K.B. 571.

Key Principle

The presumption is rebutted where the parties have separated or are about to separate when they enter into the arrangement.

MERRITT V MERRITT 1970

D, the husband, left the matrimonial home, which was in the joint names of D and P his wife. Subsequently D and P agreed that D would pay P £40 a month, out of which P should pay the mortgage. D signed an agreement that in return for P paying off the mortgage, he would transfer his share of the property to P once the mortgage was paid off.

Held

❖ (CA) P could enforce D's promise. Looking at the situation objectively parties who are no longer happily married clearly intend any agreement to be legally binding. [1970] 1 W.L.R. 1211.

Key Principle

An agreement containing financial arrangements made between a spouse and a former spouse with the intention of creating legal relations between them and which is not contrary to public policy can be enforced in the civil courts.

SOULSBURY V SOULSBURY 2007

A divorced husband paid his former wife regular maintenance pay-ments. She later agreed that in return for not receiving these payments she would be left £100,000 by her former husband in his will. He subsequently became seriously ill and on the morning of his death he married the defendant with whom he had been living for about eight years. The legal effect of the marriage was to revoke the will. The second wife, acting on behalf of her husband's estate, refused to pay the money to the first wife.

Held

❖ (CA) The agreement between the husband and his former wife was a valid enforceable contract. The court rejected the argument that the agreement was void on the ground that it ousted the jurisdiction of the court. [2007] EWCA Civ 938.

Commentary

Ward L.J. reviewed the authorities including *Merritt v Merritt* (see above) and considered that where there are negotiations to compromise a claim in the family courts for ancillary matters there is a duty to seek the court's approval and such an agreement would not normally be enforceable as a contract. (See Ch.12. Void and Illegal Contracts).

Key Principle

Where a party gives up legal rights in reliance upon a domestic arrangement the arrangement is legally binding.

TANNER V TANNER 1975

P, a married man, promised D, a single woman, that she and their two young children would be able to live in a house purchased by P until the children left school. D, in reliance on this promise moved out of her rent-controlled flat. The relationship ended. P claimed possession of the house.

Held

❖ (CA) D had a contractual licence to live in the house purchased by P, so long as the children were of school age and accommodation was reasonably required for her and the children. [1975] 1 W.L.R. 1346.

Key Principle

There is a presumption that in family arrangements the parties do not intend to create legal relations.

JONES V PADAVATTON 1969

P, a mother, offered D, her daughter, an allowance if D gave up her job in the United States and came to London to study for the Bar. D did so. Two years later P bought a house in London for D to live in and so that D could have an income from renting out spare rooms. Three years later P claimed possession of the house. D had not yet passed the Bar exams.

Held

❖ (CA) The mother and daughter were very close when the agreement was made. There was no intention to create legal relations. The arrangement was vague and uncertain. [1969] 1 W.L.R. 328.

Commentary

(1) In a dissenting judgment Salmon L.J. held that there was an intention to be legally bound. However, the agreement was only to last until the studies were completed. The implication was that they would be completed within a reasonable time.

(2) In *Hardwick v Johnson* (1978) where a mother bought a house for her son and daughter-in-law, who paid her £7.00 a week towards the purchase price, the court held that the son and daughter-in-law had a contractual licence.

Key Principle

An arrangement between members of the same household can rebut the presumption.

SIMPKINS V PAYS 1955

Three ladies, two of whom were related, lived in the same house. Every week they jointly took part in a newspaper fashion competition. They agreed to pool their entries and to share any prize money. The entry was always sent in D's name.

Held

❖ (QBD) P could recover one third of the prize money from D. There was an intention to be legally bound. [1955] 1 W.L.R. 975.

Commentary

Presumably the same approach would be adopted whether or not they lived in the same house, and would also apply to lottery or bingo winnings. In *Wilson and Another v Burnett* (2007) (unreported) the two appellants and the defendant had purchased a bingo ticket book. W and B had gone to the bingo hall together. The two appellants submitted that there was an agreement between the three of them that they would share any winnings over £10. B argued that no such agreement had been reached. The judge was not satisfied that there was an intention to create legal relations. The Court of Appeal dismissed the appellants' appeal and noted that there was also doubt as to whether the parties had in fact entered into any prior agreement.

Why do you think Marks and Spencer did not enter into a legally binding agreement with Baird Textile Holdings?

What legal advice would you give to a friend who is going to drive to South Africa with another friend and wants their agreement to share equally the cost of the purchase of a car, petrol and maintenance costs to be legally enforceable?

Privity of Contract

5

INTRODUCTION

Privity of contract means that only the parties to the contract are bound by its terms and only the parties to the contract can benefit from its terms. In other words third parties normally may not do so even where the contract is for their benefit.

However, the rigour of the doctrine has been alleviated to some extent by case law, statutory exceptions and by the **Contracts (Rights of Third Parties) Act 1999**. Other areas of law such as the law of trusts and the law of tort may, where applicable, provide a third party to a contract with legal rights other than contractual rights. The development of the tort of negligence also allows third parties to a contract to have legal rights which exist independently of the contract, as illustrated by the case of *Donoghue v Stevenson* [1932] A.C. 562.

The law of agency, which is of great practical importance, allows a principal to enforce a contract made for their benefit by their agent with a third party. In effect there is a contract between the principal and the agent, and a second contract between the agent and the third party.

A party to a contract can assign the benefit of the contract to a third party, who in certain circumstances will be able to sue the other party to the contract.

Key Principle

Contractual rights and duties can only be conferred or imposed on the parties to a contract.

> TWEDDLE V ATKINSON 1861
>
> P's father and his prospective father-in-law promised to pay P a sum of money on his marriage. His father-in-law died. P sued D, his father-in-law's personal representative, for the money.

Held

P could not recover the money. He was neither a party to the contract nor had he provided consideration for his father-in-law's promise. He could not be sued on the contract, therefore he should not be able to sue on it. [1861–1873] All E.R. Rep. 369.

Commentary

(1) There is dispute as to whether the key principle is merely a consequence of the rule that consideration must move from the promisee (see Ch.3).

(2) This case is the starting point for the doctrine of privity. Older cases dating from the seventeenth century had considered that a third party could enforce a contract made for their benefit.

WHO ARE THE PARTIES TO THE CONTRACT?

Key Principle

A collateral contract may enable a person who is not a party to the main contract to enforce that contract.

> SHANKLIN PIER V DETEL PRODUCTS LTD 1951
>
> P employed X to paint P's pier and instructed X to buy and use paint made by D. P relied on a representation made by D that the paint would last seven years. In fact it only lasted three months. X purchased the paint from D.

Held

❖ (KBD) A collateral contract existed between P and D; its main term was that the paint would last seven years. [1951] 2 All E.R. 471.

Commentary

(1) It is usually straightforward to ascertain who are the parties to a contract. However, where agents are and/or companies are involved it can be problematic.

(2) Today the plaintiff could possibly sue in tort for negligent misstatement (*Hedley Byrne v Heller* (1964)).

THE ESSENTIALS OF THE DOCTRINE

Key Principle

Only a person who is a party to a contract can sue on it.

> **DUNLOP PNEUMATIC TYRE CO LTD V SELFRIDGE & CO LTD 1915**
> P sold tyres to X on the basis that X would not resell them at less than P's list price, and that if X resold the tyres to trade buyers X would extract a similar undertaking from them. X sold tyres to D who agreed to the undertakings, and also agreed to pay P £5 for each tyre sold in breach. D supplied two tyres in breach of the undertaking. P sued for two sums of £5 as liquidated damages. P was not a party to the contract between X and D.

Held

❖ (HL) P could not recover the liquidated damages. Lord Haldane stated: "In the law of England certain principles are fundamental. One is that only a person who is a party to a contract can sue on it." [1967] 3 W.L.R. 932.

Commentary

Lord Dunedin:

(1) Concentrated on whether the plaintiff had provided any consideration for the defendant's undertaking.

(2) Considered that it would be possible for the plaintiff to have framed the agreement so as to bind the defendant.

Key Principle

The remedy of specific performance may enable a contract to be enforced for the benefit of a third party.

> **BESWICK V BESWICK 1968**
> P's husband was a coal merchant. He transferred his business to D, his nephew, in return for which D agreed to pay P an annuity of £5 per week in the event of her husband's death. After P's husband died D paid P £5 once. P sued D for arrears and for specific performance of the agreement. P sued in two capacities: (1) as widow; (2) as administrator of her husband's estate.

❖ (HL) P could not succeed as "widow", because she was a third party to the agreement. However, P could succeed as "administrator" (i.e. in place of deceased husband). An order of specific performance was granted. [1967] 3 W.L.R. 932.

Commentary ....

(1) P as "administrator" could not recover damages from D because under the agreement the money was not payable to P as administrator, and the estate had suffered no loss so only nominal damages would be recoverable.

(2) Lord Reid considered that P's inability to recover the money as "widow" could mean that the law is sadly deficient.

DAMAGES FOR THIRD PARTY'S LOSSES

Key Principle ....

As a general rule where X makes a contract with Y for the benefit of Z then X cannot recover damages for Z's losses.

> WOODAR INVESTMENT DEVELOPMENT LTD v WIMPEY CONSTRUCTION (U.K.) LTD 1980
> D agreed to buy land from P. Subsequently D purported to cancel the agreement. The main question was whether D was entitled to do so. If they were not then P could claim damages. Part of the purchase price would have been paid to X, a third party. Could P recover damages on behalf of X?

Held ....

❖ (HL) D was entitled to terminate the agreement. Even if they had not been so entitled, P could not have recovered damages on behalf of X. [1980] 1 W.L.R. 277.

Key Principle ....

In certain types of contract where X makes a contract with Y for the benefit of Z then X can recover damages for Z's losses.

JACKSON V HORIZON HOLIDAYS 1975

P booked a holiday in Sri Lanka for himself, his wife and his two children. The accommodation and facilities did not correspond with what had been promised by D.

Held

P could recover damages for the whole family's disappointment and inconvenience as well as for his own. [1975] 1 W.L.R. 1468.

Commentary

This principle has been restricted to holiday contracts and similar social activities undertaken by a group: *Woodar Investment Ltd v Wimpey* (1980) (see above).

Key Principle

Where there is a contract for a large development of property which to both parties' knowledge is going to be occupied, etc., by a third party then the assignor can recover damages for the third party's losses.

LINDEN GARDENS TRUST V LENESTA SLUDGE DISPOSALS 1993
ST MARTIN'S PROPERTY CORPN LTD V SIR ROBERT MCALPINE & SONS LTD 1993

These two cases were heard together.

In Linden Gardens, X, a lessee, entered into two contracts with D for the removal of asbestos from the leased building. Soon after the contracts had been performed X assigned the lease to P, and assigned their rights under the two contracts. P paid the market price for the lease as it was thought, wrongly in fact, that all the asbestos had been removed. X suffered no loss, and was removed as a party to the proceedings. In St Martin's, P1 assigned at full value a building development to P2, and also assigned the benefit of the building contract. The breach of the building contract had not yet occurred. In both cases there were express prohibitions against the assignment of the benefit of the contracts without both parties' consent. This consent was not obtained. P sued D for breaches of the assigned contracts.

Held

❖ (HL) The contractual prohibitions against assignment were valid. Therefore in the Linden Gardens case P, the assignee, could not sue on the contract. However, in the St Martin's case because the assignor P1 was a party to the claim and the nature of the contract was different, i.e. a large property development intended for third party occupation, P1 would be able to recover damages from D for the loss suffered by P2. [1993] 3 W.L.R. 408.

Commentary

The key principle derives from the reasoning of the majority of their Lordships, which is described as "the narrower ground". Lord Griffiths in the St Martin's case reached his decision on what has become known as "the broader ground". He held that the employer under a building contract (P1) may in principle recover substantial damages from a building contractor (D), because he has not received the performance which he was entitled to receive from the contractor under the contract. The implications of "the broader approach" were examined in detail in *Alfred McAlpine Construction Ltd v Panatown Ltd* [2001] A.C. 518 (see below).

Key Principle

Where there is a contract for the development of property which is entered into for the benefit of a third party, who was subsequently assigned the benefit of the contract, then the assignee can recover damages for losses caused by a breach of the contract.

DARLINGTON BOROUGH COUNCIL V WILTSHIER NORTHERN LTD 1995

D a building contractor entered into a contract with X, a finance company, to build a leisure centre for and on land owned by P. X then assigned all its rights under the building contract to P. P claimed that there were serious defects in the leisure centre due to defective workmanship by D.

Held

❖ (CA) P was entitled to recover damages for defects in the performance of the contract. X could not enforce the contract. The established doctrine deprived P of a remedy and allowed the contract-breaker to go scot-free. However, the present case was covered by an exception to the general rule that a plaintiff could only recover damages for his own loss. [1995] 1 W.L.R. 68.

Commentary

(1) Steyn L.J. considered that there was no doctrinal, logical or policy reason why the law should deny effectiveness to a contract for the benefit of a third party where that was the expressed intention of the parties.

Key Principle

Where substantial damages could have been claimed by the assignor, if there had been no assignment and the property had not been transferred to the assignee, an assignee can recover the same damages as the assignor could have recovered.

> TECHNOTRADE LTD V LARKSTORE LTD 2006
>
> X were owners of land on a sloping site on which they wished to build houses. In 1998 X entered into a contract with the defendants (T), whereby T produced a site investigation report, as required by the planning consent. In 1999 X sold the land to the claimants (L) with the benefit of full planning consents and including all soil investigation information. L used the report without seeking T's consent and entered into a design and build contract with Y. In 2001, while building work was being undertaken by Y, a landslip occurred which caused damage to five houses which had been built during the first phase of the development. In 2004 X assigned to L the right to T's report together with the right to sue T in respect of breaches by T of its duties and obligations. Y meanwhile had become insolvent. L relied on the assignment as the basis of its claim against T for damages for breach of contract.

Held

❖ (CA) L was entitled to claim damages from T for the losses it suffered as a consequence of any breach of contract by T in the preparation of the site investigation report. [2006] 1 W.L.R. 2926.

Commentary

(1) The contractual cause of action occurred in 1998, but no loss was suffered at that date. The damage occurred in 2001 but X was no longer the owner of the land.

(2) T argued unsuccessfully that L could only recover damages for the loss incurred by X in 2004, the date of the assignment of the cause of action, because L could not acquire from X by assignment any greater right than X had against T. Such loss was nominal because at that date X was not the owner of the land and would not be liable for any damage caused to the five houses.

(3) One difference between this case and the *Linden Gardens* and *St Martin's*

cases was that the damage occurred after the transfer of the ownership of the site from X to L but before the assignment of the cause of action.

Key Principle

A party to a contract (P), for the development of property for the benefit of a third party (X), may not recover damages from the other party to the contract (M) for losses suffered by a third party (X) where the other party (M) has entered into a separate duty of care deed with the third party.

> ### ALFRED MCALPINE CONSTRUCTION LTD V PANATOWN LTD 2001
>
> M agreed with P to construct a building and a car park on land owned by X, the third party, which was part of the same group of companies as P. M also entered into a duty of care deed with X, whereby X had a direct remedy against M, for failure to exercise reasonable care and skill in the performance of the contract with P. Serious defects were found in the building constructed by M, and X suffered financial loss as a consequence of this breach of contract by M. P suffered no loss but, as a party to the contract with M, sought to recover from M the loss suffered by X.

Held

❖ (HL) P could not recover damages from M for the loss suffered by X. P could only recover damages for loss that he himself has suffered. This case did not fall within the building contracts exception. The duty of care deed was part of a package of arrangements agreed upon by the parties to the main building contract. This package reflected the intention of all the parties that the third party should have a direct cause of action which should exclude any substantial claim by the employer P. [2001] 1 A.C. 518.

Commentary

(1) Lords Clyde, Jauncey and Browne-Wilkinson allowed the appeal by M. Lord Clyde, however, considered that the law should generally permit a contracting party to recover damages for the actual loss that he and a third party has suffered. Lord Browne-Wilkinson considered that allowing P to recover for loss suffered by X without P being liable to account to X for the damages recovered would be "another piece of legal nonsense".

(2) The legal position in the building cases is potentially affected by the Contracts (Rights of Third Parties) Act 1999. The Act did not apply to these cases because the facts arose before the Act came into force. However, in practice collateral warranties appear to be still used in most property

development and construction contracts in preference to relying on the 1999 Act.

CONTRACTS (RIGHTS OF THIRD PARTIES) ACT 1999

Key Principle

There is a rebuttable presumption that a third party may enforce a term in a contract which confers a benefit on him

> NISSHIN SHIPPING CO LTD V CLEAVES & COMPANY LTD AND OTHERS 2004
> C negotiated time charters (contracts for the hire of a ship for a fixed period) on behalf of N ship owners. The parties to each contract were N and a charterer. Each contract provided for payment of commission to C, a third party, and contained an arbitration clause. N refused to pay C the commission due. C referred the dispute to arbitration.

Held

❖ (QBD) The effect of the commission clause was to confer a benefit on C. The contract left no doubt either as to the identity of the third party to whom commission was to be made or as to the amount to be paid. The contracts between N and the charterers did not rebut the statutory presumption that C should be able to directly enforce the commission clause by arbitration, in the same way as the parties to the contract.

Commentary

(1) This is thought to be the first time that the **1999 Act** has been considered by a court.

(2) Section 1 (1)(a) provides that a third party may in his own right enforce a term of the contract if the contract expressly provides that he may.

(3) Section 1(1)(b) provides that a person who is not a party to a contract (a "third party") may in his own right enforce a term of the contract if subject to subsection (2) the term purports to confer a benefit on him.

(4) Section 1(2) provides that s.1(1) (b) does not apply where it appears that the parties did not intend the contract to be enforceable by the third party.

Key Principle

Section 1 (3) requires a third party to be expressly identified in the contract. It does not allow identification by a process of construction or implication.

The claimants entered into a contract with X Ltd for the refurbishment of two bathrooms. The work was not completed satisfactorily. The defendant partnership purchased X Ltd on April 1, 2003 and as part of the transfer agreement agreed to pay 'any liabilities properly incurred by the company as at March 31 2003'. The Court of Appeal considered whether the claimants were third parties who were entitled to enforce the transfer agreement under the **1999 Act** and recover damages from the defendants for breach of contract.

Held

❖ (CA) The relevant term of the transfer agreement did not identify any third party or class of third parties. Therefore the claimants did not come within s.1(3) of the **1999 Act** and could not bring a claim for breach of contract against the defendant. [2006] EWCA Civ 1533.

Commentary

Section 1 (3) provides that:
The third party must be expressly identified in the contract by name, as a member of a class or as answering a particular description, but need not be in existence when the contract is entered into.

EXCLUSION CLAUSES AND THIRD PARTIES

Key Principle

A third party to a contract can rely on an exclusion clause in a contract made between A and B which protects third parties where A purports to act as agent for the third party.

NEW ZEALAND SHIPPING COMPANY LTD V SATTERTHWAITE & CO LTD, THE EURYMEDON 1974

A, who was sending machinery to P in New Zealand by ship, entered into a transportation contract with B the carrier. D, stevedores in New Zealand, agreed with B to unload the goods on arrival. D negligently unloaded and damaged the machinery. A's rights under the contract having been transferred to P, P sued D. D claimed that they were entitled to the protection of the exclusion clause in the contract between A and B. The complex clause stated that no servant or agent (including any independent contractor (D), employed by the Carrier) of the Carrier (B), shall be under any liability for any loss or damages caused by any negligence on his part while acting in connection with the employment, and that every exclusion clause which protected the Carrier (B) would also protect the carrier's servants and agents (D) on whose behalf the Carrier (B) acted as agent so that D would be treated as a party to the contract between A and B.

Held

❖ (JCPC) D was protected by the exclusion clause and was not liable to P. [1974] 2 W.L.R. 865.

Commentary

(1) The exclusion clause amounted to a unilateral offer by A that anyone who was engaged by B to perform any of B's obligations under the contract with A, would be regarded as a party to that contract and would be able to benefit from the exclusion clause. D accepted that offer by unloading the goods, which was also the consideration for A's promise.

(2) The decision reflected commercial realities.

Key Principle

A third party to a contract between A and B can be bound by an exclusion clause in that contract where the third party impliedly consents to A making a contract with B on the terms normally current in the trade.

MORRIS v C.W. MARTIN AND SONS LTD 1965
P sent her mink stole to a furrier (F) for cleaning. F told her he would arrange for the fur to be cleaned by D. F contracted with D (as principal not as P's agent). One of D's employees stole the fur. D's contract conditions excluded D from liability for loss or damage to the goods during processing. P sued D.

Held

❖ (CA) P agreed that F should send her fur to D, and so consented to the exclusion clause. [1965] 3 W.L.R. 276.

Commentary

However CA also held that the wording of the exclusion clause did not apply to loss or damage which occurred before or after processing. Therefore the wording of the clause did not cover P's actual loss. (see Ch.8).

Formalities and Capacity

6

INTRODUCTION

Formalities

An oral agreement can be binding so long as there is evidence as to what the parties agreed, for example a witness or a written note made by one of the parties at the time. In most cases a written or partly written and partly oral agreement is also binding. These examples are known as simple contracts. They require an offer, an acceptance and consideration to be enforceable. A promise to give someone money is only enforceable if the promise is contained in a deed.

In practice most contract terms are wholly or partly in writing. Often such contracts are in a standard form, which may mean that one party, for example the purchaser of a package holiday, has little or no influence over the contract terms. This can also lead to a "battle of the forms" where both parties have their own standard form contract (see Ch 2).

Legislation also requires that certain contracts must be in writing. These include a contract for the sale or other disposition of an interest in land, and certain consumer credit agreements. Guarantees must be evidenced in writing. The effect of failure to comply with these formal requirements normally makes the contract unenforceable.

Capacity

An adult person in possession of their mental faculties has the legal capacity to enter into a contract. Statutory corporations, such as local authorities, only have the legal capacity to enter into contracts in accordance with the powers granted to them under statute. If they do not have the legal authority to enter the contract, the contract is void. Any money paid to them under the contract is recoverable in restitution. Minors, that is children and young people under the age of 18, have the legal capacity to enter certain types of contract.

Key Principle

An oral contract is legally enforceable except where formalities are required.

P agreed to purchase Nigerian gum arabic from D. Agreement was reached in telephone conversations made on October 17 and 19, 1994. D claimed that the terms of the contract were contained in a written contract dated October 21, 1994. A dispute arose as to the quality of the goods. P claimed that they were not bound to comply with the dispute procedures set out in the written contract.

Held

❖ (QBD) The contract was made orally on the telephone. It was final and binding. [1996] 2 Lloyd's Rep. 437.

FORMALITIES

The Sale or Disposition of an Interest in Land

Key Principle
There must be an "exchange of contracts" or one document recording the agreement.

COMMISSION FOR THE NEW TOWNS V COOPER (GREAT BRITAIN) LTD 1995
P and D agreed in a series of letters that D could have an option to require P to take an assignment of a lease from D.

Held

❖ (CA) An offer and acceptance in the course of correspondence does not satisfy the requirements of s.2 of the Law of Property (Miscellaneous Provisions) Act 1989. [1995] 2 W.L.R. 677.

Key Principle
The grant of an option must be signed by both parties to the contract.

SPIRO V GLENCROWN PROPERTIES LTD 1991
The plaintiff owner of land granted an option to purchase the property to the defendant. The defendant exercised the option but failed to complete the purchase. Both parties signed the grant of the option, but only the purchaser signed the exercise of the option.

Held

❖ (ChD) The prime purpose of s.2 of the **Law of Property (Miscellaneous Provisions) Act 1989** was to record the consent of the parties. The parties consented when the option was granted, and since both parties signed this document, the requirements of s.2 were satisfied and there was a valid contract. [1991] 2 W.L.R. 931.

Commentary

Where the subject-matter of the contract is not land, the grant of an option is normally treated as an irrevocable offer which is accepted when the option is exercised. Only then does a valid contract come into effect.

Key Principle

The interpretation of the word "signed" in s.2 of the new Act should not be encumbered with the ancient baggage of case law on earlier legislation.

> FIRSTPOST HOMES LTD V JOHNSON 1995
>
> The owner of land signed a letter and a plan which together set out her agreement to sell the land to the plaintiff. A director of the plaintiff company signed the plan, and the plaintiff's name was typed on the letter as the addressee.

Held

❖ (CA) The letter and not the plan was the document which had to be signed to satisfy the requirements of s.2(3). "Signed" meant a person writing their name with their own hand, it did not include the printing or typing of a name. [1995] 4 All E.R. 355.

Commentary

(1) The Court of Appeal considered that the **1989 Act** had a different philosophy to the Statute of Frauds and s.40 of the Law of Property Act 1925. Parliament intended that questions as to whether there was a contract and what were its terms, should be answered by looking at a single document.

(2) On electronic signatures see *Metha v J Pereira Fernandes S.A* [2006] EWHC 813 (below)

Key Principle

Where due to a drafting error the terms of the contract are contained in more than one document, then the court may order rectification of the contract.

Wright v Robert Leonard (Developments) Ltd 1994

The plaintiff agreed to buy a show flat together with its fixtures and fittings from the defendant. The exchange of contracts did not take place by the agreed date, and unknown to the plaintiff the defendants removed the furniture before the eventual exchange.

Held

❖ (CA) There was a single contract and all the terms had to be in writing to satisfy s.2, even those relating to the furniture. The contract should be rectified, so that the reference to furniture was included in the written document, and the plaintiff could recover damages from the defendant for breach of contract. [1994] N.P.C. 49.

Key Principle

Where the terms of an agreement are contained in more than one document, then the court may hold that there is a main contract which is subject to s.2 and a collateral contract which is not.

Record v Bell 1991

The plaintiff vendor wished to exchange contracts but the relevant Land Registry documents were not yet available. So, in a letter, he gave a warranty as to his title to the defendant purchaser, who then agreed to the exchange of contracts, but subsequently refused to complete the purchase.

Held

❖ (Ch D) The written warranty was an independent contract collateral to the main contract. It was not a contract for the sale of land and was not subject to s.2. The main contract was subject to and complied with s.2. Therefore both contracts were enforceable. [1991] 1 W.L.R. 853.

Key Principle

The formalities required by s.2 also apply to a variation of a term of a contract.

McCausland v Duncan Lawrie Ltd 1996

D agreed to sell a property to P. The contract complied with the requirements of s.2, but the date for completion of the purchase was subsequently changed by mutual consent evidenced in correspondence.

Held

❖ (CA) The variation was not signed by both parties and therefore did not comply with s.2. [1996] 4 All E.R. 995.

Commentary

Such a variation would have been valid under the previous legislation, but the court re-affirmed that the **1989 Act** was intended to effect a major change in the law.

Key Principle

Where a supposed bargain has been fully performed by one side and it would be inequitable to disregard the claimant's expectations the exception in s.2(5) applies.

YAXLEY V GOTT 2001

In 1991 G claimed to have purchased a house. Y entered into an oral agreement with G whereby Y would convert the house into flats and manage the property in return for becoming the owner of the ground floor flat. In fact the house was purchased by G's son. In 1995 G's son excluded Y from the property.

Held

❖ (CA) Y was entitled to a long leasehold interest under a constructive trust. [2000] Ch. 162.

Commentary

(1) Under the **Law of Property (Miscellaneous Provisions) Act 1989**, s.2(5) a constructive trust is an exception to the normal requirement that such a contract should be in writing.

(2) Beldam L.J. considered that s.2(5) also effectively excluded, from the operation of s.2, cases in which an interest in land was claimed by relying on proprietary estoppel. Robert Walker L.J. agreed that the two areas overlap, for example, in the area of a joint enterprise for the acquisition of land.

(3) However in *Yeoman's Row Management Ltd v Cobbe* [2008] UKHL 55, Lord Scott of Foscote considered that proprietary estoppel did not come within the s.2(5) exception.

GUARANTEES

An oral contract of guarantee recorded in a note or memorandum signed by the party to be charged is enforceable.

> ELPIS MARITIME CO V MARTI CHARTERING CO (THE MARIA D) 1991
> The plaintiff owners chartered a ship to the charterers. The defendants were brokers for the charterers. Telex and telephone negotiations took place between brokers for both parties, and the agreement was recorded in a written charterparty, which included a guarantee by the defendants. Subsequently, the plaintiffs were entitled to be paid compensation by the charterers under the terms of the charterparty. The money was not paid and the plaintiffs sought to recover it from the defendants, who claimed that the guarantee was unenforceable because it did not comply with the requirements of s.4 of the **Statute of Frauds 1677.**

Held

❖ (HL) The contract of guarantee was evidenced in writing as required by s.4 and was enforceable. There was either an oral agreement recorded in the written charterparty which was signed by the defendants, or alternatively the charterparty alone was a sufficient note or memorandum. [1991] 3 W.L.R. 330.

Commentary

(1) Section 4 only applies to a contract of guarantee where A promises B that if C does not discharge his liability to B, then A will do so. It does not apply to a manufacturer's guarantee of their product or to an indemnity.

(2) In *Metha v J Pereira Fernandes S.A* [2006] EWHC 813 (Ch.) the High Court held that the sender's e-mail address in the message heading did not amount to a signature. However, where the sender's name or signature of any sort appears in the body of the e-mail message this is likely to amount to a signature for the purposes of s.4. The court held that the e-mail in the case was capable of being a sufficient note or memorandum for the purposes of s.4 because it was in writing and the offer had been orally accepted.

REGULATED CONSUMER CREDIT AND CONSUMER HIRE AGREEMENTS

Key Principle

Where a regulated consumer credit agreement is not properly executed, the agreement may not be enforceable by the creditor.

DIMOND V LOVELL 2000

D's car was damaged in a road accident. D hired a replacement car from P, while her car was being repaired. P was a company which hired cars to drivers whose cars had been damaged in accidents caused by another's fault. D did not pay for the hire of the car because part of the agreement was that P would recover the cost of hire from the party at fault.

Held

❖ (HL) The agreement between P and D for the hire of the car was a regulated consumer credit agreement under the Consumer Credit Act 1974, s.65(1). The agreement was unenforceable because it did not contain a term stating the amount of credit provided to D in accordance with regulations made under s.61(1). [2000] 2 All E.R. 897.

Key Principle

Where such an agreement is not properly executed and the consumer suffers prejudice then the court may compensate the consumer.

NATIONAL GUARDIAN MORTGAGE CORP. V WILKES 1993

The plaintiff creditor sued the defendant debtor who had failed to keep up repayments on a loan agreement made with the plaintiff. The defendant's house was security for the loan, but the plaintiff in breach of **Consumer Credit Act 1974**, ss.58(1) and 62(2) had failed to give the defendant an advance copy of the unexecuted loan agreement. This deprived her of the seven-day "consideration period" which she may have used to obtain a loan at a lower rate of interest. The county court judge awarded the defendant compensation under s.127 equivalent to 40 per cent of the interest claimed by the plaintiff.

Held

❖ (CA) The court has a wide discretion and when enforcing an agreement it could compensate the defendant for the prejudice suffered by the defendant and impose such a condition on the creditor under s.136. [1993] C.C.L.R. 1.

Key principle

The parties' rights and obligations continue to exist even if the agreement is temporarily unenforceable by the creditor.

> MCGUFFICK V THE ROYAL BANK OF SCOTLAND PLC 2009
> The claimant took out a loan with the bank, which was repayable over five years in monthly instalments. The claimant fell behind with the repayments and eventually the bank informed the claimant that this would be referred to a credit reference agency. The bank had not provided the claimant with a signed statement of account as required by s.77(1) **Consumer Credit Act 1974.**

Held

❖ (QBD) The failure by the bank to provide the claimant debtor with a signed statement of account, as required by s.77(1), made the consumer credit agreement temporarily unenforceable until that failure was remedied. Reference to a credit reference agency did not amount to "enforcement" of the agreement. [2009] EWHC 2386.

Commentary

Wilson v First County Trust Limited (No 2) [2003] 3 W.L.R. 568 (see below) was distinguished.

Key Principle

Primary legislation which makes a consumer credit agreement unenforceable is not incompatible with the **Human Rights Act 1998.**

> WILSON V FIRST COUNTY LTD (NO 2) 2003
> W borrowed money from FCL and provided her car as security. The amount of credit was mis-stated in the agreement. Therefore the agreement was not a properly executed regulated agreement, and could only be enforced against the debtor on the order of the court. However, s.127(3) **Consumer Credit Act 1974** states that the court has no power to make an enforcement order where, as in this case, there is

no document signed by the debtor containing all the prescribed terms. The CA held that s.127(3) was incompatible with the **HRA 1998**.

Held

❖ (HL) The agreement was entered into before the **1998 Act** came into force. The **1998 Act** did not have retrospective effect. Therefore the court had no jurisdiction to make a declaration of incompatibility. The agreement was unenforceable. W was entitled to keep the loan, pay no interest and recover her car. [2003] 3 W.L.R. 568.

Commentary

(1) Their Lordships considered that s.127(3) was not incompatible with art.6 (right to a fair and public hearing by an independent and impartial tribunal) because it did not bar access to the court.

(2) Four of their Lordships considered that contractual rights were 'possessions' within the meaning of art.1 of protocol 1 (peaceful enjoyment of possessions).

(3) Three of their Lordships considered that Parliament was entitled to decide the appropriate way of protecting borrowers, and that s.127(3) was a proportionate means of achieving the legitimate aim of consumer protection.

(4) In *McGuffick v The Royal Bank of Scotland plc* [2009] EWHC 2386 Flaux J., noted the comments of Lawrence Collins L.J. in *Conister Trust v John Hardman & Co* [2008] EWCA Civ 841 that their Lordships in *Wilson* were divided in their reasoning as to why s.127(3) was not incompatible with art.1 of the First Protocol. Flaux J. distinguished *Wilson*. Firstly, because the judgments in *Wilson* "do not all speak with one voice". Secondly, because their Lordships were concerned with enforceability in a human rights context as opposed to a contractual context. Thirdly, their Lordships were not concerned with redeemable unenforceability.

STANDARD FORM CONTRACTS

Key Principle

The courts recognise that standard form contracts can be one-sided but have not developed specific rules to regulate their validity.

A. SCHROEDER MUSIC PUBLISHING CO LTD V MACAULAY 1974

Macaulay, a song-writer entered into a standard form exclusive services contract with the music publishers. (See Ch.12 for detailed facts.)

Held

❖ (HL) The contract was void and in restraint of trade. [1974] 1 W.L.R. 1308.

Commentary

(1) Lord Diplock identified two types of standard form contract: the first, which are normally fair, are of ancient origin such as bills of lading, and are the result of negotiation between parties of equal bargaining power; and the second, which are of comparatively modern origin, occur where one party is in a superior bargaining position and is able to impose their terms on the weaker party.

(2) Standard form contracts are very common in practice. Although not specifically regulated their terms may be subject to common law principles on restraint of trade, penalty clauses, and incorporation of terms, as well as legislative provisions, for example, the Unfair Contract Terms Act 1977 and the Unfair Terms in Consumer Contracts Regulations 1999.

CAPACITY

Key Principle

The contractual capacity of a corporation created by statute is subject to the ultra vires doctrine.

> HAZELL V HAMMERSMITH AND FULHAM LONDON BOROUGH COUNCIL 1991
> The council entered into a number of "swap agreements" between 1987 and 1989. In essence these agreements enabled the council to gamble on interest rate changes in the money market. If the rates went down the council would make money, but if they went up they would incur losses. The legality of these agreements was questioned by the district auditor when it became apparent that the council was going to incur heavy losses.

Held

❖ (HL) The agreements were void. The council's contractual capacity was limited to the powers conferred on it by statute. The agreements were not incidental to the council's power to borrow money under Local Government Act 1972, s.111. [1991] 2 W.L.R. 372.

Commentary

(1) This decision led to a number of claims based on the law of restitution (see Ch.1). Banks claimed the right to retain money held for, or recover

payments from, local authorities relating to these agreements. In *West-deutsche Landesbank Girozentrale v Islington London Borough Council* [1996] 2 W.L.R. 802, the House of Lords confirmed that the bank was entitled to recover payments made to the local authority under the swap agreements.

(2) In *Haugesund Kommune v Depfa ACS Bank* [2010] 1 C.L.C. 770 the CA held that two Norwegian municipalities did not have the legal capacity to enter into swap agreements with an Irish bank, Depfa, whereby they raised money which was used to make disastrous investments. There was no longer any general public policy ground which prevented the bank from recovering the money that it paid to the municipalities.

(3) A bank can recover the payment even where it brings its claim outside the normal limitation period (six years) if it can establish that the payment was made under a mistake of law: *Kleinwort Benson Ltd v Lincoln City Council* [1998] 3 W.L.R. 1095 (HL).

(4) The ultra vires doctrine does not apply to corporations created by Royal Charter. Nor does it any longer usually affect the contractual capacity of companies created under the Companies Act 1985.

Key Principle

A minor is bound to pay for necessaries supplied to them.

> NASH V INMAN 1908
>
> A Savile Row tailor supplied 11 fancy waistcoats and other items of clothing to a Cambridge undergraduate at a cost of £123.

Held

❖ (CA) The tailor could not recover the money because the clothes were not "necessaries", as the undergraduate already had an ample supply of clothes. [1908] 2 K.B. 1.

Commentary

(1) A "minor" is any person aged less than 18 years old. Until 1969 a "minor" or "infant" was any person aged less than 21 years.

(2) The Sale of Goods Act 1979, s.3 defines necessaries as goods which are suitable to the condition in life of the minor and to his actual requirements at the time of sale and delivery. Section 3 also provides that a minor need only pay a reasonable price for the necessaries, which may not be the contract price. Necessaries can include services such as education.

Key Principle

A minor is bound by a service contract which is for their benefit.

CHAPLIN V LESLIE FREWIN (PUBLISHERS) LTD 1966

A publisher agreed to publish a minor's autobiography which was to be written by journalists using information provided by the plaintiff minor and his adult wife. The plaintiffs approved the final proofs and received advance royalties from the defendants. Before publication the plaintiffs claimed that the book was libellous and inaccurate, and applied for an injunction to prevent its publication.

Held

❖ (CA) The contract enabled the minor to become an author and so was on the whole for his benefit. An injunction would not be granted. [1966] 2 W.L.R. 40.

Commentary

(1) A minor is not bound by all beneficial contracts, only by an employment or similar contract. In *Proform Sports Management Ltd v Proactive Sports Management Ltd and Another* [2007] 1 All E.R. 542 the High Court decided that a representation agreement entered into by the footballer Wayne Rooney, when he was 15 years old, was a voidable contract. Although the contract was beneficial it was not analogous to a contract of service, apprenticeship or education. Wayne Rooney's training contract with Everton Football Club, also made when he was a minor, was analogous to such a contract and was binding on him.

(2) See also *Proactive Sports Management Ltd v Rooney* 2010 (Ch.12).

Key Principle

Where a minor agrees to buy shares in a company then the contract is voidable at the minor's option.

STEINBERG V SCALA (LEEDS) LTD 1923

A minor applied and partly paid for shares in a company. Eighteen months after the company allotted her the shares she rescinded the contract, and sued to recover the money she paid to the company.

Held

❖ (CA) She was entitled to rescind the contract and was not liable to make any further payments for the shares. However, she was not entitled to recover the money paid because there had not been a total failure of consideration as she had been allotted the shares. [1923] 2 Ch. 452.

Commentary

(1) Restitution (see Ch.1) was the basis of her claim to recover the money paid.

(2) The company is bound by the contract. The minor is also bound, but has the option of rescinding a voidable contract during their minority or within a reasonable time of reaching the age of 18.

(3) In addition to a contract to buy shares in a company there are three other types of contract which are voidable at the minor's option: partnership agreements; contracts concerning land, e.g. leases; and marriage settlements.

(4) Contracts entered into by minors, other than contracts for necessaries, beneficial service contracts and voidable contracts, are not binding on the minor, although they may be binding on the other party. See e.g. the Minors' Contracts Act 1987 on the rights of the other party.

THINK POINT

When the requirements of s.2(1) of the **Law of Property (Miscellaneous Provisions) Act 1989** appear not to be satisfied, what options are open to the court to find that the agreement is valid?

Compare the decision of the High Court in *Proform Sports Management Ltd v Proactive Sports Management Ltd* 2007 with the decision of the Court of Appeal in *Proactive Sports Management Ltd v Rooney* 2010 (Ch.12).

Terms of the Contract

7

INTRODUCTION

The first question that has to be asked is whether a particular written or oral statement is a term of the contract or just a pre-contractual representation. If it is the latter there will be no liability if it is not complied with unless it amounts to a misrepresentation (see Ch.9) or a collateral contract.

The terms of the contract are classified as express terms or implied terms. In respect of written express terms the major issue coming before the courts is how a particular term should be interpreted and what evidence may be used to assist the court in its interpretation. Interpretation is necessary where there is an express term but its meaning is ambiguous or inconsistent. Where a mistake has clearly been made in drafting a document the court will not interpret the term in a way that does not make commercial sense.

There are four types of implied term: implied in fact, implied in law, implied by statute and implied by custom. The first two are more common. One party will state that a term should be implied because the contract does not expressly provide for what is to happen when some event occurs.The courts are unwilling to rewrite a contract and quite often such a claim is rejected so that the loss lies where it falls.

REPRESENTATIONS AND TERMS

Key Principle

A term is not a statement which is merely an incident in preliminary negotiations; it must be understood and intended by both parties to be a term of the contract.

BANNERMAN V WHITE 1861

D buyer was negotiating the purchase of hops from P seller. D asked P if any sulphur had been used in the treatment of the hops, adding that if it had, he would not even bother to ask the price. P said that no sulphur had been used. The negotiations led to a sale. Later D discovered that sulphur was used in five out of the 300 acres. D refused to go ahead with the contract. P sued D for the price.

Held

The statement "absence of sulphur" was a term of the contract, not a representation. (1861) 4 L.T. 740.

Commentary

A representation can also be a term of the contract, e.g. *Harlingdon & Leinster Enterprises Ltd v Christopher Hull Fine Art Ltd* (1990) (see below).

Key Principle

Where the interval between the making of the statement and entering into the contract is well marked the statement is likely to be a representation.

> ROUTLEDGE V McKAY 1954
> P and D were discussing P's purchase of D's motorcycle. On October 23, D said, relying on the log book, that it was a 1942 model. On October 30, P and D entered into a written contract of sale which did not refer to the date of the model. In fact it was a 1930 model. P claimed damages for breach of contract.

Held

❖ (CA) P could not recover damages for breach of contract. The date of the model was not a term of the contract because of the interval between the negotiations and the contract. [1954] 1 W.L.R. 615.

Commentary

(1) If, as in this case, an oral statement is not included in the written contract, this indicates that the statement is probably not intended to be a contractual term.

(2) Prior to the Misrepresentation Act 1967 a person in P's position would not have been able to recover damages for misrepresentation (see Ch.9) unless the misrepresentation was made fraudulently.

Key Principle

If the person who makes the statement has special knowledge or skill compared to the other party, then it is more likely that the statement is a term than a representation.

> **DICK BENTLEY PRODUCTIONS LTD V HAROLD SMITH (MOTORS) LTD 1965**
> D, car dealers, sold a car to P, a private purchaser. D told P that the car had only done 20,000 miles since the engine and gearbox had been replaced. This was not correct. D was found to have been negligent. There was no apparent interval between D's statement and the contract. The contract was not reduced to writing.

Held

❖ (CA) D was liable for breach of contract because the statement was a term of the contract. [1965] 1 W.L.R. 623.

Commentary

The court distinguished this case from *Oscar Chess v Williams* [1957] 1 W.L.R. 370, where the facts were similar except that D was a private vendor and P were car dealers. P had special skill and knowledge which they could have used to discover the age of car. In addition D was not negligent. The statement was held to be a representation not a term of the contract.

COLLATERAL CONTRACTS

Key Principle

Where A gives an undertaking to B who in reliance on that statement enters into a contract with A, then the undertaking can amount to a collateral contract.

> **CITY AND WESTMINSTER PROPERTIES (1934) LTD V MUDD 1958**
> D was a tenant of P's shop for six years. P allowed D to sleep in the shop, but did not realise that D lived in the basement. P drafted a new lease which contained a clause that in effect prohibited use of the premises other than for trade purposes. P's agent orally assured D that if he accepted the new lease D could still sleep on the premises, so D signed the lease. Subsequently P claimed forfeiture of the lease because D was still living on the premises.

Held

❖ (ChD) D had broken a term of the lease but P's oral assurance created a collateral contract. Without that assurance D would have moved and not signed the lease. [1958] 3 W.L.R. 312.

Commentary

(1) Three conditions must be satisfied for a collateral contract to come into existence:

(a) the statement must have been intended to have contractual effect;

(b) some indication is required that the parties intended the statement to take effect as a collateral contract rather than as a term of the main contract; and

(c) there must be an independent offer, acceptance and consideration.

(2) See also *Shanklin Pier v Detel Products* (1951) (see Ch.5).

EXPRESS TERMS

Parol Evidence Rule

Key Principle

Neither party can bring oral evidence to add to, vary or contradict a written contract.

> JACOBS V BATAVIA & GENERAL PLANTATIONS TRUST 1924
> P purchased 4 $AC £100 deposit notes of D's company. P relied on D's prospectus which provided for repayment of the notes in specified circumstances, in addition to the normal method of repayment. The notes did not refer to the undertaking in the prospectus. Were the contract terms just in the notes or also in the prospectus?

Held

❖ (CA) The prospectus was a collateral contract (two judges). The third judge held that the notes and prospectus should be read together as a single contract. [1924] 2 Ch. 329.

Commentary

(1) The courts have interpreted the rule less restrictively over the years.

(2) The court is not concerned with the parties' actual intention but with their manifest intention, i.e. an objective test.

EXCEPTIONS

Key Principles

Where a document is clearly designed to contain only part of the terms then the parol evidence rule does not apply.

> S.S. ARDENNES (CARGO OWNERS) V S.S. ARDENNES (OWNERS) 1951
>
> P was orange growers in Spain. D was shipowners. P shipped oranges to England relying on an oral promise by D that the ship was going straight to London. In fact it went via Antwerp, so the oranges arrived late in London and P lost a favourable market. D relied on the bill of lading (written contract) which allowed them to proceed by any route.

Held

The bill of lading was not exclusive evidence of the contract. The oral promise was also part of the contract and therefore D was in breach of contract. [1951] 1 K.B. 55.

Commentary

(1) This is the most important exception in practice.

(2) The practical effect of such a decision is to weaken the parol evidence rule. However, the rule remains a valuable rule of evidence, particularly in the context of conveyancing, as it provides certainty.

(3) In 1986 the Law Commission stated that the rule no longer existed. Whether a statement is a term of the contract is a question of the intention of the parties.

INTERPRETATION OF EXPRESS TERMS

Key Principle

The court should ascertain the "natural" meaning of the words, taking into account the factual background known to the parties and the "aim" of the transaction.

> PRENN V SIMMONDS 1971
>
> D claimed to be contractually entitled to acquire a 4 per cent interest in a company controlled by P, for the sum of £6,000. The interest was actually worth about £200,000. P disputed the claim on the ground that the contract provided that D could only acquire the interest if certain conditions were satisfied; in particular that the company (R.T.T.)

now owned by P (who had bought it from D) should make profits of not less than £300,000 in a four-year period. The profits of R.T.T. came to over £290,000. The profits of the R.T.T. group, i.e. including its subsidiary companies were more than £300,000.

Held

❖ (HL) D was entitled to the four per cent interest. The reference to "profits" meant the consolidated profits of the group controlling R.T.T. and its subsidiaries. Consolidated accounts of R.T.T. and subsidiaries reflected both normal business practice and legal requirements. This interpretation would have been an incentive for D to work for and remain with the company; and it was linguistically accurate. [1971] 1 W.L.R. 1381.

Commentary

(1) When interpreting a contract the courts refer to the "matrix of fact". This refers to the meaning the document would have to a reasonable man having all the background knowledge reasonably available to the parties at the time they entered into the contract. Evidence of pre-contract negotiations is normally not admitted as an aid to interpretation, nor is evidence of the parties' subjective intentions.

(2) See *Chartbrook Ltd v Persimmon Homes Ltd* [2009] 1 A.C. 1101 below.

(3) In *Sirius International Insurance Co v FAI General Insurance Ltd and others* (2004) 1 W.L.R. 3251; (2005) 1 All E.R. 191; [2004] UKHL 54 Lord Steyn noted at para.19 that: "There has been a shift from literal methods of interpretation [of contracts] towards a more commercial approach". This means that an interpretation should not lead to a conclusion that flouts business common sense.

(4) In *Re Sigma Finance Corporation* [2009] UKSC 2 the Supreme Court emphasised the need to construe an agreement which was part of a series of agreements by taking into account the overall scheme of the agreements and reading sentences and phrases in the context of that overall scheme. Lord Collins stated that: "In this type of case it is the wording of the instrument which is paramount. The instrument must be interpreted as a whole in the light of the commercial intention which may be inferred from the face of the instrument and from the nature of the debtor's business. Detailed semantic analysis must give way to business common sense".

Key principle ....

The process of interpretation is to decide what a reasonable person would have understood the parties to have meant by using the language which they did.

CHARTBROOK LTD V PERSIMMON HOMES LTD 2009

The claimants (C) owned land in south London. Following negotiations, which included a letter dated May 24, 2001 which informally set out their agreement, they entered into a contract with the defendant builders (PH) on October 2001 for the development of the site, whereby PH would obtain planning permission for the site and bear the cost of building a mixed residential and commercial development. Once the leases of individual premises were granted, PH would receive the proceeds from the sale of these premises, and pay C an agreed price for the land as well as a "balancing payment" which included an "additional residential payment" (ARP) . The ARP was "23.4% of the price achieved for each residential unit in excess of the minimum guarantees residential unit value less the costs and incentives". A dispute arose as to how the ARP was to be calculated. C calculated it as meaning that they should be paid £4.5m, whereas PH's interpretation resulted in a payment of £0.9m.

Held ....

❖ (HL) Both the judge and the majority of the CA were wrong on the question of construction. The definition of ARP was defective as a piece of drafting. PH's appeal was allowed. [2009] 1 A.C. 1101.

Commentary ....

(1) Lord Hoffman considered that previous negotiations may be relevant, but that there was no clearly established case for departing from the exclusionary rule clearly reaffirmed in *Prenn v Simmonds*. The rule only excludes the use of such evidence for the purpose of drawing inferences about what the contract meant.

(2) In *Chartbrook* Lord Hoffmann set out the principles applicable where the drafting had been careless or a mistake made.

(3) Baroness Hale of Richmond noted that the House was aware of the agreement which the parties had reached on this aspect of the bargain during the negotiations which led to the formal contract. She considered that evidence of negotiations where consensus is reached is very helpful indeed.

(4) In *Re Sigma Finance Corporation* [2009] UKSC 2 Lord Collins stated that:

"... this is not the type of case where the background or matrix of fact is or ought to be relevant, except in the most generalised way. I do not consider, therefore, that there is much assistance to be derived from the principles of interpretation re-stated by Lord Hoffmann ... . Where a security document secures a number of creditors who have advanced funds over a long period it would be quite wrong to take account of circumstances which are not known to all of them".

(5) See also Ch.10 (Mistake) in respect of rectification of the contract.

IMPLIED TERMS

Terms Implied in Fact

Key Principle

The court will imply a term into a particular contract to give efficacy to the transaction.

> THE MOORCOCK 1889
>
> D were wharfingers who agreed to allow P shipowner to discharge his ship at their jetty for a fee. The jetty extended into the Thames and, as both parties realised, the ship must ground at low water. This occurred but the ship settled onto a ridge of hard ground below the mud, and was damaged.

Held

❖ (CA) There was an implied undertaking by D that the river bottom was, as far as reasonable care could provide, in such a condition as not to endanger the ship. [1886–1890] All E.R. Rep. 530.

Commentary

(1) The court looks for the presumed intention of parties.

(2) The principle was further explained in *Shirlaw v Southern Foundries* (1926) Ltd [1939] 2 All E.R. 113 where MacKinnon L.J. proposed the "officious bystander" test.

(3) The term should be necessary to give business efficacy to the contract.

(4) Implied terms normally impose an obligation to take reasonable care.

(5) For recent examples of vessels damaged at a loading berth see *George v Coastal Marine 2004 Ltd* [2009] EWHC 816 (Admlty) which the judge

described as a "classic *Moorcock* situation"; and *Mediterranean Salvage & Towage Ltd v Seamar Trading and Commerce Inc* [2009] EWCA Civ 531.

Key principle
An implied term spells out in express words what the contract, read against the relevant background, would reasonably be understood to mean.

A-G OF BELIZE V BELIZE TELECOM LTD 2009
The government of Belize privatised the provision of telecommunications services in Belize, which had previously been provided by a publicly owned body. To this end the government formed a company, BTL, the first defendant. BTL owned one "special" share and 37.5 per cent of the ordinary C class shares. This entitled BTL to appoint two of the four directors allocated to the C shareholders. After a year, BTL found itself in financial difficulties and no longer owned the C shares, but the two directors remained in place. The claimants sought a declaration that the articles of association, which set out the classes of shares and who was entitled to be a director, should be interpreted as containing an implied term that in these circumstances the directors concerned would cease to be directors.

Held
❖ (JCPC) There was an implied term that directors would vacate office when there was no longer any shareholder with a shareholding appropriate to authorise their appointment. The overriding purpose of the machinery of appointment and removal of directors was to ensure that the board reflected the appropriate shareholder interests in accordance with the scheme set out in the articles. [2009] 1 W.L.R. 1988.

Commentary
(1) Lord Hoffman, who gave the opinion of the JCPC, stated that the court has no power to improve upon the instrument, whether it is a contract, a statute or articles of association. It cannot introduce terms to make it fairer or more reasonable.

(2) The court is concerned only to discover what the instrument means. This is an objective test.

(3) Lady Justice Arden stated in *Groveholt v Hughes* [2010] EWCA Civ 538 at para.45 that Lord Hoffman "rebases the doctrine of implied terms within the principles of contractual interpretation".

(4) In *Mediterranean Salvage & Towage Ltd v Seamar Trading and Commerce Inc* [2009] EWCA Civ 531, Sir Anthony Clarke M.R. considered that Lord Hoffman's analysis is extensive and likely to be much quoted. He thought it sufficient to say that the implication of a term is an exercise in the construction of the contract as a whole.

Terms Implied in Law

Key Principle

Such terms are legal incidents of particular types of contracts, e.g. between employer and employee.

> LISTER V ROMFORD ICE & COLD STORAGE CO LTD 1957
>
> P's son was employed by D as a lorry driver. P was his mate on the lorry. While backing his lorry, P's son drove negligently and injured P, who sued D. D were held vicariously liable for P's negligence. D claimed an indemnity from P's son who was in breach of his contract of employment with D.

Held

❖ (HL) The son was in breach of an implied term in his contract of employment that he would use reasonable care and skill in the performance of his duties. [1957] 2 W.L.R. 158.

Key Principle

It is an implied term in a contract of employment that an employer should take reasonable care not to injure an employee's health.

> JOHNSTONE V BLOOMSBURY HEALTH AUTHORITY 1991
>
> P was employed by D as a junior doctor. It was a term of the contract of employment that P should work "40 hours per week and be available for overtime of further 48 hours per week on average".

Held

❖ (CA) D was in breach of the implied term. [1991] 2 W.L.R. 1362.

Key Principle

A landlord should take reasonable care to keep in reasonable repair and usability the common parts of a high rise block of flats.

P owned a tower block. D were tenants of flats in the block. They refused to pay rent because of the poor state of the block, which was partly due to vandals and partly to D's non-cooperation. P sought an order for possession.

Held

❖ (HL) P was not in breach of an implied obligation to keep the lifts in working order, the stairs lit, and the rubbish chutes cleared. [1977] A.C. 239.

Commentary

The implied obligation must be necessary for the agreement to work. Lord Denning's view that the court could imply any terms it thought reasonable was rejected by HL.

TERMS IMPLIED BY STATUTE

Key Principle

A statement that a painting was by a particular artist would amount to a sale by description where the buyer relies on the statement.

HARLINGDON & LEINSTER ENTERPRISES LTD V CHRISTOPHER HULL FINE ART LTD 1990

D sold a painting by a German expressionist artist, Gabriele Munter, to P who were dealers in German art. D had made it clear that he was not familiar with the artist's work, and that he was not an expert in regard to the painting. D's invoice described the painting as the work of Gabriel Munter. Two months later P discovered that the painting was a forgery. P sued D for:

(i)   breach of three statutory implied terms: ss. 13(1), 14(2) and (3) **Sale of Goods Act 1979**; and

(ii) misrepresentation.

The judge found for D. P appealed to CA on the s.13(1) and s.14(2) grounds.

Held

❖ (CA) There was no breach of s.13(1) the parties could not have reasonably contemplated that P were relying on D's statement that the painting was by Gabriele Munter. Similarly there was no breach of s.14(2). The picture was of merchantable quality. It was fit for its purpose in that it could be resold or admired. [1990] 3 W.L.R. 13.

TERMS IMPLIED BY CUSTOM

Key Principle

A term can be implied by custom, so long as it is compatible with the contract.

> HUTTON V WARREN 1836
> A tenant was bound to farm his land in certain manner. On quitting the tenancy of his farm the tenant claimed to be entitled to fair allowance for seed and labour on the arable land.

Held

The lease should be construed in the light of this custom which was proved to exist. (1836) 1 M. & W. 466.

Commentary

Trade usage can also be implied into commercial contracts such as marine insurance contracts and collective agreements. See e.g. *British Crane Hire Corporation v Ipswich Plant Hire Ltd* 1975 (Ch.8).

THINK POINT

How does the approach to be adopted by the court when interpreting an express term differ from the approach used by the court when deciding whether a statement amounts to an offer?

What difference does it make, if any, that Lord Hoffman has "rebased the doctrine of implied terms within the principles of contractual interpretation"?

Exclusion and Limitation Clauses

8

INTRODUCTION

An exclusion or exemption clause is a term of the contract which excludes or restricts a party's liability or remedies for breach of a term of the contract. Such clauses are used to allocate risk between the parties. This will affect the price paid for goods and services. For example, if the seller of goods is liable under the contract for damage to the goods while they are being delivered to the buyer, the seller will bear the loss or the costs of insuring against such loss.

A limitation clause normally limits the amount of damages that may be recovered by the injured party for a breach of contract.

Exclusion and limitation clauses have been regulated to some extent by the **Unfair Contract Terms Act 1977** and the **Unfair Terms in Consumer Contract Regulations 1999,** which replaced the **1994 Regulations,** and which give effect to Council Directive 93/13/EEC on unfair terms in consumer contracts. The Regulations give powers to the Office of Fair Trading to investigate and complain to the courts about the use of unfair terms in consumer contracts.

Exclusion and limitation clauses are frequently found in standard form contracts. Consumers often have no choice but to agree to such clauses if they wish to obtain the goods or services. The courts interpret such clauses restrictively against the party wishing to rely upon them (*contra proferentem* rule).

For an exclusion or limitation clause to be effective:

(1) it must be incorporated as a term of the contract either by signature, notice, or course of dealing;

(2) the wording of the clause must apply to the particular breach; and

(3) the clause must

    (a) satisfy the requirements of the **1997 Act** or the **1999 Regulations;** or

    (b) where the legislation does not apply, reflect the clear and unambiguous intention of the parties that the clause is to apply where there has been a serious breach.

INCORPORATION BY SIGNATURE

Key Principle

When a document containing contractual terms is signed then in the absence of fraud or misrepresentation, the party signing it is bound.

> **L'ESTRANGE V GRAUCOB LTD 1934**
> P bought a slot machine from D. P signed an order form which contained a clause excluding D's liability for any breach of collateral warranties. P claimed that she had not read the form and did not know what it contained.

Held

❖ (KBD) P was bound by the clause. It was wholly immaterial whether she had read the document or not. [1934] All E.R. 16.

Commentary

This principle applies to all terms not just exclusion clauses. See *Curtis v Chemical Cleaning & Dyeing Co* 1951 where there was misrepresentation. (Ch.9).

INCORPORATION BY NOTICE

Key Principle

An exclusion clause in an unsigned document will be incorporated if the parties intend the document to have contractual force.

> **CHAPELTON V BARRY UDC 1940**
> P hired a deck chair from D for three hours. P paid 2d and was given a ticket which P did not read. The ticket excluded D from liability for negligence. The deckchair collapsed as a result of D's negligence.

Held

❖ (CA) The ticket was a mere receipt. It was not intended to have contractual force. Therefore the exclusion clause on the ticket was not incorporated into the contract. [1940] 1 All E.R. 356.

Commentary

Reasonable notice of the clause is also required.

Key Principle

An exclusion clause will be incorporated by giving reasonable notice that the document contained writing.

> **PARKER V SOUTH EASTERN RAILWAY 1877**
> P deposited a bag in the cloakroom at D's station. P paid 2d and was given a ticket. On the front of the ticket was written "see back". On the back, there was a limitation of liability clause.

Held

❖ (CA) Mellish L.J. said: if a person receiving a ticket:
  (1) did not see or know that there was writing on the ticket, they are not bound by the clause;
  (2) knew that there was writing and knew and believed that writing contained conditions then they are bound by them; and
  (3) knew that there was writing on the ticket, and the delivery of the ticket to him was in such a manner as to amount to reasonable notice that the writing contained conditions, then he is bound by them whether or not he knew or believed that the writing contained conditions. (1877) 2 C.P.D. 416.

Key Principle

Whether reasonable notice is given is a question of fact determined objectively.

> **THOMPSON V LM & S. RLY CO 1929**
> P's niece purchased a railway ticket from D for P. P could not read. The ticket was issued subject to conditions which included a clause which excluded D from liability for any injury suffered by passengers. There was only one free copy of the conditions at the station. P was injured and sued D.

Held

D had taken reasonable steps to bring the conditions to public's notice. It was irrelevant that P could not read. [1929] All E.R. 474.

Key Principle

The more unusual or unexpected a particular term the higher will be the degree of notice required to incorporate it.

THORNTON V SHOE LANE PARKING LTD 1971

P parked his car in D's car park, and when he collected it he was injured in an accident which was partly D's fault. At the entrance to the car park a notice stated: "All cars parked at owner's risk". As P drove in he took a ticket from a machine. The ticket had writing on it, including a clause which referred to conditions which were displayed inside the garage. These conditions excluded D from liability for injury to customers.

Held

❖ (CA) P was not bound by the exclusion clause. The contract was made when the machine issued the ticket. The ticket was a mere receipt. The contract could not be altered by words on the ticket. [1971] 2 W.L.R. 585.

Commentary

Lord Denning said: In any event the exclusion clause is "so wide and so destructive of rights that the court should not hold any man bound by it unless it is drawn to his attention in the most explicit way ... In order to give sufficient notice it would need to be printed in red ink on the face of the document with a red hand pointing to it or something equally startling."

Key Principle

The principle of reasonable notice also applies to other types of onerous clauses.

INTERFOTO PICTURE LIBRARY LTD V STILETTO VISUAL PROGRAMMES LTD 1988

P hired 47 photographs to D. They were sent round in a jiffy bag with a delivery note. The delivery note contained nine conditions including a clause which provided that £5.00 per transparency per day must be paid, when they were kept more than 14 days. D did not use photos, and forgot about them. P sued D for £3,783.50.

Held

❖ (CA) P had done nothing to draw D's attention to the particular unreasonable and extortionate condition. Therefore it was not a term of the contract. [1988] 2 W.L.R. 615.

Commentary

(1) Note the similarity between this clause and a penalty clause (see Ch.15) and **U.T.C.C. Regs 1999.**

(2) In *O'Brien v MGN Ltd*, *The Times*, August 8, 2001, the Court of Appeal applied the judgments of Bingham L.J. and Dillon L.J. in Interfoto to a newspaper scratchcard game. The rules of the game provided that where there were more winners than prizes a simple draw would take place. Their Lordships held that the newspaper had fairly and reasonably brought the rules to the notice of the claimant, and that the rule was neither particularly onerous nor unusual. Hale L.J. considered that the issue would make an excellent question in a contract law examination.

Key Principle

The clause must be brought to the other party's attention before or at the time of contracting.

> OLLEY V MARLBOROUGH COURT 1949
> An exclusion clause was in a notice in P's hotel bedroom. P's luggage was stolen.

Held

P not bound by the exclusion clause. The contract was made at the reception desk. [1949] 1 All E.R. 127.

INCORPORATION BY COURSE OF DEALING

Key Principle

An exclusion clause can be incorporated by a long continuous and consistent course of dealing between the two parties.

> KENDALL (HENRY) & SONS V WILLIAM LILLICO & SONS LTD 1968
> There were three or four contracts a month for feeding-stuff between P and D over a period of three years. An oral order to buy was placed and the seller would send a contract note soon afterwards. The note contained conditions one of which stated that the buyer would be responsible for latent defects. Young pheasants died as a result of defective feeding-stuff being supplied.

Held

❖ (HL) The exclusion clause was incorporated in the particular transaction even though the usual steps to incorporate the clause were not taken. [1968] 2 All E.R. 444.

Commentary

However, HL also held that the wording of the clause did not cover the particular breach.

Key Principle

A term may also be implied into a contract because of a general course of dealing amounting to a trade custom or usage.

> BRITISH CRANE HIRE CORPORATION LTD v IPSWICH PLANT HIRE LTD 1975
> P and D both hired out earth-moving equipment. D urgently needed a drag-line crane and orally agreed to hire one from P, who sent D a printed form for D's signature. Before D signed it the crane sank in marshy ground. The printed form contained terms whereby D would be liable to indemnify P for the loss of the crane.

Held

❖ (CA) The indemnity clause was a term of the contract. Both parties understood that the hire would be on normal trade terms. [1974] 2 W.L.R. 856.

Commentary

(1) CA distinguished *Hollier v Rambler Motors* (1972) (see below) where there were three or four transactions over a five-year period and where one party was a consumer.

(2) This case involves an indemnity clause, but Treitel considers that the principle is equally applicable to exclusion clauses.

INTERPRETATION OF EXCLUSION CLAUSES

Key Principle

An exclusion clause will always be construed narrowly against the party who put it forward.

Andrew Bros (Bournemouth) Ltd v Singer & Co Ltd 1933

P was appointed as dealers for "new Singer cars" by D. P contracted to buy cars under an agreement which provided inter alia that "all conditions, warranties and liabilities imposed by statute, common law or otherwise are excluded". D delivered a car which was not strictly a "new" car, as it had already been driven a considerable mileage to be shown to another customer.

Held

❖ (CA) D could not rely on the exclusion clause, because it dealt only with implied terms. The obligation to deliver a new car was an express term. [1933] All E.R. 479

Commentary

This principle is known as the contra proferentem rule. See also *Morris v C.W. Martin & Sons* (1965) at Ch.5.

Key Principle

The contra proferentem rule is not applied so strictly to a limitation clause.

Ailsa Craig Fishing Co Ltd v Malvern Fishing Co 1983

D2 agreed to provide a security service for D1's fishing boats in Aberdeen harbour. D2 were negligent and as a result D1's boat and a boat belonging to P (Malvern) sank. P sued D1 who claimed against D2. However, in the contract between D1 and D2 there was a clause which limited D2's liability to £1,000. D1's actual loss was £55,000.

Held

❖ (HL) D2 was able to rely on the limitation clause. The clause was clear and unambiguous. It was not unlikely that a party would agree to such a clause. [1983] 1 W.L.R. 964.

Commentary

Lord Fraser stated that limitation clauses are not regarded "with the same hostility" as exclusion clauses. The court should consider the risks to which the defending party may be exposed, the remuneration which he receives, and the possibility of insurance by the other party.

EXCLUSION OF NEGLIGENCE LIABILITY

Key Principle

General words will not usually exclude liability for negligence where the party could be liable irrespective of negligence.

> #### WHITE V JOHN WARWICK & CO LTD 1953
> P hired a bicycle from D. A clause in the agreement stated that "nothing in this agreement shall render the owners liable for any personal injuries". P was injured because of defective saddle.

Held

D was liable for negligence. The clause excluded strict liability in contract but not the tortious duty to take reasonable care. [1953] 1 W.L.R. 1285.

Commentary

(1) Under **UCTA 1977**, s.2(1) it is no longer possible to exclude liability for negligence which causes death or personal injury. However, it is still possible to exclude liability for negligence which causes damage to property so long as the exclusion clause is reasonable (**UCTA 1977**, s.2(2)).

(2) The court will look at the wording of the clause to see if the intention of the party to exclude liability for negligence has been made sufficiently clear to the other party.

Key Principle

It is advisable to use "negligence" or a synonym to exclude liability for negligence.

> #### DORSET COUNTY COUNCIL V SOUTHERN FELT ROOFING 1990
> D, a building contractor, was engaged to repair a school belonging to P. During the work the school caught fire. The contract provided that P would "bear the risk of loss or damage in respect of ... the existing structure ... by fire, lightning, explosion, aircraft and other aerial devices." D argued that this was an exclusion clause.

Held

❖ (CA) An exemption clause could exclude liability for negligence. However, by including events other than fire which might occur without human fault, the clause was intended to cover heads of liability other than negligence and so the clause could not operate to exclude liability in negligence. [1990] 48 B.L.R. 96.

Commentary

In *Shell Chemicals UK Ltd v P & O Roadtanks Ltd* [1995] 1 Lloyd's Rep. 297, CA held that "all claims and demands whatever" was not sufficiently clear and unambiguous to cover negligence liability. In *Monarch Airlines Ltd v London Luton Airport Ltd* [1997] C.L.C. 698 QBD held that the words "neglect or default" were wide enough to exclude such liability.

Key Principle

General words will not always exclude liability for negligence even where the only possible liability is in negligence.

HOLLIER V RAMBLER MOTORS (AMC) LTD 1972

D orally agreed to repair P's car. The car was damaged by a fire caused by D's negligence. On two previous occasions P had signed an invoice which contained a condition excluding D from liability for damage caused by fire to customers' cars.

Held

❖ (CA) The wording of the clause did not exclude liability for a fire caused by D's negligence. In every case it comes down to a question of construing the exclusion clause but the wording has to be clear for negligence to be excluded. [1972] 2 W.L.R. 401.

Key Principle

Where a party to the contract has committed a particularly serious breach then the court will only permit the exclusion clause to apply where there is a clear and unambiguous intention that it should do so.

PHOTO PRODUCTION LTD V SECURICOR TRANSPORT LTD 1980

D agreed to provide a night patrol service for P's factory at a weekly charge of £8.75. One of D's employees started a small fire which got out of control so that the factory, worth £650,000, was destroyed. The contract contained a clause which stated that in no circumstances would D be liable for the acts of its employees.

Held ....

❖ (HL) D could rely on the exclusion clause. The words of the exclusion clause were clear. [1980] 2 W.L.R. 283.

Commentary ....

(1) The courts will take into account:
  (a) the importance of the term broken;
  (b) the manner of the breach; and
  (c) the seriousness of the consequences of the breach.

(2) See also *Ailsa Craig Fishing Co Ltd v Malvern Fishing Co Ltd* (1983) where D was able to rely on a limitation clause despite a "total" breach; and *George Mitchell (Chesterhall) Ltd v Finney Lock Seeds* (1983).

(3) This rule of construction remains important in the context of commercial and other contracts, whose exclusion clauses are not subject to **UCTA**'s reasonableness test or to the **UTCCR 1999**. See, for example, *Internet Broadcasting Corp Ltd (t/a NETTV) v MAR LLC (t/a MARHedge)* [2009] EWHC 844 (Ch) where the court held that the exclusion clause did not apply because there would have to be clear strong language which indicated that the parties intended the clause to apply to a deliberate repudiatory breach of contract.

....

UNFAIR CONTRACT TERMS ACT 1977

Meaning of "Exemption Clause"

Key Principle ....

A contract term which states that a buyer cannot refuse to pay for incorrect or defective goods is an exemption clause and is subject to the Act.

> STEWART GILL LTD V HORATIO MYER AND CO LTD 1992
> D entered into a contract with P for the supply and installation of an overhead conveyor system. D withheld the final 10 per cent of the contract price claiming that P was in breach of contract. It was a term of the contract that "the Customer shall not be entitled to withhold payment of any amount due to the Company under the Contract by reason of any counterclaim, etc."

Held ....

❖ (CA) The clause was an exclusion clause and was unreasonable under **UCTA**, s.3. Therefore it was invalid. [1992] Q.B. 600.

(1) **UCTA**, s.13, defines exemption clauses more widely than clauses which just exclude or limit liability.

(2) A customer who receives incorrect or defective goods is normally entitled to refuse payment for them (see Ch.14).

Key Principle

A clause which transfers liability in negligence from the owner to the hirer of machinery is an exclusion clause.

PHILLIPS PRODUCTS LTD V HYLAND 1987

P hired a JCB and a driver (D1) from D2 on standard form conditions of hire. One clause provided that drivers would be regarded as servants or agents of the hirer (P) who would alone be responsible for claims arising from the operating of plant by drivers, etc. The driver negligently damaged P's building. D2 argued that they were not vicariously liable for D1's negligence because of the clause, and that the clause transferred rather than excluded liability.

Held

❖ (CA) The clause was an exclusion clause. It was subject to s.2(2) of UCTA. It was unreasonable in relation to this particular contract because of the particular facts of the case. In particular P was not in the business of hiring; the hire was arranged at short notice; P had no opportunity to obtain insurance; and P had no say in the choice of driver. [1987] 2 All E.R. 620.

Commentary

The same clause was held not to be an exclusion clause in *Thompson v Lohan (Plant Hire) Ltd* (1987) where the claim was brought by a third party.

Key Principle

A disclaimer which purports to exclude liability for negligent misstatement is subject to UCTA 1977.

SMITH V ERIC S. BUSH 1989

P purchased a house in reliance on a valuation given by a surveyor. HL held that the surveyor was liable to P under the tort of negligent misstatement. Was a disclaimer of liability for negligence effective?

Held

❖ (HL) The disclaimer did not prevent a duty of care arising in the first place; it excluded liability. It was subject to s.2(2) of UCTA. The disclaimer was unreasonable. The court took into account that: the purchaser had no power to object to the clause; he should not be expected to obtain a second valuation; D should take responsibility for a straightforward valuation; and the decision would only have a marginal impact on insurance premiums. [1989] 2 All E.R. 514.

Commentary

Liability for the tort of negligent misstatement was established in *Hedley Byrne & Co v Heller & Partners* [1963] 3 W.L.R. 101 (see Ch.9).

"DEALING AS A CONSUMER"

Key Principle

Where a business enters into a contract which is incidental to its business then it is dealing as a consumer.

> R & B CUSTOM BROKERS CO LTD V UNITED DOMINION TRUST LTD 1988
>
> P, a company, bought a car from D for its directors. The contract excluded liability for breach of **SGA 1979**, s.14 (implied conditions as to fitness and quality). Under **UCTA**, s.6 the exclusion clause was invalid if P was dealing as a consumer. The company was not in the business of car dealing. The car leaked.

Held

❖ (CA) The car was not fit for its purpose (**SGA 1979**, s.14(3)). The company was dealing as a consumer. The transaction was not an integral part of its business. Such a transaction would only be done in the course of business if there was a degree of regularity. [1988] 1 W.L.R. 321.

Commentary

(1) "Dealing as a consumer" is relevant in deciding whether the reasonableness test referred to in **UCTA 1977**, ss. 3, 4, 6, and 7 is applicable. It is defined in s.12 **UCTA** as amended by the Sale and Supply of Goods to Consumers Regulations 2002 reg. 14.

(2) The decision has been criticised because it applies however large and complex the business.

REASONABLENESS TEST

Key Principle
The relative bargaining strength of the parties, the opportunity to purchase without an exclusion clause, and commercial practice are all factors relevant to the reasonableness of an exclusion clause.

> GEORGE MITCHELL (CHESTERHALL) LTD V FINNEY LOCK SEEDS LTD 1983
> D, seed merchants, agreed to supply P, a farmer, with Dutch winter cabbage seed for £192. A term of the contract purported to limit D's liability if the seed supplied was defective. D's liability was limited to replacing the seed and refunding the price. D was not liable for other loss or damage. P planted 63 acres but the seed was the wrong kind. It was unmerchantable and the crop was a total failure. P claimed £63,000 for lost production.

Held
❖ (HL) The exclusion clause covered the loss but it was unreasonable. [1983] 2 A.C. 803.

Commentary
(1) In CA Kerr L.J. listed the following factors as being relevant to reasonableness:
  (a) any fault was wholly on D's part;
  (b) P should not be expected to insure against such loss, whereas D could;
  (c) there was a grossly disproportionate and unreasonable allocation of respective risks, which was not negotiated but imposed by D;
  (d) the clause was not normally relied upon where there was a genuine and justified claim; and
  (e) the meaning and effect of the clause was obscure.

(2) Consider also *Philips v Hyland* (1987); *Smith v Eric S. Bush* (1989) (see above).

Key Principle
Commercial parties of equal bargaining strength are generally capable of making contracts of their own choosing and should be bound by their terms.

> GRANVILLE OIL AND CHEMICALS LTD V DAVIS TURNER & CO LTD 2003
> DT was an international freight forwarder. They entered into a BIFA standard form contract with GOC to carry a consignment of paint from

Kuwait to Rotherham and to arrange insurance. The paint was damaged in transit. DT had failed to arrange adequate insurance. It was a term of the contract that any claim by GOC against DT had to be brought within nine months. GOC failed to bring a claim against DT for failure to insure within the time limit. The question was whether the time limit clause satisfied the requirement of reasonableness under s.3 **UCTA**.

Held

❖ (CA) The nine month time limit satisfied the reasonableness test. [2003] 2 Lloyd's Rep. 356.

Commentary

CA confirmed that the Sch.2 guidelines on the reasonableness test should be taken into account even though the contract in this case was not a contract for the sale or hire purchase of goods.

Key Principle

Where a clause limits liability to a specific sum of money, the sum specified should be justifiable.

ST ALBANS CITY AND DISTRICT COUNCIL V INTERNATIONAL COMPUTERS LTD 1996

D, a computer company entered into a contract on its standard terms and conditions with P, a local authority, to supply a database for the community charge register. A clause limited the company's liability for loss to £100,000. P's actual loss was £1,314,846.

Held

❖ (CA) The clause was unreasonable under ss.3 and 11 of **UCTA 1977**. [1996] 4 All E.R. 481.

Commentary

(1) The Court of Appeal upheld the QBD decision on reasonableness. The clause was unreasonable because:
  (a) the parties were of unequal bargaining power;
  (b) D could not justify the figure of £100,000; it was small considering the potential and actual loss; and
  (c) D was insured £50 million worldwide; and was better able to insure against such loss than P.

(2) See also *Watford Electronics Ltd v Sanderson CFL Ltd* [2001] 1 All E.R.

(Comm) 696 where the Court of Appeal held that neither an exclusion clause nor a limitation clause in a contract for the supply of computer hardware and software was unreasonable under s.11 **UCTA 1977**.

Key Principle

A limitation clause may be unreasonable where it is difficult and expensive for the other party to insure against loss.

> SALVAGE ASSOCIATION V CAP FINANCIAL SERVICES 1995
>
> In 1987 P, a marine surveying company, entered into a contract with D for the design, development and supply of computer accounting software. By July 1989 the software was not complete and contained numerous errors. P sued D for breach of contract claiming approximately £850,000. D relied on clauses in the contract which limited their liability to £25,000.

Held

❖ (QBD) D was under a contractual obligation to exercise reasonable care and so the limitation clause was subject to the reasonableness test in s.2(2). The limitation clause was unreasonable because P unlike D was effectively unable to insure, and D could not justify the limit of £25,000. [1995] F.S.R. 654.

Commentary

(1) The contract came within **UCTA** and was not excluded from its operation by Sch.1, para.1(c) (creation of intellectual property rights).

(2) The contract was based on D's standard terms but P had considered and received advice on each of its standard terms, so the contract did not fall within **UCTA,** s.3.

UNFAIR TERMS IN CONSUMER CONTRACTS REGULATIONS 1999

Key Principle

The twin requirements of good faith and significant imbalance will in practice be the factors which determine the unfairness or otherwise of a non-negotiated contract term.

DIRECTOR GENERAL OF FAIR TRADING V FIRST NATIONAL BANK PLC 2001

A term in a standard form loan agreement permitted the bank to charge additional interest where a borrower defaulted on the repayment of the loan and agreed to pay off the debt by instalments over a longer period. Regulation 3(2)(b) of the **1994 Regulations** provided that contract terms relating to the adequacy of remuneration were not subject to the fairness test.

Held

❖ (HL) Regulation 3(2)(b) should not be interpreted broadly and did not exempt the term in question from the fairness test, because the term was concerned with the consequences of a borrower defaulting rather the adequacy of the interest charged. The term was not unfair. [2001] 3 W.L.R. 1297.

Commentary

(1) The **1994** and **1999 Regulations** implement **Council Directive 93/13/EEC** on unfair terms in consumer contracts.

(2) Their Lordships considered that good faith implies "open and fair dealing".

(3) In considering "significant imbalance" the court should look at the position of the consumer at the time they entered the contract. The obligation to pay additional interest was clearly and unambiguously expressed. There was nothing unbalanced or detrimental to the consumer in the obligation.

(4) In *Mylcrist Builders Ltd v Buck* [2008] EWHC 2172 (TCC) the High Court applied this key principle to an arbitration clause in a builder's standard term contract and held that it was not binding on his lay customer because it was unfair under para.1 (q) of Sch.2 of the **1999 Regulations**. The arbitration award was not enforced.

(5) The **UTCCR 1999** do not apply to terms implied in fact (*Baybut v Eccle Riggs Country Park* 2006, *The Times*, November 13, 2006).

(6) **UCTA** 1977 ss.6 & 7 apply to certain statutory implied terms.

(7) In February 2005 the Law Commission published a final report on **Unfair Terms in Contracts** (Cm 6464), as well as a draft bill. The aim was to replace **UCTA** and the **UTCC Regs** with a single Act.

Key principle ....
Any monetary price or remuneration payable under a non-negotiated term of a contract comes within reg.6(2)(b).

> OFFICE OF FAIR TRADING V ABBEY NATIONAL PLC 2009
> Most UK banks levy bank charges on personal current account customers in respect of unauthorised overdrafts. The question before the Court was whether the OFT could challenge as excessive the fairness of such bank charges in relation to the services supplied to customers. In particular whether such a challenge was excluded by reg.6(2) of the **1999 Regulations,** which provides that "the assessment of fairness of a term shall not relate —
> (a) to the definition of the main subject matter of the contract, or
> (b) to the adequacy of the price or remuneration, as against the goods or services supplied in exchange".

Held ....
❖ (SC) The banks' "Relevant Terms and Relevant Charges" fall squarely within reg.6 (2) (b).The charges for unauthorised overdrafts were money paid for the package of services supplied to current account customers. So long as the terms setting out the charges were in plain and intelligible language, an assessment of the fairness of those terms in respect of the "adequacy" of the price was excluded. [2009] 3 W.L.R. 1215.

Commentary ....
(1) The SC distinguished the decision of the HL in *OFT v First National Bank plc* 2001 (above) because it was concerned with a default provision. Ancillary payments may also be covered by reg.6(2).

(2) "Adequacy" means "appropriateness" in this context.

(3) Lord Phillips noted that the SC's decision did not close the case on the OFT's investigations and may well not resolve the cases brought by customers who challenge the charges imposed on them as excessive for the services to which they relate. This is because reg.6(2) could apply to a complaint that the banks' charges overall are unfair since those who pay them pay an excessive amount in exchange for the package of services received.

Key principle

The court has the power to grant an injunction and/or a declaration in rela-tion to existing contracts which contain unfair terms

> OFFICE OF FAIR TRADING V FOXTONS LTD 2010
> The OFT sought first a declaration that the standard terms used by the defendant estate agent in contracts with private landlords were unfair and not binding because they were not expressed in plain language; and second an injunction to prevent the defendants enforcing those terms in the existing contracts.

Held

❖ (CA) Regulation 12 of the **1999 Regulations** did not restrict the availability of such remedies to future contracts. The fact that the case was brought by the OFT rather than an individual landlord (the consumer) was not a bar to the court granting a declaration. [2010] W.L.R. 663.

Key principle

A national court is under an obligation to consider whether a term in a contract is unfair under Directive 93/13 where the necessary legal and factual elements are present.

> PANNON GSM ZRT V SUSTIKNE GYORFI (C-243/08)
> The national court was asked to resolve a dispute between a Hungarian consumer who had entered into a subscription contract with a mobile phone provider. The standard form contract stated that where there was a dispute it should be heard in the court where the provider had their place of business, which was about 275 km from where the consumer lived. The court referred the case to the ECJ because it was uncertain whether it could raise on its own initiative the question of whether this amounted to an unfair term. The consumer was in receipt of invalidity benefit and had limited means of transport.

Held

❖ (ECJ) It was not necessary for the consumer to have explicitly raised the question of unfairness. The role of the national court is not just to rule on the possible unfairness of a contractual term. Where it considers the term to be unfair, it must not apply it, unless the consumer opposes the non-application.

(1) This preliminary ruling may have significant implications for the role of the judiciary in England and Wales.

(2) The EU Directive and case law are important aids to construction of the domestic UK regulations.

EXCLUSION CLAUSES AND THIRD PARTIES

Key Principle

An exclusion clause can protect a third party to the main contract where the exclusion clause creates a collateral contract.

> NEW ZEALAND SHIPPING V SATTERTHWAITE, THE EURYMEDON 1974
> (see facts in Ch.5).

Key Principle

A third party may be bound by an exclusion clause in a contract to which they are not party.

> MORRIS V C.W. MARTIN & SONS LTD 1965
> (see facts in Ch.5).

THINK POINT

Draft an exclusion clause which legally excludes a multi-storey car park from liability for any damage howsoever caused to a customer's car.

Identify the main differences between the **UCTA 1977** and **UTCCR 1999** in respect of:
(a) the types of contract to which each applies;
(b) the types of contract term to which each applies; and
(c) the factors which determine the fairness of a particular contract term.

Misrepresentation

9

INTRODUCTION

A representation is a pre-contractual statement made, for example, in the course of negotiations, which may or may not become a term of the contract (see Ch.7). Where such a statement does not become a term of the contract the person making it may be legally liable where it amounts to a misrepresentation.

A misrepresentation is a false statement of fact which induces the other party (the representee) to enter a contract with the person making the statement (the representor).

An actionable misrepresentation makes the contract voidable. "Voidable" means that there is a valid contract unless the representee rescinds the contract, that is brings the contract to an end. Rescission is an equitable remedy and is only available in certain circumstances. The representee may also be able to recover damages at common law under the tort of deceit or under the **Misrepresentation Act 1967**, as amended by the **Unfair Contract Terms Act 1977**.

There are three types of misrepresentation:

(1) Fraudulent, which is based on the tort of deceit.
(2) Negligent, which was introduced by the **Misrepresentation Act 1967**.
(3) Innocent, which equity recognised as unlawful and provided the remedy of rescission.

If the misrepresentation is also a term of the contract, a claimant may claim for breach of contract as well as misrepresentation.

Negligent misstatement is a tort (*Hedley Byrne v Heller* 1963) which may also apply where there is a misrepresentation. Normally it is more advantageous to claim negligent misrepresentation than negligent misstatement.

MISREPRESENTATION

Key Principle

An actionable misrepresentation is a false statement of existing fact.

> ### EDGINGTON V FITZMAURICE 1885
>
> D, a director of a company, issued a prospectus inviting loans from the public, which stated that the money would be used in the improvement of buildings and the extension of the business. This was untrue since the evidence showed that company intended to use the loans to discharge existing liabilities. P lent D money in reliance on the statement in the prospectus.

Held

❖ (CA) The prospectus was a fraudulent misrepresentation of fact, even though it was a statement of intention. "The state of a man's mind is as much a fact as the state of his digestion" (Bowen L.J.). [1881–1885] All E.R. Rep. 59.

Commentary

(1) A representation may be made by conduct as well as by words. In *Spice Girls Ltd v Aprilia World Service BV, The Times*, April 5, 2000, the High Court held that the participation by the Spice Girls in making a film advertising motor scooters constituted a representation by conduct of the group's intention that it would not break up during the advertising contract.

(2) A false statement as to future intention is not a statement of existing fact.

(3) An actionable misrepresentation makes the contract voidable.

(4) Misrepresentations of law as well as fact amount to actionable misrepresentations following *Kleinwort Benson Ltd v Lincoln City Council* [1999] 2 A.C. 349; see e.g. Tedd J. in *Pankhania v Hackney London Borough Council* [2002] N.P.C. 123.

Key Principle

An opinion is not usually a statement of fact.

> ### BISSET V WILKINSON 1926
>
> The vendor of land in New Zealand, which had not previously been used as a sheep farm, told a prospective purchaser that in his judgement the land could carry 2,000 sheep.

Held

❖ (JCPC) It was an honest statement of opinion as to the capacity of the farm. It was not a representation as to its actual capacity. [1926] All E.R. 343.

Key Principle

An opinion which is either not held or could not be held by a reasonable person with the speaker's knowledge is a statement of fact.

> SMITH V LAND AND HOUSE PROPERTY CORP. 1884
> Vendor described his property as being let to a "most desirable tenant" on certain terms "thus offering a first class investment". In fact the penultimate quarter's rent had been paid in instalments under pressure, and the previous quarter's rent had not been paid.

Held

The description "most desirable tenant" was not a mere expression of opinion, it was an untrue assertion that nothing had occurred which made the tenant undesirable. (1884) 28 Ch.D. 7.

Commentary

(1) See also *BG Plc v Nelson Group Services (Maintenance) Ltd* [2002] EWCA Civ 547.

(2) Criminal liability will also arise where a statement is a false trade description under the Trade Descriptions Act 1968.

Key Principle

If a party makes a statement on some matter, it must be a full and frank statement, not partial and misleading.

> CURTIS V CHEMICAL CLEANING & DYEING CO 1951
> D, a dry cleaner, accepted a wedding dress for cleaning. D asked P, the customer, to sign a receipt, and explained that it contained an exclusion clause which exempted him from liability for damage to beads and sequins. In fact the clause stated that the company would not be liable for "any damage howsoever arising".

....

❖ (CA) D's statement conveyed a false impression which amounted to a misrepresentation; so the exclusion clause was ineffective. [1951] 1 All E.R. 631.

Commentary ....

A party to a contract is generally under no obligation to say anything. However, even saying "No" in response to a question may amount to a misrepresentation (See e.g. *Banks v Cox*, 2000 (unreported)).

Key Principle ....

If a true representation is falsified by later events, then the change in circumstances should be communicated.

WITH V O'FLANAGAN 1936

Negotiations took place between P and D for the sale of D's medical practice said to be worth £2,000. Four months later, a contract of sale was entered into, by which time the practice had become worthless because of D's intervening illness.

Held ....

❖ (CA) D ought to have communicated this change in circumstance to P. Therefore, the contract could be avoided. [1936] 1 All E.R. 727.

Commentary ....

(1) The general rule is that silence does not amount to misrepresentation. See e.g. the House of Lords decision in *Hamilton v Allied Domecq Plc* [2007] UKHL 33.

(2) Exceptions to the general rule in addition to the two cases above are:
  (a) Contracts uberrimae fidei (of the utmost good faith) where one party alone knows the full facts and must make full disclosure of all material facts, e.g. contracts of insurance.
  (b) Where there is a special relationship between parties to the contract, of a confidential or fiduciary nature, e.g. principal/agent.

(3) If the parties enter into the contract under a misapprehension, then the contract may be invalidated under the doctrine of mistake (see Ch.10).

Key Principle

The false statement of fact must have been intended to cause and have in fact caused the representee to enter the contract.

> HORSFALL V THOMAS 1862
>
> B purchased a gun with a defect. After six rounds being fired, the gun blew to pieces. It was not clear why this happened. It appears that S, the seller, had concealed the defect. B had not examined the gun. B claimed that the contract induced by S's fraud and misrepresentation.

Held

B could not succeed because the attempt to conceal the defect had produced no effect upon his mind. (1862) 1 H. & C. 90.

Key Principle

The false statement should have affected the representee's judgment.

> SMITH V CHADWICK 1884
>
> A company prospectus contained a false statement that one Grieve was a director of the company. P bought shares relying on the prospectus, but admitted that he had never heard of "Grieve" and was, therefore, in no way influenced by the statement.

Held

❖ (HL) P could not avoid the contract. (1884) 9 App. Cas. 187.

Key Principle

The representee should have relied on the statement.

> J.E.B. FASTENERS LTD V MARKS BLOOM & CO 1983
>
> P took over a company having seen its accounts. They were inaccurate, having been negligently prepared by D. However, P had not relied on the accounts. The evidence showed that P took over the company to obtain the services of two of its directors, The state of its accounts was irrelevant.

Held

❖ (CA) P's claim for damages was unsuccessful. [1983] 1 All E.R. 583.

Key Principle

The onus is on the representee to show that he was induced by the statement to enter the contract.

> **MUSEPRIME PROPERTIES V ADHILL PROPERTIES 1990**
>
> P bought three commercial properties at an auction in reliance on representations that revised rents were yet to be agreed. On discovering that in the case of two of the properties the rents had been fixed at a level which P considered to be too low, P refused to complete the purchase because of the misrepresentation. P considered, perhaps unreasonably, that they would have been able to negotiate higher rents if the rents had still been under review.

Held

❖ (Ch D) P could rescind because they had been induced by the representations, even if a reasonable person would not have been similarly induced. [1990] 36 E.G. 114.

Key Principle

The false statement should be the main reason for entering into the contract.

> **ATTWOOD V SMALL 1838**
>
> The vendor of a mine made exaggerated and unreliable claims about its earning capacities. The buyer wanted verification of these claims and appointed experienced agents who reported that they were accurate.

Held

The buyer could not rescind the contract. He did not rely on the vendor's statements but on the report of his own agents. [1835–1842] All E.R. Rep. 258.

Key Principle

Actual and complete knowledge of the true facts will defeat the representee's claim.

> **REDGRAVE V HURD 1881**
>
> P, an elderly solicitor, advertised for a younger partner who would also buy P's house. D purchased P's house in reliance on P's statements

about the value of the practice. P also showed D papers concerning the value of the practice but D did not examine them. D discovered after entering into a contract to buy the house that the value of the practice was less than P claimed. P claimed specific performance of the contract.

Held

❖ (CA) D was found to have relied on P's statement, even though D had an opportunity to examine the papers. The onus of proof was on P to show that D had actual knowledge of the true facts. [1881–1885] All E.R. Rep. 77.

THREE TYPES OF MISREPRESENTATION

Key Principle

A fraudulent misrepresentation is a statement made:
  (1)   knowingly; or
  (2)   without belief in its truth; or
  (3)   recklessly, careless whether it be true or false.

DERRY V PEEK 1889

A company, after submitting plans to a government department, obtained the passage of an Act of Parliament authorising it to run trams in Plymouth. The plans proposed the use of steam power for the trams. However, the Act as passed stated that the trams would be moved by animal power or, if the government department consented, by steam or mechanical power. The directors of the company believed that the consent would be given as a matter of course and issued a prospectus stating that the company had the right to use steam power instead of horses. P took shares in the company in reliance upon this statement. However, the government department refused its consent. The company was wound up.

Held

❖ (HL) P's action in the tort of deceit against the directors must fail. The directors honestly believed the statement in the prospectus to be true. (1889) 14 App. Cas. 337.

Commentary

(1) The claim for damages for fraudulent misrepresentation is strictly an action in the tort of deceit.

(2) The equitable remedy of rescission is also available (see below).

(3) In practice fraudulent misrepresentation is rarely alleged because it is difficult to prove; and since 1967 damages have been available for negligent misrepresentation.

Key Principle

A negligent misrepresentation is a statement made without reasonable grounds for believing it to be true.

HOWARD MARINE & DREDGING CO LTD v A. OGDEN & SONS (EXCAVATIONS) LTD 1978

P quoted D a price for the hire of two sea-going barges, and told D the cubic capacity of the barges. Subsequently P told D that the carrying capacity of each barge was about 1800 tonnes. P gave this figure because that was the weight given in Lloyd's Register. In fact the carrying capacity was correctly stated in the shipping documents as 1055 tonnes. D hired the barges. They subsequently refused to pay the hire charges when they became aware of the reduced carrying capacity and claimed damages because of P's misrepresentation.

Held

❖ (CA) P did not have an objectively reasonable ground to disregard the figure in the ship's documents and rely on the Lloyd's Register figure. [1978] 2 W.L.R. 515.

Commentary

(1) Note that, under s.2(1) of the **Misrepresentation Act 1967**, P had to disprove negligence rather than D prove it.

(2) Counterclaims were made by D under s.2(1) of the **Misrepresentation Act 1967**; the tort of negligent misstatement; and breach of collateral warranty. The second and third counterclaims were not successful.

(3) P's exclusion clause was held to be unreasonable under **Misrepresentation Act 1967**, s.3.

Key Principle

An innocent misrepresentation is a false statement of existing fact which is made neither fraudulently nor negligently.

GOVERNMENT OF ZANZIBAR V BRITISH AEROSPACE (LANCASTER HOUSE) LTD 2001

In 1992 Z purchased a corporate jet from BAe(LH). In 1998 Z issued a writ claiming that the contract should be rescinded because of misrepresentation or alternatively that damages should be awarded under s.2(2) or 2(1) of the **Misrepresentation Act 1967**. The misrepresentations alleged to have been made by BAe(LH) related to the airworthiness, reliability, design and construction of the aircraft.

Held

❖ (QBD) Summary judgment was given in favour of BAe(LH). Rescission was no longer available as a remedy to Z because of delay. [2000] 1 W.L.R. 2333.

Commentary

See below on damages for innocent misrepresentation.

REMEDIES FOR MISREPRESENTATION

Key Principle

A misrepresentation may become a term of the contract.

LEAF V INTERNATIONAL GALLERIES 1950

In May 1944 P purchased a painting called Salisbury Cathedral from D for £85. D represented that the artist was John Constable. Five years later P tried to sell the painting and was told that it was not painted by Constable. P brought an action for rescission of the contract to recover the purchase price.

Held

❖ (CA) The representation was a term of the contract. P had accepted the goods and could not rescind for breach of contract. Even if P's claim was for innocent misrepresentation, P had left it too late to claim rescission. [1950] 1 All E.R. 693.

Commentary

It is not clear why P did not claim damages for breach of contract.

RESCISSION

Key Principle
Where a representor cannot be traced a representee can record their intention of rescinding the contract by doing some overt act that is reasonable in the circumstances.

> ### CAR & UNIVERSAL FINANCE CO LTD v CALDWELL 1964
> D sold and delivered a car to X in return for a cheque which bounced the next day, by which time both the car and X had disappeared. D immediately notified the police and the AA requesting them to find the car. Meanwhile X sold the car to Y car dealers who had notice of X's defective title. Y sold the car to P, who bought it in good faith.

Held
❖ (CA) D, by asking the police and the AA to find his car, had indicated an intention to rescind the contract and from that time the title of the car reverted to D. Therefore no title to the car passed to P. [1964] 2 W.L.R. 600.

Commentary
(1) Rescission does not require a court order, but note that rescission is an equitable remedy, i.e. available at the discretion of the court.

(2) Normally the representees should communicate their decision to rescind to the representor within a reasonable time.

LIMITS TO THE RIGHT OF RESCISSION

Key Principle
Where the representee has affirmed the contract the right to rescind is lost.

> ### LONG v LLOYD 1958
> D, a haulage contractor, advertised a lorry, which he described as being in exceptional condition. P who was also a haulage contractor noticed some defects but still purchased the lorry having been assured by D that he had told him about all its defects. Two days after the purchase P became aware of more defects. D agreed to pay half the cost of a reconstructed dynamo but denied any knowledge of a leaking oil seal. The repairs were carried out but four days later the lorry had broken down again and P asked for the return of his money.

Held

❖ (CA) P's continued use of the defective lorry and agreeing to D's offer to share the cost of repairs amounted to affirmation of the contract. [1958] 2 All E.R. 402.

Key Principle

Where there has been a lapse of time between the making of the contract and the decision to rescind the right to rescind is lost.

LEAF V INTERNATIONAL GALLERIES 1950
(see facts above).

Held

❖ (CA) P should have rescinded within days of making the contract rather than after five years.

Key Principle

Where the parties are not able to be restored to their original position the right to rescind is lost.

CLARKE V DICKSON 1858
P purchased shares in a company in reliance on a misrepresentation. The company was being wound up and P discovered the misrepresentations and tried to rescind the contract to recover the money he paid.

Held

P could not rescind because he could not return the shares in the company now that it was being wound up. (1858) 120 E.R. 463.

Key Principle

Where a third party's rights would be affected, the right to rescind is lost.

PHILLIPS V BROOKS 1919
P sold a ring to X thinking that he was Sir George Bullough. X pawned the ring to D.

Held

❖ (CA) The contract was voidable for fraud, but not void for mistake. An innocent third party (D) acquired the jewellery in good faith for valuable consideration. The contract between P and X could not be rescinded. [1918–1919] All E.R. 246.

DAMAGES

Key Principle

In a claim for fraudulent misrepresentation the defendant is bound to make reparation for all the actual damages directly flowing from the fraudulent inducement.

> DOYLE V OLBY (IRONMONGERS) LTD 1969
>
> P purchased a business from D in reliance on statements made by D during the pre-contractual negotiations. D made fraudulent representations that the business made a healthy annual profit and that two-thirds of the business was done through the shop. The implication being that P would not need to employ a salesman to visit wholesale purchasers. Despite P's best endeavours he suffered considerable losses and eventually sold the business. P was left with debts of £4,000. The trial judge assessed damages as if the representations were contractual promises and awarded P damages of £1,500.

Held

❖ (CA) P was awarded damages of £5,500. The object of damages is to compensate P for all the loss he has suffered. Damages for fraud are assessed differently from damages for breach of contract. [1969] 2 All E.R. 119.

Commentary

(1) The House of Lords in *Smith New Court Securities Ltd v Scrimgeour Vickers (Asset Management) Ltd* [1996] 3 W.L.R. 1051 approved and applied this principle. In addition Lord Browne-Wilkinson set out seven principles which should be applied by the courts when assessing damages for fraudulent misrepresentation. In particular he stated that the damage must directly flow from and have been directly caused by the transaction entered into as a result of the misrepresentation; and that the plaintiff is entitled to damages for any consequential losses.

(2) In a claim for breach of contract, the damages are normally limited to what

may reasonably be supposed to have been in the contemplation of the parties.

(3) Damages for fraudulent misrepresentation can include modest damages for anxiety and distress: *Kinch v Rosling* [2009] EWHC 286 (QB).

Key Principle

The aim of damages in the tort of deceit is to put the representee in the position they would have been in if the deceit had not been perpetrated.

SMITH KLINE & FRENCH LABORATORIES LTD V LONG 1989

P, pharmaceutical drug manufacturers, were induced to sell quantities of drugs by means of fraudulent misrepresentations. D paid the "ex-factory" price. P sued D for damages in the tort of deceit.

Held

❖ (CA) P was entitled to the difference between that price and the market price. Damages were measured at the market value of the goods, not the lesser cost of replacement. [1989] 1 W.L.R. 1.

Key principle

Damages can be awarded for loss of the use of money which resulted from the fraudulent inducement

PARABOLA INVESTMENTS LIMITED AND ANOTHER V BROWALLIA CAL LIMITED AND ANOTHER 2010

The claimant was a company set up by one person for the purpose of trading in stocks, shares, and derivatives. The defendant was a company trading on the London Stock Exchange and other world markets. Over a ten-year period the claimant consistently made profits from its trading except for the period between July 2001 and February 2002 when it was trading primarily through the defendant. During this period it was the victim of a systematic fraud perpetrated by one of the defendant's employees, a senior futures broker, who induced the claimant to continue its course of trading by repeated false assurances that the trading was profitable. The employee also lied about how much money was in the claimant's account stating in October 2001 that there was £9.27m when in fact there was about £2.8m. In February 2002 the claimant was told the true position by another of the defendant's employees, which was that there was £817,000 in the account. The defendant appealed against the award of damages (£12.15m) for loss of use of the claimant's trading fund between the date the fraud was discovered in February 2002 and the date of the trial.

Held

❖ (CA) The claimant was entitled to damages to reflect the fact that it was likely to have traded more profitably with a larger fund between February 2002 and March 2008. The fraud had a continuing effect on the claimant's ability to trade profitably. The court does not apply the same balance of probabilities approach as it would to the proof of past facts. Rather it estimates the loss by making the best attempt it can to evaluate the chances. [2010] EWCA Civ 486.

Key Principle

In a claim for negligent misrepresentation the measure of damages for negligent misrepresentation is the same as for fraudulent misrepresentation.

ROYSCOT TRUST LTD V ROGERSON 1991

D1 bought a car from D2. The car was bought on hire-purchase through P, a finance company. D1 and D2 represented to P that D1 had paid a 20 per cent deposit of £1,600 and so the total purchase price was £8000, when in fact D1 had paid a deposit of £1,200 and the total purchase price was £7,600. As a result P paid D2 £6,400, when it would have only been prepared to pay £4,800. D1 sold the car to X who obtained good title.

Held

❖ (CA) P was able to recover £3,625 being the difference between the amount paid by it to D2 and the amount received from D1 before he defaulted on the payments. The measure of damages under **Misrepresentation Act 1967**, s.2(1) was the measure of damages for fraudulent misrepresentation. Therefore, P was able to recover from D2 any loss which flowed directly from D's misrepresentation. [1991] 3 All E.R. 294.

Commentary

(1) This means unforeseeable losses are recoverable. However, on the facts the court considered that D1's act of selling the car was not unforeseeable.

(2) The judgments refer to innocent misrepresentation, but discuss the award of damages under **Misrepresentation Act 1967**, s.2(1) which is concerned with negligent misrepresentation.

(3) In *Smith New Court Securities Ltd v Scrimgeour Vickers (Asset Management) Ltd* [1996] 3 W.L.R. 1051, Lords Browne-Wilkinson and Steyn implied that the decision in this case was not correct. Arguably in a claim for negligent misrepresentation damages should only be awarded for loss that is reasonably foreseeable.

(4) In *Laws v The Society of Lloyd's* [2003] EWCA Civ 1887 the CA considered that a claim for negligent misrepresentation was not an "action for damages for negligence" within s.14A Limitation Act 1980. See also *Thomson v Christie Manson & Woods Ltd* [2004] EWHC 1101 (QB).

Key Principle

Damages are measured at the time the negligent misrepresentation was discovered not at the time the contract was entered into.

NAUGHTON V O'CALLAGHAN 1990

P purchased a young racehorse at the Newmarket sales in reliance on a description of the horse's pedigree in the sales catalogue. The price paid was £31,500. Almost two years later P discovered that, because of a mix-up at the stud where the horse had been born, the horse's pedigree was not that of a thoroughbred racehorse but an American dirt track race horse. The value of the horse at the time the contract was made was about £24,500. However, its value when the misrepresentation was discovered was about £1,500. P sued D, the seller, to recover the purchase price as well as training fees and expenditure.

Held

❖ (QBD) P recovered the damages claimed. The horse they purchased was altogether different from what they expected. It was reasonable to train and race the colt after the purchase. The horse's fall in value related to its particular circumstances not to a general fall in the market. [1990] 3 All E.R. 191.

Key Principle

The court has the power to award damages under s.2(2) **Misrepresentation Act 1967** only where the contract is subsisting and the right to rescind has not been lost.

Government of Zanzibar v British Aerospace (Lancaster House) Ltd 2001

Z agreed to buy a corporate jet from BA(LH). Z claimed that the contract should be rescinded or that damages should be awarded under s.2(2) **Misrepresentation Act 1967** because of misrepresentation(s) made by BA(LH) relating to the airworthiness and reliability of the aircraft.

Held

❖ (QBD) Rescission was no longer available as a remedy to Z. Therefore they were not entitled to damages under s.2(2). [2000] 1 W.L.R. 2333.

Commentary

The court declined to follow *Thomas Witter Ltd v T.B.P. Industries Ltd* [1996] 2 All E.R. 573 where the court held that the power to award damages under s.2(2) did not depend on a subsisting right to rescission. It only depended upon a right having existed in the past.

Key Principle

The measure of damages in a claim for innocent misrepresentation is the difference between the actual value of the subject-matter at the time of the contract and the misrepresented value of the subject-matter.

William Sindall Plc v Cambridgeshire County Council 1994

D sold land for housing to P for £5 million. In reply to a pre-contractual enquiry as to whether D was aware of any undisclosed easements affecting the land, D had answered "not so far as the vendor is aware". In fact there were sewer pipes under the land.

Held

❖ (CA) There was no actionable misrepresentation. If there had been, the measure of damages under s.2(2) of the **Misrepresentation Act 1967** would be the difference between the actual value of the land at the time of the contract and the value of the land as represented. [1994] 1 W.L.R. 1016.

Commentary

(1) Damages should not take into account the decline in market value since the contract was made. The value of the land in fact halved.

(2) Measure of damages is assessed differently under s.2(2) from s.2(1).

Key Principle
Under section 2(2) of the **Misrepresentation Act 1967** the court is required to undertake a balancing exercise when deciding which remedy would be equitable in the circumstances.

> UCB CORPORATE SERVICES LTD V THOMASON 2005
> The bank (UCB) claimed £2.9 million from the respondent, a Conservative MP, and his wife either under two guarantees entered into in 1990, or alternatively as damages for breach of a 1997 agreement under which the bank agreed to accept the lesser amount of £34,000. The bank had been induced to enter into the waiver agreement as a consequence of misrepresentations made by the respondents during negotiations undertaken with the aim of avoiding the respondents being made bankrupt. The bank claimed rescission of the waiver agreement, which would have the effect of reviving the guarantees, or damages in lieu under s. 2(2) of the **Misrepresentation Act 1967**.

Held
❖ (CA) First, the court would not order rescission of the waiver agreement because the evidence did not indicate that the bank would in fact have been in a financially better position had it not entered into the agreement. Second, the bank was not entitled to damages because it did not suffer any significant loss as a consequence of the misrepresentations. [2005] EWCA Civ 225.

Commentary
(1) Latham L.J. considered that loss in s.2(2) included financial loss and other "detriment".

(2) The "loss" suffered by the bank as a consequence of the misrepresentations was the lost chance of obtaining more money had the appellants told the truth before entering into the waiver agreement; not the full amount of the guaranteed debt.

EXCLUSION CLAUSES AND MISREPRESENTATION

Key Principle
A limitation on the apparent authority of an auctioneer is not an exclusion clause.

Overbrooke Estate Ltd v Glencombe Properties Ltd 1974

P instructed auctioneers to sell a property. The particulars of sale stated that "neither the auctioneer nor any person in the employment of the auctioneer has any authority to make or give any representation or warranty". D, who were the highest bidders at the auction, alleged that three days before auction they asked the auctioneer questions to which inaccurate answers were given which amounted to misrepresentations.

Held

❖ (Ch D) Even if there were misrepresentations, the question was not whether the clause was reasonable under s.3 of the **Misrepresentation Act 1967**. Section 3 was irrelevant because the clause was a limitation on the apparent authority of auctioneers, not an exclusion clause. D knew or ought to have known that nothing told them by the auctioneer could bind P. [1974] 3 All E.R. 511.

Key Principle

The court will look behind the clause to see whether it is designed to avoid liability.

Cremdean Properties v Nash 1977

P purchased property from D. P then claimed rescission of the contract because of a misrepresentation about the amount of rentable office space. In the contract of sale D disclaimed responsibility for the accuracy of the particulars of sale and stated that no misdescription would annul the contract.

Held

❖ (CA) The disclaimer was subject to the reasonableness test if P could show that they in fact relied on the particulars of sale, and the effect of the disclaimer was to exclude D from liability. (1977) 244 E.G. 837.

Key Principle

A term in an agreement which excludes liability for representations is invalid unless reasonable.

LEASE MANAGEMENT SERVICES V PURNELL SECRETARIAL SERVICES 1994

P leased a photocopier, making it clear that the machine supplied should be able to produce "paper plates". It did not have this feature. The lease excluded liability for representations made about the machine.

Held

❖ (CA) The exclusion clause was unreasonable. It was overridden by representations made to P by the copier salesman. [1994] C.C.L.R. 127.

Commentary

The reasonableness test is to be found in s.3 **Misrepresentation Act 1967** as substituted by s.8 **Unfair Contract Terms Act 1977**. See also *Curtis v Chemical Cleaning & Dyeing Co* (1951), and *Howard Marine & Dredging Co Ltd v A. Ogden & Sons (Excavations) Ltd* (1978).

NEGLIGENT MISSTATEMENT

Key Principle

Precontractual statements made negligently can give rise to liability in the tort of negligent misstatement.

ESSO PETROLEUM CO LTD V MARDON 1976

P made statements to D, during pre-contractual negotiations, estimating the likely quantity of petrol a filling station would sell over a three-year period. The estimates were over optimistic and D lost money. P sued for possession of the site and D claimed damages for the false representations.

Held

❖ (CA) P recovered damages under the tort of negligent misstatement. P owed D a duty of care. P had a financial interest in the advice they were giving and knew that D was relying on their knowledge and expertise. P was in breach of the duty of care. [1976] 2 W.L.R. 583.

Commentary

(1) CA also held that Esso had given a contractual warranty that their opinion was carefully formed.

(2) The facts arose before the **Misrepresentation Act 1967** became law. Therefore, D could not claim under s.2(1).

(3) The tort of negligent misstatement derives from the decision of the House of Lords in *Hedley Byrne & Co v Heller & Partners* [1963] 3 W.L.R. 101.

(4) Different limitation periods may apply to a claim for negligent misstatement rather than negligent misrepresentation under s.2(1) **MA 1967**. See e.g. *Thomson v Christie Manson & Woods Ltd* [2004] EWHC 1101 (QB).

THINK POINT

When may an opinion amount to an actionable misrepresentation?

If the misrepresentation in *Parabola Investments Limited and another v Browallia Cal Limited and Another* 2010 had been negligent instead of fraudulent, what difference would that have made to the remedies available to the claimant?

Mistake

10

INTRODUCTION

Mistake is not often the basis of a claim. The central issue for the common law was whether the mistake was of such a nature or degree that it destroyed the basis of consent on which the contract rests. Mistake has links with certainty (See Ch.2). A case of unilateral mistake may also include a misrepresentation (see Ch.9).

There are three types of mistake which can make the contract either void or voidable. "Void" means that the contract never had any legal effect, so that, for example, if A sells a painting to B and the contract is void for mistake, B acquires no property rights in the painting.

If the contract is "voidable" for mistake B would normally acquire property rights in the painting, which means that B can transfer those rights on the sale of the painting to C, so long as A has not avoided the contract, that is brought it to an end.

The three types of mistake are:

(1) Common.
(2) Mutual.
(3) Unilateral.

This classification is the one most commonly used by the courts. The remedies for mistake do not include damages. Equitable remedies, such as rescission and rectification, prevail.

Key Principle
The mistake must occur at the time of making the contract.

> AMALGAMATED INVESTMENT AND PROPERTY CO LTD V JOHN WALKER & SONS LTD 1976
>
> P was negotiating to buy a warehouse from D. D knew that P intended to redevelop the property. Both P and D knew that P required planning permission to do so. P asked D if the property was of special historical or architectural interest. On August 14, D truthfully replied that it was not. Unknown to P and D, the Department of Environment planned to make the warehouse a listed building. On September 26, P entered into

a contract to buy the property for £1.71 million. On September 27, the Department of Environment made it a listed building, and it became worth £210,000.

Held

❖ (CA) P could not rescind for common mistake. The parties were not mistaken about the nature of the building at the date of the contract. [1976] 3 All E.R. 509.

Commentary

Mistakes of law as well as fact affect the validity of a contract following *Kleinwort Benson Ltd v Lincoln City Council* [1998] 2 A.C. 349; see Morland J. in *Brennan v Bolt Burden*, *The Times*, November 7, 2003.

COMMON MISTAKE

Key Principle

Where unknown to both parties the specific subject matter of the agreement is in fact non-existent then the contract is void for common mistake.

> COUTURIER V HASTIE 1856
> There was a contract for the sale of a cargo of corn thought to be in transit from Salonika to the UK. Unknown to both parties the corn had fermented and was sold by the master of the ship in Tunis.

Held

❖ (HL) It was a contract to buy specific goods, which in fact did not exist. The buyer did not have to pay for the corn. The contract was in effect void. [1843–1860] All E.R. Rep. 280.

Commentary

(1) This is known as res extincta.

(2) Both parties make the same mistake.

(3) **Sale of Goods Act 1979** states that a contract for sale of specific goods which have perished is void.

Key Principle

Where A agrees to buy property from B, which both A and B believe is owned by B, but which in fact belongs to A, then the contract is void for common mistake.

> COOPER V PHIBBS 1867
>
> A man erroneously believed that he owned a fishery, and told his nephew that he did. After his uncle's death his nephew leased the fishery from his uncle's daughters. In fact the nephew owned the fishery.

Held

❖ (HL) The contract was set aside, but the daughters were given a lien on the fishery for such money as they had spent on it. (1867) L.R. 2 HL 149.

Commentary

(1) This is known as res sua.

(2) Both parties make the same mistake.

Key Principle

Where parties have entered into a contract which is impossible to perform at the time the agreement was made, the contract is void for common mistake.

> GREAT PEACE SHIPPING LTD V TSAVLIRIS (INTERNATIONAL) LTD 2002
>
> The Cape Providence, a ship, suffered serious damage in the Indian Ocean. The defendant agreed to provide salvage services. The claimant owned the Great Peace, which was thought by both parties to be about 12 hours sailing time away from the CP. The claimants agreed that the GP would alter course and stand by to assist the crew of the CP. Soon afterwards the defendant discovered that the GP was in fact about 39 hours sailing away from the CP. The defendant cancelled the contract and refused to pay the contract fee.

Held

❖ (CA) The contract was not void for common mistake. The fact that the vessels were further apart than both parties had appreciated did not mean that it was impossible to perform the contract. [2002] W.L.R. 1617

(1) The CA considered that common mistake is analogous to the doctrine of frustration.

(2) The CA held that five elements must be present if common mistake is to avoid a contract:
  (a) A common assumption as to the existence of a state of affairs.
  (b) No warranty by either party that the state of affairs exists.
  (c) The non-existence of the state of affairs is not attributable to the fault of either party.
  (d) The non-existence of the state of affairs renders performance of the contract impossible.
  (e) The "state of affairs" refers to a vital factor which must be present in order for the contractual adventure to be performed.

(3) The CA suggested that there is scope for legislation to give greater flexibility to the law of mistake than the common law allows.

Key Principle
Where both parties enter into a contract under a false and fundamental assumption then as a general rule the contract is valid.

BELL V LEVER BROTHERS 1932
P, Lever Brothers, made D, the managing director of a subsidiary company, redundant. P agreed to pay D £30,000 compensation. After paying D the money P discovered that they could have dismissed D for breach of his duties as a director. Therefore P sued D for the return of the £30,000 on the basis of common mistake.

Held
❖ (HL) The fundamental assumption that the contract was not terminable turned out to be false but this did not affect the validity of the contract. [1932] A.C. 161.

Commentary
In *Great Peace Shipping Ltd v Tsavliris (International) Ltd* (see above) the CA held that it was impossible to reconcile *Solle v Butcher* [1949] 2 All E.R. 1107 with *Bell v Lever Bros*. The CA refused to follow Lord Denning in *Solle v Butcher* and held that the courts do not have a general equitable jurisdiction to grant rescission of a contract on the ground of common mistake where the contract is not void at common law.

MISTAKE

Key Principle

Where a contract is not void for mistake the court may exercise its equitable jurisdiction and rectify the written contract because it does not give effect to an antecedent agreement.

JOSCELYNE V NISSEN 1970

P, the father, sued D, his daughter, for breach of a written contract whereby he agreed to transfer his business to D in return for being allowed to occupy his flat in his daughter's house free from rent and other outgoings. D paid the gas, electricity and coal bills until a dispute arose between the parties.

Held

❖ (CA) The court ordered rectification of the contract so that these items were specifically mentioned, because there was convincing proof that the written contract did not represent the parties' common intention. [1970] 1 All E.R. 1213.

Commentary

(1) The court retains this jurisdiction after *Great Peace Shipping Ltd v Tsavliris (International) Ltd* (see above) because the CA stated that the case was not concerned with this type of mistake.

(2) In *Chartbrook Ltd v Persimmon Homes Ltd* [2009] 1 A.C. 1101 (see Ch.7), Lord Hoffman stated that there was a prior consensus between the parties, based on the May letter, and that both parties were mistaken in thinking that the subsequent contractual documents reflected that consensus. If the House of Lords had not allowed PH's appeal on the issue of construction, PH would have been entitled to rectification of the contract.

MUTUAL MISTAKE

Key Principle

Where there is no genuine agreement between the parties because they are at cross-purposes, there is no binding contract.

SCRIVEN BROS & CO V HINDLEY 1913

P sold goods at auction to D. P was selling both hemp and tow in two lots, but they were not clearly distinguished. D thought both lots were hemp which was more expensive than tow. So D paid a much higher price for the tow than was necessary. Therefore P intended to sell tow, but D intended to buy hemp.

Held

❖ (KBD) There was no binding contract because there was no certainty as to what was the subject matter of the contract. [1913] 3 K.B. 564.

Commentary

Note the overlap with contract formation.

Key Principle

Where there is a mutual mistake which does not invalidate the contract, an equitable remedy may be available.

> DENNY V HANCOCK 1870
>
> D purchased a house and grounds. Before entering into the contract to buy the property he had inspected the property with a plan and believed that three magnificent trees were within the boundaries. He then discovered that they were not. D refused to proceed with the purchase and P sued for specific performance.

Held

There was a binding contract. However, the court declined to make a decree of specific performance because the plan was confusing and the physical boundary was misleading when physically inspected. (1870) L.R. 6 Ch. App. 1.

UNILATERAL MISTAKE

Key Principle

Where P could not have reasonably supposed that the offer reflected D's real intention the contract is void for mistake.

> HARTOG V COLIN & SHIELDS 1939
>
> D offered to sell hareskins to P at 101/4d per pound. Preliminary negotiations with P had taken place on the basis of 101/4d per piece. In the hareskin trade skins were always sold per piece. There were about three pieces to the pound so D's offer amounted to 31/4d per piece, whereas three weeks earlier the price had been 101/4d per piece.

Held

❖ (QBD) P must have realised D's mistake, therefore the contract was void. [1939] 3 All E.R. 566.

Commentary

(1) Most cases involving unilateral mistakes arise because of mistaken identity usually involving a "rogue".

(2) In order to make the contract void the mistake as to identity must be fundamental.

(3) The onus is on the person deceived to rebut the presumption that there is valid contract.

Key Principle

At the time of negotiating the contract, the identity of the other party must be of crucial importance to the mistaken party and this must be apparent from their conduct during the negotiations.

CUNDY V LINDSAY 1878

A rogue, "Blenkarn", writing from 37 Wood Street, Cheapside, offered to buy goods from P. The rogue signed his letters so that the signature looked like "Blenkiron & Co", which was a respectable firm at 123 Wood Street, Cheapside. The rogue intended to mislead because his address was a single room, and the street entrance was in an adjoining street. P knew of Blenkiron and without checking sent goods to Blenkiron, 37 Wood Street. The rogue sold them to D who took them in good faith. P sued D for conversion.

Held

❖ (HL) P intended to sell to Blenkiron not to the person who traded at 37 Wood Street. Therefore, the contract was void for unilateral mistake, and P could recover the goods from D. [1878] 3 App. Cas. 459.

Key Principle

The mistaken party must prove that he intended to deal with some person other than the person with whom he apparently made the contract.

Wallis, with deception in mind, set up in business as Hallam & Co. Using impressive headed notepaper, he ordered goods on credit from P, which W then sold to D. There had been previous dealings between W & P. W did not pay for the goods. P tried to recover the value of goods from D on the grounds that the contract between P and W was void, since P mistakenly believed that such a firm as Hallam & Co existed. Therefore, the title to the goods still remained with them.

Held

❖ (CA) P was unsuccessful. P intended to contract with the writer of the letter. P was unable to show that they meant to contract with Hallam & Co rather than with W. [1897] 14 T.L.R 98.

Commentary

The contract was voidable for fraud but, because it had not been avoided at the time of the sale by W to D, D had good title to the goods.

Key Principle

In a written consumer credit agreement a mistake as to the identity of one of the parties is likely to be fundamental and make the contract void.

Shogun Finance Ltd v Hudson 2003

A rogue claiming to be "Mr Patel" wanted to buy a new car from a car dealer on hire purchase. The rogue produced a genuine driving licence as evidence of his name and address. The dealer telephoned SFL, the claimant finance company, which in a few minutes checked "Mr Patel's" identity and creditworthiness, as well as comparing faxed copies of the rogue's signature with the signature on the driving licence. SFL told the dealer that the finance was available to "Mr Patel", and the dealer on receipt of a 10 per cent deposit handed over the car and its documentation to the rogue. The rogue sold the car to D who bought the car as a private purchaser in good faith. The claimant sought to recover the car from D.

Held

❖ (HL) The rogue's contract with SFL was void for mistake. SFL intended to enter into a hire purchase agreement with "Mr Patel", not with the rogue. Therefore the rogue was not "the debtor" under the hire purchase agreement and D could not rely on s.27 of the Hire Purchase Act. As a consequence D had not acquired title to the car, and either had to return the car or its value to the claimant, SFL. [2003] W.L.R. 1371.

Commentary

(1) The **Hire Purchase Act 1964**, s.27, as substituted by the **Consumer Credit Act 1974**, provides that a private purchaser who buys a car in good faith from someone (the debtor), who acquired the care under a hire purchase agreement, obtains a good title to the car.

(2) Lords Hobhouse, Phillips (M.R.) and Walker emphasised that the main issue was the construction of the written hire-purchase agreement. This made it clear that SFL intended to contract with "Mr Patel". This was not a face-to-face agreement.

(3) Lord Hobhouse considered that in a consumer credit transaction the identity of the customer is fundamental to the whole transaction because it is essential to the checking of the credit rating of the applicant borrower.

(4) Lord Nicholls and Lord Millet gave powerful dissenting judgments and considered that *Cundy v Lindsay* (see above) should be overruled. Where two individuals deal with each other by whatever medium and agree terms of the contract, but one party deceives the other as to their identity the contract should be voidable for fraud but not void for mistake.

(5) Lord Millet thought that the law should protect innocent third parties, such as D.

Key Principle
The mistaken party must prove that the other party was aware of the mistake.

> HARDMAN v BOOTH 1863
> P called at the place of business of Gandell & Co and was fraudulently persuaded by a clerk, Edward Gandell, that he had authority to act for the firm. P sold and delivered goods to Gandell & Co, but they were intercepted by EG who pledged the goods to D. P sued D in the tort of conversion.

Held

P could recover the goods from D. No contract came into existence because P's offer was to the company, as EG knew, but EG tried to accept the offer for himself. EG, therefore, acquired no title to the goods which he could transfer to the innocent D. [1863] 1 H. & C. 803.

Key Principle

In a face to face transaction, the mistaken party must take reasonable steps to verify the identity of the person with whom they are dealing.

LEWIS V AVERAY 1972

A rogue, pretending to be the actor Richard Greene (Robin Hood), offered to buy P's car and did so with a worthless cheque. P saw Richard Greene's identity pass for Pinewood Studios. P handed over the car to the rogue who sold it to D. P sued D for conversion.

Held

❖ (CA) P had concluded a contract with the rogue. P intended to sell to the person in front of him. P had done little to verify the rogue's identity. [1973] 1 W.L.R. 510.

Commentary

(1) There are two earlier CA decisions on this point. *Phillips v Brooks Ltd* (1919) [1918–1919] All E.R. Rep. 246 (see Ch.9) was followed; the court expressed disagreement with the decision in *Ingram v Little* [1960] 3 W.L.R. 504. In *Shogun Finance Ltd v Hudson* 2003 (see above) Lords Millett and Walker considered, obiter, that *Ingram v Little* should not be followed.

(2) In *Shogun* Lord Nicholls and Lord Millet (dissenting) considered that the same principles should apply irrespective of whether the transaction was negotiated face to face or at a distance. In particular where two individuals deal with each other by whatever medium and agree terms of the contract, but one party deceives the other as to their identity, the contract should be voidable for fraud but not void for mistake.

Key Principle

Where a contract is not void for unilateral mistake, the court may exercise its equitable jurisdiction and rectify the written agreement.

THOMAS BATES AND SON V WYNDHAMS (LINGERIE) LTD 1981

P, landlords, sought rectification of a lease. D had been tenants of P under two previous leases, which gave D an option to renew the lease and provided for arbitration in the event of P and D being unable to agree the new rent. The third lease by an oversight did not include a provision for fixing the rent by arbitration if the parties could not agree.

Held

❖ (CA) P could obtain rectification. P could show that they thought the lease contained such a term; D was aware of the omission and knew that it was a mistake on P's part; D did not draw the mistake to P's attention; the mistake benefited D. [1981] 1 All E.R. 1077.

Key Principle

A successful rectification claim based upon unilateral mistake will usually require the defendant to have knowledge of the claimant's mistake and to have acted dishonestly.

> GEORGE WIMPEY UK LTD V VI CONSTRUCTION LTD 2005
>
> W, which had vast experience of residential developments, sought rectification of a contract to purchase land from VIC, which had no relevant experience, because of an error included in the written contract relating to the calculation of the price to be paid to VIC. VIC were aware of W's mistake but said nothing.

Held

❖ (CA) Rectification of the contract was not granted. W had failed to provide convincing evidence that VIC had acted dishonestly. [2005] EWCA Civ 77.

Commentary

"Knowledge" of the mistake means (i) actual knowledge as well as (ii) "wilfully shutting one's eyes to the obvious", and (iii) "wilfully and recklessly failing to make such inquiries as an honest and reasonable man would make".

NON EST FACTUM

Key Principle

Where A is induced by the false statement of B to sign a written document containing a contract that is fundamentally different in character from that which A contemplated, then A is not bound by the contract.

> SAUNDERS V ANGLIA BUILDING SOCIETY 1970
>
> P, a widow aged 78, gave the deeds of her house to her nephew so that he could raise money using the house as security. P made it a condition that she could stay in the house until she died. A document was

prepared which assigned the leasehold not by way of gift to the nephew, but by way of sale to the dishonest D. P signed the document. She did not read it because she had broken her glasses, and her nephew told her that it was a deed of gift to him. D, who paid no money to P or to her nephew, mortgaged the house to the building society, but failed to pay any mortgage instalments. P sued D and the building society, pleading *non est factum* on the ground that she intended to give the house not sell it.

Held

❖ (HL) This distinction was not fundamental. The assignment was not totally different in character and nature from what she had in mind. Its object was to enable her nephew to raise a loan. [1970] 3 W.L.R. 1078.

Commentary

(1) HL considered that plea of *non est factum* is not limited to deeds. It is applicable to other documents.

(2) There is a heavy burden of proof on the person raising the plea.

Key Principle

The plea of non est factum applies where without negligence a person fails to scrutinise a document which they have signed.

LLOYDS BANK V WATERHOUSE 1990

D was illiterate and signed a bank guarantee without reading it or telling the bank that he could not read, but in reliance on the bank's misrepresentations about its nature.

Held

❖ (CA) D was entitled to rely on defence of non est factum, as well as on the bank's negligent misrepresentation. The Independent, February 27, 1990.

THINK POINT

What is the difference between:
(a) common mistake;
(h) mutual mistake; and
(c) unilateral mistake?

MISTAKE

If the facts of *Lewis v Averay* 1972 were to arise now, do you think, bearing in mind later cases, that the court would reach the same decision as it did in 1972?

Unfair Pressure

11

INTRODUCTION

Where one party is pressured to enter into a contract by, for example, physical threats or by psychological or economic pressure, the contract may be voidable.

There are three main types of pressure which may affect the validity of a contract:

(1) duress;

(2) undue influence; and

(3) economic duress.

Duress, which requires physical intimidation, is relatively rare.

Undue influence has its roots in equitable principles. Recent case law has primarily been concerned with the effect of undue influence, often by a husband on a wife, on the rights of third parties such as banks. For example, a bank lends a husband money for his business, using the matrimonial home as security for the loan with his wife's agreement. The business fails, the husband is unable to repay the loan, and so the bank wishes to take possession of the matrimonial home.

Economic duress has been developed by the courts since the 1970s. However, there is a thin line between unlawful economic pressure and ordinary commercial pressure which is not unlawful. English law does not recognise a general principle of unconscionability. EU law indirectly impinges on this area of law, for example, art.82 of the EC Treaty (abuse of a dominant position) and the **Unfair Terms in Consumer Contracts Directive 93/13/EEC** (see Ch.8).

DURESS

Key Principle

At common law, actual violence or threats of violence to the person to pressurise that person into entering into a contract make the contract voidable and possibly void.

BARTON V ARMSTRONG 1975

P, was the managing director of a company. He arranged that the company would pay money to D, the chairman of the company, in order to get him off the board. P did this partly for commercial reasons, and partly because D had threatened to have P killed if P did not make the arrangement. P applied to the court to have the contract set aside for duress.

Held

❖ (JCPC) P might have entered into the arrangement even if there had been no threats or unlawful pressure from D, but the threats and unlawful pressure contributed to his decision to enter into the arrangement. Once the fact of duress was established the burden was on D to show that the duress did not in fact induce the contract. [1975] 2 All E.R. 465.

UNDUE INFLUENCE

Actual Undue Influence

Key Principle

Where a contract is induced by improper pressure, not amounting to duress, it is voidable.

WILLIAMS V BAYLEY 1866

P's son had given D promissory notes on which he had forged his father's signature. P was threatened with the criminal prosecution of his son and so agreed to make an equitable mortgage in favour of D in exchange for the return of the promissory notes.

Held

❖ (HL) The agreement could be cancelled. P did not make a free and voluntary decision. (1866) L.R. 1 H.L. 200.

Key Principle

Where actual undue influence is proved it is not necessary to establish manifest disadvantage.

Held

❖ (HL) Where a wife was induced by the undue influence of her husband to charge the matrimonial home as security for a loan made to them jointly, the lender would not be affected by the undue influence if the husband was not his agent and if the lender had no actual knowledge of the undue influence, nor was there any indication that the transaction was anything other than a normal loan to a married couple for their joint benefit. [1993] 4 All E.R. 433.

Commentary

(1) D was able to set aside the agreement she made with her husband because of his actual undue influence. However, she was not able to set aside the mortgage as against P.

(2) In *Daniel v Drew*, *The Times*, May 18, 2005, a forceful and insensitive nephew obtained his vulnerable 85-year old aunt's agreement to resign as a trustee from the family trust, which owned the family farm. This left the nephew and his brother as the only trustees. The CA confirmed that the aunt's agreement was obtained by actual or express undue influence and considered that in such cases it is appropriate to inquire what prompted the relevant decision taken by the donor.

PRESUMED UNDUE INFLUENCE

Where a Special Relationship Exists Between the Parties

Key Principle

Where a special relationship exists between the parties there is a presumption that one party acted under a pressure which they could not resist.

During that period she gave £7,000 to the sisterhood. By the time she left £1,671 had been spent. 6 years after P left she sought to recover the £1,671 on the grounds of undue influence.

Held

❖ (CA) P could not recover the money because she did not claim immediately after leaving the sisterhood. There was undue influence. Although no personal pressure was placed on P, and no unfair advantage taken of her, the gifts were made under a pressure she could not resist. [1886–1890] All E.R. Rep. 90.

PRESUMED UNDUE INFLUENCE

Where no Special Relationship Exists Between the Contracting Parties

Key Principle

The burden of proving that undue influence has been exercised normally lies on the party challenging the validity of the agreement.

> LLOYDS BANK V BUNDY 1974
> D was an elderly farmer, whose home and only asset was a farm house. D, his son, and the son's company all banked at the same branch of P's bank. The son's company ran into financial difficulties. D guaranteed his son's overdraft with a charge on the farm house together with a subsequent guarantee and charge. In total the amount charged against the house was £7,500. The house was worth £10,000. D was advised by his solicitor that he should not commit himself further, but P's assistant manager arranged for another charge which would increase the total to £11,000. He told D that this was the only way P could support his son's company. In May 1970 receivers were appointed to the company and P attempted to enforce the guarantee and charges.

Held

❖ (CA) The guarantee and charges were set aside. D looked to P for financial advice and placed confidence in it. It was in P's interest to obtain the guarantee. P should have ensured that D received independent advice. [1974] 3 All E.R. 757.

Key Principle ....

The presumption will be raised where a transaction is large or improvident and the person giving effect to the transaction places great trust and confidence in the recipient.

> GOLDSWORTHY V BRICKELL 1987
>
> P, aged 85, let his farm at a very low rent to D, with a favourable option to purchase. D was a neighbouring farmer whom P came to trust and depend on for advice and help in running the farm.

Held ....

❖ (CA) The agreement was set aside. Their relationship raised a presumption of undue influence. P had not entered the agreement after full, free and informed thought. [1987] 2 W.L.R. 133.

Key Principle ....

There are two elements to establishing presumed undue influence: (1) the complainant placed trust and confidence in the other party; and (2) the transaction is not readily explicable by the relationship of the parties.

> ROYAL BANK OF SCOTLAND PLC V ETRIDGE (NO.2), BARCLAYS BANK PLC V HARRIS, MIDLAND BANK PLC V WALLACE, NATIONAL WESTMINSTER BANK PLC V GILL, UCB HOME LOANS CORPORATION LTD V MOORE, BARCLAYS BANK PLC V COLEMAN, BANK OF SCOTLAND V BENNETT, KENYON-BROWN V DESMOND BANKS & CO 2001
>
> The House of Lords heard these eight appeals together. In each case a wife had agreed to the matrimonial home being used as security for a loan by a bank to her husband or to her husband's company. Subsequently in seven of the cases the bank sought possession of the matrimonial home because the loan was not repaid. Each wife resisted the bank's application on the ground that her agreement had been obtained by her husband's undue influence and that she had not received independent legal advice before agreeing to the matrimonial home being used as security for the loan. In three of the seven cases the court had rejected the wife's defence at a preliminary stage. In the other four cases the wife had been unsuccessful at the trial. The eighth case concerned a claim by a wife for damages from a solicitor who advised her before she entered into the transaction.

Held

❖ (HL) The appeals in three cases (Harris, Wallace, Moore) were allowed on the ground that the wife had an arguable defence that the bank had not taken reasonable steps to satisfy itself that the wife had received independent legal advice as to the nature and effect of the transaction she entered into. The appeal by the wife in Bennett, one of the four cases that went to trial, was successful as was the appeal by the solicitor in the eighth case (Kenyon-Brown). The appeals in the other three cases (Etridge, Gill, Coleman) were dismissed, either because the wife failed to establish at trial that she had been subject to undue influence, or because constructive notice of undue influence could not be imputed to the bank. [2001] 3 W.L.R. 102.

Commentary

(1) Lord Nicholls stated that undue influence means that influence has been misused. Reasonable or even exaggerated statements by a husband would not usually amount to undue influence or misstatements. Inaccurate explanations or decisions taken by a husband on his wife's behalf which are in his interest rather than hers are likely to amount to an abuse of his influence.

(2) Lord Nicholls considered that the label "manifest disadvantage" which had been used for the second element of presumed undue influence was ambiguous in the context of wives guaranteeing payment of their husband's business debts, and should be discarded. He considered that the label may still be apt when applied to straightforward transactions such as a substantial gift or a sale at an undervalue.

(3) Lord Scott argued that it is the combination of relationship and the nature of the transaction that gives rise to the presumption.

(4) Where both elements are established the law reverses the burden of proof and requires the other party to provide an explanation for the transaction which may or may not rebut the presumption of undue influence.

EQUITABLE REMEDY OF RESCISSION

Key Principle

The court can set aside the contract in such a way that justice can be achieved in the particular case.

O'SULLIVAN V MANAGEMENT AGENCY AND MUSIC LTD 1984

P, Gilbert O'Sullivan, was a young unknown composer and performer when he entered into a management agreement with D. P had no business experience and completely trusted D. As a consequence P entered into various agreements put forward by D without any independent advice. D also had a financial interest in the agreements.

Held

❖ (CA) D was in a fiduciary relationship with P, and the agreement could be set aside because of the undue influence, even though restitutio in integrum was not strictly possible. D was entitled to be paid for the work he had undertaken on P's behalf. [1984] 3 W.L.R. 448.

Commentary

(1) This case is also relevant to contracts in restraint of trade (see Ch.12).

(2) In *Halpern and Another v Halpern and Others* (No.2) [2007] 3 All E.R. 478 the Court of Appeal considered that the same principle applied whenever rescission was sought, including for common law duress. Carnwath L.J. stated that for the purposes of "practical justice", the primary objective may not always be to restore *both* parties to their previous positions.

(3) See also *Samuel (professionally known as Seal) v Wadlow* [2007] EWCA Civ 155 where Seal unsuccessfully argued that the settlement agreement that he entered into with his former manager in 1995 was voidable because of undue influence and should be rescinded.

Key Principle

The aim of the court is to achieve practical justice for both parties.

CHEESE V THOMAS 1994

There was an agreement between P and D, his great-nephew. P gave D £43,000 which was to be put towards the cost of a house for them both. D bought the house in his sole name for £83,000. P had the right to live in the house for the rest of his life. D defaulted on the mortgage. The house was sold for £55,400. It was accepted that P had entered into the transaction as a result of D's undue influence. P claimed £43,000.

Held

❖ (CA) P could only recover the same proportion of the selling price of £55,400 as he had contributed towards the purchase (i.e. just over half). [1994] 1 W.L.R. 129.

Commentary

(1) The payment was accepted to be for purchase of property in which P would have rights rather than a loan.

(2) The equitable remedy of rescission aims to restore both parties to their original position. Note other bars to rescission (see Ch.9).

Key Principle

The wife's right to set aside the transaction is an "all or nothing" process.

> TSB BANK PLC V CAMFIELD 1995
> The bank had constructive notice of a misrepresentation by H which had induced W to charge the matrimonial home so that a loan could be made to his business. H had innocently misrepresented that the loan was limited to £15,000 when in fact it was unlimited. P claimed they could recover £15,000.

Held

❖ (CA) W could have the whole transaction set aside. Terms should not be imposed on W as a condition of her obtaining equitable relief. In any event W had nothing to return to the bank as she had received nothing from the bank. [1995] 1 All E.R. 951.

Commentary

However, in *Barclays Bank Plc v Caplan*, *The Times*, December 12, 1997, the court (Ch D) held that setting aside was not invariably an all or nothing process. The court could not rewrite an agreement, but where part of a document was tainted by undue influence it could be severed and set aside leaving the remainder of the agreement valid.

THIRD PARTY RIGHTS

Key Principle

A creditor will have constructive notice of undue influence where a wife offers to stand surety for her husband's debt, the transaction is not to her financial advantage and there is a substantial chance that the husband has committed a legal or equitable wrong in procuring his wife's agreement.

BARCLAYS BANK PLC V O'BRIEN 1993

H and W jointly owned their matrimonial home. H's company had an overdraft. P required security for the overdraft from H. This included a mortgage on the matrimonial home which had to be agreed to and signed by W. W signed the mortgage and an accompanying explanatory letter at the bank in the presence of H. H had told W that the mortgage was for £60,000 and would last three weeks when in fact it was unlimited on both counts. P sought possession of the matrimonial home. W claimed that she was induced to sign the mortgage as a result of H's undue influence and misrepresentations. The undue influence claim was rejected by the trial judge. The hearing in HL was on the misrepresentation and constructive notice points.

Held

❖ (HL) P was fixed with constructive notice of the wrongful misrepresentations made by H to W who was therefore entitled as against P, to have the mortgage set aside. [1993] 4 All E.R. 417.

Commentary

(1) Lord Browne-Wilkinson stated that the same principles are applicable to any case where there is an emotional relationship between the cohabitees, whether heterosexual or homosexual, or any other relationship based on trust and confidence, and the bank is aware of the relationship.

(2) In *Royal Bank of Scotland plc v Etridge* (No.2) [2001] 3 W.L.R. 1021 Lord Nicholls preferred the phrase "put on inquiry" to "constructive notice". He considered that a bank is put on inquiry whenever a wife offers to stand surety for her husband's debts, or for the debts of a company whose shares are held by her and her husband. Where money is advanced to a husband and wife jointly, the bank is not put on inquiry unless it is aware that the loan is being made for the husband's purposes as distinct from their joint purposes (see *CIBC Mortgages Plc v Pitt* 1994, above).

(3) Lord Nicholls also considered that the key principle (above) constituted the underlying rationale but did not amount to factual conditions that must be proved in each case before a bank is put on inquiry.

Key Principle

A creditor may have constructive notice of undue influence exercised over an employee by an employer.

CREDIT LYONNAIS BANK NEDERLAND N.V. v BURCH 1997
D, an employee, agreed to her employer's request to put up her flat as
security for a £20,000 extension to his company's overdraft. P advised
D in writing to obtain independent legal advice, which she declined to
do. In fact D provided P with an unlimited guarantee of her employer's
debts.

Held

❖ (CA) The mortgage and guarantee were set aside. The transaction was so
manifestly to D's disadvantage that the bank could not claim to have taken
reasonable steps to avoid being fixed with constructive notice of the
employer's undue influence. [1997] 1 All E.R. 144.

Commentary

In *Royal Bank of Scotland Plc v Etridge* (No.2) [2001] 3 W.L.R. 1021, Lord
Nicholls confirmed that the *O'Brien* principle was of wider application. He
stated that as a general principle banks should be "put on inquiry" in every
case where the relationship between the surety and the debtor is non-
commercial, as in *Burch* or, for example, where there is a parent-child
relationship.

Key Principle

The bank should be expected to take reasonable steps to satisfy itself that
the wife understood the nature and effect of the transaction she was entering
into.

ROYAL BANK OF SCOTLAND PLC v ETRIDGE (NO.2) 2001
**(See facts above). Each wife resisted the bank's application for pos-
session of the matrimonial home on the ground that she had not
received independent legal advice before agreeing to the matrimonial
home being used as security for the loan to her husband or his
company.**

Held

❖ (HL) (see above). The appeals in three cases (Harris, Wallace, Moore) were
allowed on the ground that the wife had an arguable defence that the bank
had not taken such steps. [2001] 3 W.L.R. 1021.

(1) Lord Nicholls set out what amounted to reasonable steps. He stated that in future a bank should (1) check directly with the wife (W) the name of the solicitor she wishes to act for her, and (2) should inform W that it requires written confirmation from the solicitor that W has been independently advised of the legal and practical implications of the proposed transaction.

(2) The bank should not proceed with the transaction until it has received from W the name of her solicitor.

(3) The solicitor acting for W may also act for the bank or for H, unless there is evidence of undue influence or other impropriety by H.

NATURE AND EXTENT OF INDEPENDENT LEGAL ADVICE

Key Principle ....
The wife's solicitor is under a duty to satisfy themselves that their client understands the nature and effect of the transaction and is willing to enter into it.

> ROYAL BANK OF SCOTLAND PLC V ETRIDGE (NO.2) 2001
> See facts above.

Held ....
❖ (HL) See above. [2001] 3 W.L.R. 1021.

Commentary ....
(1) The aim is to ensure that W receives true independent advice from her solicitor as to the nature and effect of the transaction so that she is able to give genuine consent. The solicitor is not under a duty to satisfy themselves of the absence of undue influence.

(2) The wife's solicitor is under a duty is to explain to W (1) the legal and practical effect of the transaction, (2) that W has the choice whether or not to proceed, and (3) that the solicitor is required to confirm to the bank that W has been so advised

(3) An informed wife is not to be stopped from entering into a financially unwise transaction should she wish to do so, and she should not be able to subsequently plead that the bank had constructive notice of any undue influence.

(4) The bank should provide the solicitor with detailed financial and other

relevant information so that the solicitor can ensure that W appreciates the seriousness of the risks she is taking, and can identify any reasons why the transaction may not be in her best interests.

(5) The solicitor's discussion with W should take place at a face to face meeting in the absence of H.

(6) Normally a bank should be able to rely upon the written confirmation from W's solicitor that she has been properly advised, unless the bank has reason to suspect that such advice has not been given.

(7) Where the solicitor wrongly advises W or wrongly confirms to the bank that she has received independent advice, W's remedy will be against the solicitor.

ECONOMIC DURESS

Key Principle
Economic duress renders a contract voidable.

> PAO ON V LAU YIU LONG 1979
> P threatened to break a contract with X company unless D who were shareholders in the company gave P a guarantee against loss resulting from the performance of that contract. D thinking that the risk of such loss was small, gave the guarantee to avoid the adverse publicity which the company might suffer if the contract was not performed.

Held
❖ (JCPC) In the circumstances there was no coercion of the will so the guarantee was not vitiated by duress. [1980] A.C. 614.

Commentary
Lord Scarman stated that the basis of economic duress is that it must always amount to a coercion of will, which vitiates consent.

Key Principle
The right to set the contract aside for economic duress can be lost by affirmation.

D agreed to build a ship for P. The price was to be paid in US dollars over five instalments. After P paid the first instalment, there was a steep decline in the value of the dollar. D demanded a 10 per cent increase in price and threatened not to complete the ship if they were not paid. P agreed. Eight months after completing the payments P claimed repayment of the excess.

Held

❖ (QBD) In principle this was a case of economic duress, since the threat not to build the ship was wrongful and highly coercive of P's will. However, P had lost the right to set the contract aside by not bringing the claim more promptly. [1979] 3 W.L.R. 419.

Key Principle

Economic duress vitiates one party's consent and renders the contract voidable.

UNIVERSE TANKSHIPS OF MONROVIA V ITWF, THE UNIVERSE SENTINEL, 1982

Trade union officials threatened to induce the crew of a ship to break their contract of employment so as to prevent the ship leaving port unless P made payments to D's welfare fund. If implemented the threats would have catastrophic financial consequences for ship-owners. Therefore it was conceded that the threats amounted to economic duress.

Held

❖ (HL) P's consent to make payments was vitiated by D's economic duress. P could recover the money paid. [1982] 2 W.L.R. 803.

Commentary

(1) Thus HL assumed the existence of a doctrine of economic duress based on illegitimate economic pressure.

(2) In *Borrelli v Ting* [2010] UKPC 21 the JCPC confirmed that economic duress arises where one party exerts illegitimate economic or similar pressure on another

Key Principle

Illegitimate pressure will amount to economic duress.

> **DIMSKAL SHIPPING CO S.A. V ITWF 1990**
>
> P, shipowners, were coerced into contracting with and making payments to D, an international trade union, by D's threatened and actual "blacking" of their ship while berthed in a Swedish port.

Held

❖ (CA) P were entitled to avoid the contracts (which were governed by English law) and recover the payments, notwithstanding that the industrial action was permitted under Swedish law. [1990] 1 Lloyd's Rep. 319.

Commentary

(1) The court preferred to talk of legitimate or illegitimate pressure not just coercion of will, i.e. to look at the pressure as well as the effect on the individual.

(2) The case went to the House of Lords in 1991 ([1991] 3 W.L.R. 875) where the main discussion was whether the legality of the industrial action should be determined by English or Swedish law. It was accepted that there was illegitimate pressure.

Key Principle

The illegitimate pressure vitiates the consent to be bound.

> **ATLAS V KAFCO 1989**
>
> D was under contract to supply baskets to branches of Woolworth's. D entered into a contract with P whereby P would deliver the baskets at an agreed price. However, P over-estimated the number of cartons which could be loaded onto one trailer and had set the price per carton too low. P then tried to vary the price agreed and ultimately stated that unless D agreed to pay a new increased price per load P would not deliver the baskets. D considered that they would be unable to find an alternative carrier. D felt compelled to sign the new agreement, but soon after the deliveries were completed they refused to pay the additional sums on grounds of economic duress.

Held

❖ (QBD) D was not liable to pay the increased price. P put illegitimate pressure amounting to economic duress on D. [1989] 3 W.L.R. 389.

Commentary ....

Two recent examples of illegitimate pressure in a commercial context are:

(1) *Adam Opel GmbH v Mitras Automotive (UK) Ltd* [2008] EWHC 3205 (QB), where the court held that an agreement by a car manufacturer to pay compensation to a supplier of front bumper mounts, because of its decision to terminate the supply contract, was void for economic duress because the manufacturer had only agreed to make the payment because the supplier had threatened to immediately stop supplying the parts if it did not do so.

(2) *Kolmar Group AG v Traxpo Enterprises Pvt Ltd* [2010] EWHC 113 (Comm) where the court held that the agreement by a purchaser of methanol to accede to the seller's demand to pay a higher price and accept a lesser amount was voidable. The purchaser was entitled to restitution of the additional £1.4 million paid because they had no practical choice but to agree to pay the increased price for the methanol, which was being purchased to supply a major client who required it urgently. The seller's demands amounted to economic duress.

Key Principle ....

Economic duress would not be proved in the context of arm's length commercial dealing between two companies.

> CTN CASH AND CARRY V GALLAHER 1994
>
> P bought cigarettes from D who delivered them by mistake to the wrong address, from where they were stolen. D invoiced P for the cigarettes and threatened to cut off P's credit facilities if they did not pay. P paid the invoice and then brought an action to recover the money on the grounds that it had been paid under economic duress.

Held ....

❖ (CA) P could not recover the money. Commercial parties are free to withdraw credit facilities without that amounting to economic duress. [1994] 4 All E.R. 714.

Key Principle ....

To exert ordinary commercial pressure to obtain payment is not a breach of Art.82 (formerly 86) of the EC Treaty.

LEYLAND DAF LTD V AUTOMOTIVE PRODUCTS PLC 1993

P manufactured motor vehicles but became insolvent, and receivers were appointed. D supplied parts. P owed D substantial sums of money. D threatened to stop supplying brakes and clutches if the receiver did not pay P's pre-receivership debts (which they were not legally obliged to do). In practice there was no alternative source of supply. If the receivers did not pay then production would be brought to a halt. The receivers sought an injunction to compel D to continue to supply parts.

Held

❖ (CA) Under common law principles a court would not order D to trade with P. Under art.82 (formerly 86) of the **EC Treaty** abuse of a dominant position meant using methods different from normal commercial operations. This was not the case here. [1993] B.C.C. 389.

Commentary

Compare *Adam Opel GmbH v Mitras Automotive (UK) Ltd* [2008] EWHC 3205 (QB) (see above) where the claimants, having calculated that they only had enough supplies for 24 hours production and having unsuccessfully applied for an injunction to compel the suppliers to continue to supply the front bumper mounts, agreed to the supplier's demands to pay them compensation.

UNCONSCIONABILITY

Key Principle

The elements of unconscionability exist in English law.

LLOYDS BANK V BUNDY 1974

(For facts see above).

Held

❖ (CA) Two of the judges set aside the guarantee on the grounds of undue influence, but Lord Denning suggested that a single thread runs through various categories in English law, including undue influence and undue pressure; that thread is inequality of bargaining power.

Key Principle

There is no need for a general principle of unconscionability in English law.

> NATIONAL WESTMINSTER BANK V MORGAN 1985
> D's family home was owned jointly by H and W(D). It was mortgaged to a building society. H was unable to meet the mortgage repayments and the building society started repossession proceedings. H wanted to remortgage the house to P. A bank manager visited W at home to obtain her signature. W stated that she had no confidence in H's business schemes. The bank manager incorrectly told her that the new mortgage was in effect for the same amount as the old one. In fact the mortgage was to be unlimited so that all of H's liabilities could be charged against the house. W signed the documents. W received no independent legal advice. P claimed possession of the house. W claimed that the mortgage was obtained as a result of P's undue influence.

Held

❖ (HL) A special relationship did not exist between a banker and customer. The mortgage was not obtained as a result of P's undue influence. [1985] 2 W.L.R. 588.

Commentary

(1) In Lord Scarman's opinion there is no general principle of inequality of bargaining power in English law. It is relevant in some cases of undue influence. There is no need for a general principle. Where necessary legislation has been enacted to protect the weaker party, e.g. **UCTA** 1977.

(2) The idea of a general principle has received a more enthusiastic reception in the USA, Australia, and Canada. English courts tend to accept hard but fair bargaining as legitimate.

THINK POINT

(a) what must a lender establish; and
(b) what steps must a lender take
to ensure that it is able to recover possession of the matrimonial home where a wife has agreed to it being used as security for a loan by the lender to her husband or her husband's company?

Is there a clear principle of law which distinguishes economic duress from ordinary commercial pressure?

Void and Illegal Contracts

12

INTRODUCTION

The principle of freedom of contract continues to permeate English contract law.

As a consequence the courts will rarely intervene and strike a contract down on public policy grounds. However, the law may refuse to give full effect to a contract because the contract involves the commission of a legal wrong or is in some other way contrary to public policy.

There is no agreed classification of such contracts. Generally the important question is what effect does the illegality have on the parties' rights.*

This chapter concentrates on one particular type of illegal contract: contracts in restraint of trade. Clauses or terms in restraint of trade occur fairly frequently in practice. They are an example of contracts which are void on grounds of public policy. The public policy identified by the courts varies according to the context. In the nineteenth century such a clause might be valid because it protected British trade, whereas in the twentieth century freedom of competition and the right of an individual to earn a living is balanced against an employer's interest in protecting their trade secrets and customer base legitimate.

Key Principle

A contract which appears legal may be illegal if one party has an illegal purpose in mind.

> #### PEARCE V BROOKS 1866
>
> D hired a new carriage, which was unusually designed, from P. D was a prostitute and she intended to use the carriage to attract customers. P was aware that this was her intention. After paying one instalment D returned the carriage. P sued D for damages under the agreement.

Held

P could not recover the money because P knew that D had hired the carriage to attract customers. [1861–1873] All E.R. Rep. 102.

* See The Law Commission (LAW COM NO 320) The Illegality Defence, March 2010.

Commentary

(1) If P had not been aware of D's activities they would not have been implicated in the illegality and would have been able to recover damages.

(2) In *Armhouse Lee v Chappell*, *The Times*, August 7, 1996 the CA held that the defendants were contractually bound to pay for the placing of telephone sex line advertisements in magazines. The contracts were not immoral or illegal on grounds of public policy.

(3) In *Blue Chip Trading Ltd v Helbawi* (2008) a foreign student claimed that his employer had not paid him the minimum wage. The EAT (UKEAT/0397/08/LA) held that the contract of employment between the student and a security company was illegal during those periods when the student worked more than 20 hours a week during term time in breach of the immigration restrictions placed on the student under the UK immigration rules. It was possible to sever the legal from the illegal part of the contract (see Severance below). The claimant was entitled to recover additional wages for those weeks that he worked when he was not in breach of his immigration conditions.

Key Principle

Although an illegal contract cannot be enforced by a guilty party, a claim which arises out of the contract, under for example the law of trusts, may be upheld.

TINSLEY V MILLIGAN 1993

P and D, who were lovers, ran a lodging house as a business. They purchased a new house using money from a previous house. Although the house was in P's sole name, they regarded the house as belonging to both of them. P and D agreed that the house was to be in P's name alone so that D could fraudulently claim money from the Department of Social Security by stating that she did not own a house and that P was her landlady. P and D quarrelled. P moved out of the house and claimed possession. D claimed that the property was held by P on trust for them both in equal shares.

Held

❖ (HL) D had established that a resulting trust existed. She was entitled to recover under the resulting trust. She did not have to rely on the illegal contract, even though the rights she acquired under the trust arose from the performance of the illegal contract. [1993] 3 W.L.R. 126.

Commentary

Similarly, if a breach of contract also amounts to a tort a guilty party may be able to recover money by suing in tort.

Key Principle

A contract in restraint of trade is prima facie void, unless the restriction is reasonable from the point of view of the parties themselves and the public at large.

> NORDENFELT V MAXIM NORDENFELT GUNS AND AMMUNITION CO 1894
>
> D, a manufacturer of guns and other weapons, sold his business to P. The contract provided that D would not for 25 years engage in:
>
> "any business involving the gun trade, or *in any business competing or liable to compete in any way with that for the time being carried on by the company.*"

Held

❖ (HL) The clause was valid except for the part italicised. It was valid because D had sold his gun business, so he should not be able to set up in competition. The clause kept the business in England, which was in the public interest. Nevertheless, the latter part of the clause was too wide and was not necessary to protect P's proprietary interests. That part of the clause was declared void and severed from the contract. [1891–1894] All E.R. Rep. 1.

Commentary

(1) The burden of proving that the clause is reasonable rests on the party seeking to uphold the clause.

(2) Note the clause was worldwide in effect.

Key Principle

A restraint of trade clause is more likely to be upheld in a contract for the sale of a business, than in a contract of employment.

> MASON V PROVIDENT CLOTHING AND SUPPLY CO LTD 1913
>
> D, an agent, was employed to canvass for orders and collect debts in Islington. D was not permitted by a clause in his contract with P to trade within 25 miles of London for three years after ceasing employment with P.

Held

❖ (HL) The clause was void. In a contract of employment the employer is normally in a stronger bargaining position than the employee. [1911–1913] All E.R. Rep. 400.

Commentary

In a contract for the sale of a business the parties are more likely to be of equal bargaining power. Purchasers need to be able to protect their investment. They buy goodwill, and obtain a proprietary interest.

Key Principle

A clause which restrains an employee from competition is always void as being unreasonable unless there is some exceptional proprietary interest owned by the employer which needs protection.

MORRIS (HERBERT) LTD V SAXELBY 1916

D, an employee, had spent all his working life in the employment of P, which manufactured hoisting machinery in the United Kingdom. A clause in his contract of employment forbade him from working in a similar business in the United Kingdom and Ireland for seven years after leaving P's employment.

Held

❖ (HL) The clause was void. If upheld it would mean that an employer could force an employee to use a skill developed in his employment exclusively for the benefit of the employer. [1916–1917] All E.R. Rep. 305.

Commentary

In *Wrn Ltd v Ayris* [2008] EWHC 1080 (QB) the court held that a clause in a contract of employment which purported to prevent a former employee from having contact with any customer of his former employer for six months after leaving the employment was unreasonable and in restraint of trade. If the clause had prevented the former employee from having contact with customers of his former employer with whom he personally had dealings that would have been reasonable.

Key Principle

The doctrine of restraint of trade is not limited to contracts for the sale of a business and contracts of employment.

> ESSO PETROLEUM CO LTD V HARPERS GARAGE (STOURPORT) LTD 1967
>
> D owned two garages. They entered into two solus agreements with P; an agreement for each garage. Both agreements contained the following clauses:
> 1. a "tying covenant" by which D agreed in return for a discount to sell only P's brand of petrol;
> 2. a "compulsory trading covenant" which obliged D to keep the garage open at reasonable hours and to provide the public with an efficient service; and
> 3. a "continuity covenant" which required D, if they sold the business, to procure the acceptance of the agreement by the purchaser.
>
> The first agreement was to operate for four years five months and the second for 21 years. In addition under the second agreement the garage was mortgaged to P for £7,000. The mortgage was to be repaid over 21 years and could not be redeemed earlier. D was in breach of the first clause and P sought an injunction to prevent further breaches.

Held

❖ (HL) Both agreements fell within the category of contracts in restraint of trade. D's freedom to trade was limited. The restrictions (1.)–(3.) were reasonable because both parties benefited. However, although the 4 ½-year period was reasonable the 21-year period was unreasonable because it was excessive and not in the public interest. Therefore, the first agreement was valid, but the second was void. [1967] 1 All E.R. 699.

Commentary

(1) The House of Lords considered that the following approach should be used: is the contract/clause so restrictive of the promisor's liberty to trade that it must be treated as prima facie void? If yes, can the clause be justified as reasonable? If yes, then valid.

(2) The court should look at current commercial practice. Solus agreements for garages were not established practice in the trade at this time.

(3) Public interest appears to be the court's notion of what is appropriate, e.g. free competition should be encouraged.

(4) Tying agreements are also common in the brewery trade where pubs are "tied houses". These agreements may also be invalid under art.81 (formerly 85) of the **EC Treaty**. See, for example, *Courage Ltd v Crehan, The Times*, October 4, 2001 (ECJ).

(5) The doctrine of restraint of trade applies also to exclusive service agreements (see below), partnerships, franchises (see e.g. *ChipsAway International Ltd v Kerr* [2009] EWCA Civ 320) and agency agreements (see e.g. *BCM Group Plc v Visualmark Ltd & Anor* [2006] EWHC 1831 (QBD)).

CONTRACTS FOR THE SALE OF A BUSINESS

Key Principle
Some proprietary interest of the purchaser must be protected by the clause.

> BRITISH REINFORCED CONCRETE ENGINEERING CO LTD V SCHELFF 1921
> D sold his business making "loop" road reinforcements to P who made BRC road reinforcements. There was a clause to restrain D from making road reinforcements.

Held
❖ (Ch D) The clause was void. P could only stop D making "loop" road reinforcements. Only the actual business sold by D to P was entitled to protection. [1921] 2 Ch. 563.

Commentary
(1) When considering the reasonableness of the covenant, the court will also consider the area and duration of the restraint as well as the public interest (e.g. *Nordenfelt v Maxim Nordenfelt* (1894), see above). See also the cases under contracts of employment below.

(2) It is not uncommon for manufacturers or traders to form an association with the object of restricting the output or maintaining the selling price of certain commodities. At common law such restrictive trading agreements are subject to the restraint of trade doctrine, but for the most part such agreements are now covered by the Competition Act 1998 (which replaces the Restrictive Trade Practices Act 1976 and the Resale Prices Act 1976) and art.81 (formerly 85) of the **EC Treaty**.

In principle covenants in restraint of trade contained in a contract for the sale of a business are subject to art.81 (formerly 85) of the EC Treaty.

> REMIA B.V. VERENIGDE BEDRIJVEN NUTRICIA NV V EC COMMISSION 1987
> Nutricia, a Dutch company, sold its sauce business to another Dutch business. It was a term of the agreement that neither N nor another subsidiary would engage directly or indirectly in the production or sale of sauces on the Dutch market for 10 years. N notified the EC Commission of this and various other related agreements. N's request for exemption from art.85 was refused. N appealed against this finding.

Held

❖ (ECJ) The agreement affected inter-state trade although it related to a purely Dutch activity. The 10-year non-competition clause was too long, four years was sufficient. [1987] 1 C.M.L.R. 1.

Commentary

(1) Article 81 (formerly 85) treats as invalid all agreements between undertakings which may affect trade between Member States and which have as their object or effect the restriction or distortion of competition within the common market.

(2) In *Days Medical Aids Ltd v Pihsiang Machinery Manufacturing Co Ltd* [2004] 1 All E.R. (Comm) 991 (QBD) the court considered that where an exclusive distribution agreement in Europe and the UK infringes the common law restraint of trade doctrine, but is not in breach of art.81, Community law prevails and the contract would not be void.

CONTRACTS OF EMPLOYMENT

Key Principle

The clause in restraint of trade must protect a legitimate interest of the employer.

> FITCH V DEWES 1921
> D was a solicitor's managing clerk. In his contract of employment there was a lifelong restraint not to practise within seven miles of P's office in Tamworth Town Hall.

Held
The clause was valid because of the contact D had with P's clients. [1921] 2 A.C. 158.

Commentary
(1) Where there is an express term in the contract of employment it is more likely to be enforced where it relates to trade secrets, or customer information and contacts.

(2) Disputes usually arise once the employee has left the employment.

Key Principle
The court will be reluctant to find for a construction of a clause which deprives of all practical utility in circumstances where all parties were familiar with the background to and the aim of the clause.

> BECKETT INVESTMENT MANAGEMENT GROUP LTD & ORS V GLYN HALL & ORS 2007
> D was a financial adviser, who worked for BFS a subsidiary company of BIMG. His contract of employment with BIMG, contained a "non-dealing" clause aimed at preventing him doing business with any of the Beckett Group's clients for a period of 12 months after his employment with BIMG ceased. H joined a competitor company and BIMG sought to enforce the restrictive covenant.

Held
❖ (CA) The fact that clients dealt with BFS, rather than BIMG, was not fatal to BIMG being able to rely on the clause. BIMG had a legitimate business interest to protect by the restrictive covenant. The covenant against dealing was reasonable in the circumstances of this case. The 12 month period was reasonable between the parties and in the interests of the public, having regard to D's seniority and importance, the evidence about business patterns in the particular business, the logistics of replacing D, and the evidence of an industry standard of 12 months. [2007] EWCA Civ 613.

Commentary
(1) The first issue which a court deals with in this type of case is the inter-pretation or construction of the clause (see Ch.7). In this case the trial judge held that the clause only protected D's employers, BIMG, the holding com-pany, not BFS a subsidiary company. BIMG did not provide advice to clients

and so the clause was of no practical use to BIMG. The Court of Appeal disagreed with the judge's interpretation.

(2) The extended definition of "relevant client" in the contract of employment was held to be unreasonably wide and was severable from the primary definition (see Severance below).

(3) "Non-dealing" clauses have become popular, particularly in specialist areas such as the financial sector, because it is easier for an employer to show that an ex-employee is in breach of a 'non-dealing' clause than a "non-solicitation" clause.

(4) The court has the discretion to issue an injunction against the employee where the clause is held to be valid (See e.g. *TFS Derivatives Ltd v Morgan* [2004] EWHC 3181 (QBD)).

Key Principle

The clause will not be valid if it merely protects an employer against competition from an ex-employee.

> MARSHALL V NM FINANCIAL MANAGEMENT LTD 1997
> P was a sales agent for D, selling mainly life assurance and pensions. It was a term of P's contract with D that if on termination of the contract P did not become a representative or employee of "any company or organisation which may directly or indirectly be in competition with the company", then D would pay P renewal commission due from business he obtained before the termination.

Held

❖ (CA) The clause was void because it was in restraint of trade. No legitimate interest of the defendant was protected by it. P's business as an agent arose from his reputation and connections and was his property. The anti-competition part of the clause could be severed so that the right to commission remained enforceable. [1997] 1 W.L.R. 1527.

Key Principle

An anti-competition clause may be upheld where an employee entered into a contract of employment and it was likely that the employee would be exposed to trade secrets or other information of equivalent confidentiality.

THOMAS V FARR PLC AND ANOTHER 2007

T, had been the managing director of F, his employer. His contract of employment included an anti-competition clause, which stopped him working in the social housing insurance sector in England and Wales for 12 months. He left F and obtained employment with a competitor.

Held

❖ (CA) As part of his employment T had been in possession of confidential pricing and financial information which F was entitled to require to be kept confidential after the termination of T's employment The non-solicitation clause in the contract was not adequate alone to protect T's interests because it would be difficult to enforce and not all the confidential information was client specific. The anti-competition clause was reasonable in the circumstances. [2007] EWCA Civ 118.

Key Principle

The court will uphold freedom of contract against third parties as well as the parties to the contract.

EASTHAM V NEWCASTLE UNITED FOOTBALL CLUB LTD 1964

P, a football player, entered into a contract with D which provided for the "retain and transfer" system. This meant that D had the right to keep P as a player and that P could not transfer to another club without D's consent.

Held

The clause was void. It neither protected D's trade secrets, nor had P obtained influence over D's customers, the fans. The court issued a declaration not only against D but also against the F.A. [1964] Ch. 413.

Commentary

In the *Bosman* case ([1996] All E.R. (EC) 97) the European Court of Justice held that National Football Association rules, which prevented a footballer transferring to a football club in another Member State unless the club paid a transfer fee, were in breach of Art.48 (now 39) of the EC Treaty on the freedom of movement of workers.

The clause must be reasonable as to its geographical area.

> **MASON v PROVIDENT CLOTHING AND SUPPLY CO LTD 1913**
> (See facts above).

Held ....

❖ (HL) The clause restricting D's freedom to trade was void. The area covered by the clause was 10,000 times larger than where D was employed. [1911–1913] All E.R. Rep. 400.

Key Principle ....
The clause must be reasonable as to its duration.

> **FELLOWES & SON v FISHER 1976**
> D, a solicitor's clerk, entered into a contract of employment with P, a firm of solicitors in Walthamstow in east London. A clause of the contract provided that if D left the firm he would not for five years be directly or indirectly employed in the legal profession within the postal districts of Walthamstow and Chingford, an area of 12 square miles with a population of about 150,000. He left his employment and after working in the City of London for six months he obtained a post in Chingford. P applied for an interlocutory injunction to restrain D from breaking the clause.

Held ....

❖ (CA) The application for an injunction was refused. D was more likely to succeed than P at any full trial. [1976] Q.B. 122.

Commentary ....
It is unlikely that a lifelong restraint in a prescribed area would now be upheld (compare *Fitch v Dewes*, see above).

Key Principle ....
The clause must be reasonable and fair as between the parties.

> **OFFICE ANGELS LTD v RAINER-THOMAS 1991**
> D were two employees of P, an employment agency with 34 branches. It was a term of their contracts of employment that:

(a) D would not for six months after the termination of their employ-ment, solicit custom from any person who had been a company client during their employment; and

(b) D would not within six months of their employment engage in or undertake the trade or business of an employment agency in Greater London within a 1km radius of the branch at which they had been employed. D were employed at a branch in the City of London, before leaving to set up their own employment agency within the 1km radius and in the City of London.

Held

❖ (CA) Clause (a) was void. It was too wide because it applied to clients at any of the 34 branches not just the branch where D were employed. Clause (b) was also void. It merely protected P's trade connections with its clients by preventing D from operating an office within the 1km radius. It did not spe-cifically protect P's trade secrets or confidential information. It went further than was reasonable. [1991] I.R.L.R. 214.

Commentary

Generally, the court will take into account the adequacy of the consideration in relation to the extent of the restraint, and the relative bargaining strength of the two parties.

Key Principle

The covenant should not prejudice the public interest.

WYATT v KREGLINGER AND FERNAU 1933

P was a wool broker. When he retired D, his employers, paid him a pension which was conditional upon him not unfairly competing with his former employers. Subsequently they ceased to pay the pension and he sued to recover the arrears.

Held

❖ (CA) The agreement to pay P a pension was in restraint of trade and he could not recover the arrears. The clause was unreasonable because it deprived the community of P's services, which might be of benefit to the community. [1933] 1 K.B. 793.

See also *Bull v Pitney-Bowes Ltd* [1967] 1 W.L.R. 273 and *Marshall v NM Financial Management Ltd* (see above).

Key Principle
Where legislation restricts a person's use of their skills, only in exceptional cases will additional contractual restraints be in the public interest.

DRANEZ ANSTALT AND OTHERS V HAYEK AND OTHERS 2003
H invented a ventilator for the treatment of patients with breathing problems. He obtained a patent and in 1984 set up a number of companies to develop, manufacture and market the ventilator world-wide. In 1994 investors invested $5m in the business. H agreed with the investors that he would only carry on this business through existing companies and would not compete with the business. In 1995 H's employment with one of the companies was terminated, and he set up his own company to produce and sell a new ventilator which he had invented and patented. H appealed against the judge's decision that H was in breach of the agreement.

Held
❖ (CA) The restraint of competition was unenforceable against H on grounds of public policy. [2003] 1 B.C.L.C. 278.

Commentary
(1) The investors were protected under the Patents Act 1977 from competition which infringed the 1984 patent rights owned by the claimant companies. CA considered that powerful reasons would be required to justify the imposition of further restrictions upon H's freedom to exploit his skill and expertise as an inventor.

(2) CA noted that H was a pioneer in a field of medical science, and that his work appeared to have an obvious public benefit.

Key Principle
If an employer, in breach of contract, dismisses an employee then a covenant in restraint of trade cannot be enforced by the employer.

BRIGGS V OATES 1991

D, a solicitor, was employed by P and his partner in a firm of solicitors. It was a clause of D's contract of employment that D would not for five years after its termination practise as a solicitor within five miles of the firm's offices or solicit any persons who were clients of the firm while he was employed there. The partnership was dissolved and D obtained alternative employment which was in breach of the clause.

Held

❖ (QBD) P's application for an injunction was refused. The dissolution of the partnership was a breach of D's contract of employment and brought it to an end, so the clause was no longer binding on D. [1991] 1 All E.R. 407.

Key Principle

There is an implied duty of fidelity in every contract of employment.

FACCENDA CHICKEN V FOWLER 1986

P, a company, marketed fresh chickens. P employed D as a sales manager. D devised a marketing system for P. D left P's company, and set up a similar business in the same area employing a number of P's staff. There was no express clause in D's contract of employment which restricted the activities of P's former employees. P applied for injunction to restrain D from using confidential sales information.

Held

❖ (CA) P's application was not successful. Sales information was not a trade secret, and therefore was not protected. [1986] 3 W.L.R. 288

Commentary

(1) The court considered that:

(a) Ex-employees do not owe the same duty of fidelity as a current employee in relation to information short of trade secrets (unless that information could be memorised or recorded). Such information could not be protected in any event.

(b) In deciding whether information amounts to a trade secret, the court should take into account:

(i) the nature of the employment and the status of the employee;

(ii) the nature of the information;

(iii) whether the employer had stressed the confidentiality of the information to the employee; and

(iv) whether the information could be collated from other non-confidential information.

(2) An express clause will more readily be applied to ex-employees.

EXCLUSIVE SERVICE AGREEMENTS

Key Principle
An exclusive service agreement is subject to the doctrine of restraint of trade.

A. SCHROEDER MUSIC PUBLISHING CO LTD V MACAULAY 1974
P, a young and unknown song-writer, entered into a contract with D, a music publishing company, on D's standard terms. Under the contract, P assigned the world copyright in his musical compositions to D who did not undertake to exploit all or indeed any of them. D would pay P royalties if D did exploit them. The five-year agreement could be automatically extended by D for a further five years if P's royalties reached £5,000. D could terminate the agreement at any time on giving one month's notice. P had no such right.

Held
❖ (HL) Such an agreement fell within the doctrine of restraint of trade. The contract was unreasonable because it was very one-sided. [1974] 1 W.L.R. 1308.

Commentary
(See also Ch.6).

Key Principle
Where the terms of an agreement are prescribed by an outside body then such a contract is subject to the restraint of trade doctrine.

WATSON V PRAGER 1991
P was a professional boxer. He entered into a British Boxing Board of Control boxer-manager agreement with D for three years. D had the right to P's exclusive services. D was also a boxing promoter. The agreement provided that:
(a) D had a right to extend the contract for a further three years if P won a championship fight;
(b) D could stipulate the terms on which P would fight matches.

Held

❖ (Ch D) The clauses were unreasonable because D could impose on P the terms on which he had to fight, and the option to renew was for too long a period. [1991] 1 W.L.R. 726.

Key Principle

An exclusive services agreement will not be in restraint of trade where the parties are of equal bargaining power.

PANAYIOTOU V SONY MUSIC ENTERTAINMENT (UK) 1994

In 1988 P, George Michael (Panayiotou), entered into an agreement with CBS Records whereby he agreed to: deliver eight albums of music in 15 years; only record for CBS; and receive around 20 per cent of the sale price in royalties. CBS obtained copyright to the work, but were under no obligation to promote it. CBS's recording business was then taken over by D. P claimed that the contract he entered into was void because it was an unreasonable restraint of trade, and it was void under art.85(2) (now art.81) of the **EC Treaty**.

Held

❖ (Ch D) It was not in restraint of trade because:
  (a) P had received expert legal advice from his solicitors at all times.
  (b) There was a public interest in upholding a compromise such as the 1988 agreement.
  (c) P had affirmed the agreement in 1990 when he obtained an advance payment.
  (d) There was no breach of art.85 because there was no Community-wide market for the services of UK recording artists in the field of popular music and so the agreement did not affect trade between Member States. The relevant market for P's services was the UK market not a Community-wide market. The Times, June 30, 1994

Commentary

In contrast in *Proactive Sports Management Ltd v Rooney* [2010] EWHC 1807 (QB), the High Court held that the image rights agreement entered into by Wayne Rooney was unenforceable because it was an unreasonable restraint of trade. Under the agreement the claimant company had the exclusive right to exploit Rooney's image. In reaching his conclusion the judge took into account the following factors: the agreement gave the claimant exclusive rights; the claimant was entitled to 20 per cent of the income produced without any cap on the total amount; the terms were not negotiated; the agreement was for eight years which is a long time in a footballer's career; Rooney was only just 17-years old when he entered into the agreement; and Rooney and his family had no commercial experience and had not taken independent legal advice before entering into the agreement.

SEVERANCE

Key Principle

Where the contract is partly void and partly valid, the court may (1) sever the void part of the contract (without otherwise adding to or modifying the wording), provided that (2) the remaining terms continue to be supported by adequate consideration, and (3) the severance does not radically change the character of the contract.

> MARSHALL V NM FINANCIAL MANAGEMENT LTD 1995
> (For facts see above).

Held

❖ (CA) The question as to consideration was one of substance not form. The two clauses in restraint of trade could be struck out (although only the first was of relevance to P). The remainder of the contract was valid, and so P could recover the post termination commission to which he was entitled under the contract.

Commentary

(1) This is known as the "Blue pencil" test.

(2) The courts also severed the void clause in, e.g. *Nordenfelt v Maxim Nordenfelt Guns and Ammunition Co* (above), *British Reinforced Concrete Engineering Co Ltd v Schelff* (above). See also *Blue Chip Trading Ltd v Helbawi* (2008) (above).

(3) In *Beckett Investment Management Group v Glyn Hall* [2007] EWCA Civ 613, Kay L.J. considered that the three-fold test applied in *Marshall* in relation to severance should be adopted.

THINK POINT

What does the term *prima facie void* mean in the content of a restraint of trade clause?

What "legitimate interests" of an employer can be protected by a restraint of trade clause in an employee's contract?

Discharge by Agreement and by Frustration

13

INTRODUCTION

A contract may be terminated or "discharged" in a number of ways:
  (1) by agreement;
  (2) by frustration;
  (3) by performance; and
  (4) by breach.

This chapter sets out the main principles applicable to the first two types of discharge.

Discharge by agreement

When parties enter into a contract each is bound to perform their side of the bargain. Once they have done so their rights and obligations come to an end.

They may, however, decide that they do not wish to proceed with the contract. In this situation they may agree to discharge the contract, that is bring it to an end. In order for such agreement to have legal effect there must be an agreement supported by consideration, which is referred to in this context as accord and satisfaction.

Discharge by frustration

Frustration arises where an unforeseen external event occurs which makes it impossible for the parties to perform the contract or makes the performance radically different from that agreed. Such an event includes a serious fire, a natural disaster, outbreak of war or a change in the law. Most commercial contracts will contain terms which set out how the parties' contractual rights and obligations will be affected should such an event occur. These are often referred to as *force majeure* clauses. In this situation the doctrine of frustration will not apply because the event is not unforeseen

Where a contract is discharged by frustration neither party will be able to claim damages for breach of contract. Their right to recover money paid before the frustrating event, or not pay money due to be paid afterwards, is normally governed by the Law Reform (Frustrated Contracts) Act 1943.

BY AGREEMENT

Key Principle

Unless there is fresh consideration for a promise to release one party from their obligations, the promise to release will not be enforceable.

> ### FOAKES V BEER 1884
>
> P had obtained judgment against D for £2,090. However, she agreed to allow D to pay her by instalments and not to take any proceedings to enforce the judgment. A judgment debt attracts interest from the date of the judgment. D paid the debt, but P then claimed the interest.

Held

❖ (HL) P was entitled to recover the interest (see Ch.3). [1881–1885] All E.R. Rep. 106.

Commentary

If P had agreed to forgo the interest and D had provided consideration for her promise this would be an example of unilateral discharge.

Key Principle

A promise not to insist on exact performance may be effective as a waiver, even without consideration.

> ### HUGHES V METROPOLITAN RAILWAY 1877
>
> In October 1874, a landlord gave his tenant six months' notice to repair the property. In November the landlord started negotiations to buy the remainder of the lease from the tenant. The negotiations broke down in December. The tenant did not carry out any repairs. At the end of the six-month period the landlord claimed that the lease was forfeited.

Held

The landlord was not entitled to forfeit the lease. The tenant had failed to carry out the repairs because the landlord had started negotiations to buy the remainder of the lease. (1877) 2 App. Cas. 439.

Commentary

(1) The tenant had not provided any consideration for the landlord's promise. The landlord's right to forfeit was suspended not lost.

(2) The equitable principle of waiver was used to support the creation of the doctrine of promissory estoppel (see *High Trees* case, Ch.3).

Key Principle

A promise not to insist on exact performance can be revoked by giving reasonable notice.

CHARLES RICKARDS V OPPENHEIM 1950

In July 1947 D agreed to take delivery of a new Rolls Royce car from P within "six months or, at the most, seven months". The car was not ready in time and D agreed to wait another three months. When it was still not ready then D gave notice that if the car was not ready within four weeks he would cancel the order, which he did.

Held

❖ (CA) D was entitled to refuse to take delivery of the car. Although he had waived his right to take delivery of the car by a particular date, he had reasserted this right when requiring the car to be ready within four weeks. [1950] 1 All E.R. 420.

Commentary

(1) P was in breach of contract by failing to deliver the car on time. The court considered that "time was of the essence", which meant that D was entitled to treat the contract as discharged or terminated by P's failure to deliver on time.

(2) Denning L.J. considered that D's waiver was a type of estoppel similar to that in the *High Trees* case (see Ch.3). D was entitled by the giving of reasonable notice to make time of the essence once again.

Key Principle

Discharge by agreement may be inferred from prolonged inactivity in certain circumstances.

THE HANNAH BLUMENTHAL 1983

In 1972 the buyers of a ship referred a dispute with the sellers to arbitration in accordance with the contract of sale. Letters were occasionally exchanged between the parties until 1980 when the buyers proposed fixing a date for the arbitration hearing. The sellers claimed that the arbitration agreement had been discharged by a mutual agreement to abandon the arbitration.

Held

❖ (HL) Whether or not a contract is abandoned is a question of fact, and in this case there was no mutual agreement to abandon the arbitration agreement. [1983] 1 All E.R. 34.

Commentary

(1) Where two parties agree to release each other from their respective obligations under a contract this is a bilateral discharge.

(2) In this case their Lordships agreed that there could be "tacit abandonment by both parties". However, three different views were expressed as to what would amount to "tacit abandonment". Lord Brightman's view reflects the traditional objective approach to contract formation. He considered that the sellers must show that the buyers so conducted themselves as to entitle the sellers to assume, and that the sellers did assume, that the contract was to be abandoned without any further communication.

BY FRUSTRATION

Key Principle

Frustration occurs where a contractual obligation has become incapable of being performed because external circumstances have caused the performance to be radically different from that agreed.

DAVIS CONTRACTORS LTD V FAREHAM URBAN DISTRICT COUNCIL 1956
P contractors agreed to build 78 houses for D for £92,425 within eight months. Due to a shortage of skilled labour and building materials the work took 22 months and cost £111,076. P claimed that the contract was frustrated by the long delay and claimed the additional costs on a quantum meruit basis.

Held

❖ (HL) The contract was not frustrated because the cause of the delay was not unforeseeable, and delay did not have the same significance for both parties. [1956] 3 W.L.R. 37.

Commentary

(1) The change in circumstances should not be the fault of either party.

(2) "Frustration is not to be lightly invoked as the dissolvent of a contract", per Lord Radcliffe.

(3) In *The Sea Angel* [2007] 1 C.L.C. 876, [2007] 2 Lloyd's Rep 517 (see below) Rix L.J. stated that:
  (a) "the application of the doctrine of frustration requires a multi-factorial approach";
  (b) some of these factors exist at the time of the contract such as the terms of the contract, its matrix or context, the parties' knowledge, expectations, assumptions and contemplation in particular as to risk. Other factors are post-contractual and include the nature of the supervening event and the possibility of future performance in the new circumstances; and
  (c) the demands of justice provide the ultimate rationale of the doctrine.

Key Principle

The doctrine of frustration will apply to leases, but only in exceptional circumstances.

NATIONAL CARRIERS V PANALPINA 1981
In January 1974 P leased a warehouse to D for 10 years. In May 1979 the local authority closed the only access road to the warehouse because of the dangerous condition of a listed building. The closure was likely to last 18 months. P claimed rent due. D claimed the lease was frustrated by the closure.

Held

❖ (HL) The denial of access to the warehouse was not sufficiently serious to frustrate the contract. [1981] 2 W.L.R. 45.

Commentary

(1) Lord Hailsham considered that the shorter the lease the more likely it would be that the doctrine would be applicable.

(2) If a hotel was built on a cliff which slipped into the North Sea and the property was leased then the lease would be frustrated.

Key Principle

Where performance of the contract becomes impossible because of the destruction of the subject-matter of the contract then the contract is frustrated.

TAYLOR V CALDWELL 1863

D hired out the Surrey Gardens and Music Hall to P for a series of concerts. Six days before the first concert the Hall was destroyed by an accidental fire.

Held

D was not liable to P for wasted advertising and other expenses. (1863) 122 E.R. 309.

Commentary

(1) The court's view was that there was an implied term in the contract that excused the parties.

(2) The destruction of something other than the subject-matter of the contract will still cause the contract to be discharged by frustration if the result is that the main purpose of the contract is defeated.

Key Principle

Where performance of the contract becomes impossible because a person or object which is essential for performance is unavailable then the contract may be frustrated.

THE EVIA (NO.2) 1982

In November 1979 P, the owners of the ship, chartered their vessel to D for 18 months. In September 1980 the ship unloaded its cargo in Basrah but was detained in the Shatt-Al-Arab waterway because of the outbreak of the Iran/Iraq war. The ship was still trapped in July 1982 when HL heard the case. D claimed that the charterparty had been frustrated when it became clear that the hostilities would not be shortlived. P claimed that D were in breach of the charterparty by sending the ship to Basrah when it was not "a safe port".

Held

❖ (HL) D was not in breach of the charterparty. The decision of the lower courts, that the performance of the charterparty became impossible and the contract was frustrated on October 4, 1980, was accepted. [1982] 3 All E.R. 350.

Commentary

See also *Jackson v Union Marine Insurance Co Ltd* (1874) which involved a voyage charter rather than a time charter. A ship was chartered by D for a voyage from Liverpool to San Francisco via Newport where a cargo was to be loaded. The ship ran aground before arriving at Newport. It took more than eight months for the ship to be refloated and repaired. The court held that the voyage the parties contemplated had become impossible. There was an implied condition that the ship should arrive in time to load the cargo. (1874) L.R. 10 C.P. 125.

Key Principle

Where the method of performance of the contract becomes impossible then the contract is frustrated.

NICKOLL & KNIGHT V ASHTON EDRIDGE & CO 1901

In a contract for the sale of cottonseed, it was provided that the cottonseed would be shipped on a named ship from a specified port during a particular month. Before the loading date the ship went aground.

Held

❖ (CA) Since the contract did not provide for any alternative method of performance, e.g. a different ship, the contract was frustrated. [1901] 2 K.B. 126.

Key Principle

Where substituted performance is possible under the contract, then the contract is not frustrated.

TSAKIROGLOU & CO LTD V NOBLEE THORL 1961

P agreed to buy groundnuts from D, who was to ship them to Hamburg from Port Sudan. It was contemplated by both parties that the ship would use the Suez canal. The canal was then closed to shipping, and the sellers did not deliver the goods claiming that the contract was frustrated.

Held

❖ (HL) The contract was not frustrated. The goods could have been shipped via the Cape of Good Hope, which would not have been commercially or fundamentally different from what was agreed. [1961] 2 W.L.R. 633.

Key Principle

Where a change in circumstances radically affects the purpose of the contract then the contract will be frustrated.

> KRELL V HENRY 1903
>
> D hired rooms in Pall Mall for two days in order to see Edward VII's coronation procession as it passed along Pall Mall. No reference to the procession was made in the written agreement. The coronation was postponed because of the king's illness.

Held

❖ (CA) The contract was frustrated. The taking place of the processions was regarded by both parties as being the foundation or basis of the contract, and their postponement prevented performance of the contract. [1903] 2 K.B. 740.

Commentary

See also *Chandler v Webster* (1904) (see below).

Key Principle

A change in circumstances which only incidentally affects the purpose of the contract will not frustrate the contract.

> HERNE BAY STEAMBOAT CO V HUTTON 1903
>
> D chartered a steamboat from P in order to take paying passengers to see the royal naval review at Spithead and for a day's cruise round the fleet. The naval review was cancelled because of the king's illness.

Held

❖ (CA) The naval review was not the foundation of the contract so the contract was not frustrated when it was cancelled. [1900–1903] All E.R. Rep. 627.

Commentary

See also *WJ Tatem Ltd v Gamboa* (1938) (see below).

Key Principle

A change in circumstances which makes the contract impracticable for one party will not frustrate the contract.

> BRITISH MOVIETONEWS LTD V LONDON & DISTRICT CINEMAS LTD 1952
> During the Second World War P and D entered into an agreement for the supply of newsreels. D argued that the contract was frustrated because the war was over and there was no longer any need to show these particular newsreels.

Held

❖ (HL) The contract was not frustrated just because it was no longer commercially viable for one party. [1952] A.C. 166.

Key Principle

If a valid contract becomes illegal because of a change in the law then the contract is frustrated.

> FIBROSA SPOLKA AKCYJNIA V FAIRBAIRN LAWSON COMBE BARBOUR LTD 1942
> In July 1939 D sold machinery to P, a Polish company in Gdynia. An advance payment of £1,000 was paid. In September 1939, before the machinery was due to be delivered, Great Britain declared war on Germany and Germany occupied Gdynia. P requested the return of the £1,000, but D refused because they had carried out a considerable amount of work on the machinery.

Held

❖ (HL) The contract was frustrated because when war is declared it becomes illegal to trade with the enemy. P was entitled to recover the £1,000 because there had been total failure of consideration. [1942] 2 All E.R. 122.

Key principle ....

A contract may be partially frustrated by illegality

ISLAMIC REPUBLIC OF IRAN SHIPPING LINES V STEAMSHIP MUTUAL
UNDERWRITING ASSOCIATION (BERMUDA) LIMITED 2010

The claimant insured its ships with the defendant against a wide range
of risks including pollution. The insurance policy included a clause
which provided that the defendant would indemnify the claimant in
respect of claims brought by third parties for pollution damage from the
escape of bunker oil from a ship, as required by an international
convention (the Bunkers Convention). The UK government passed legislation which prohibited transactions and business relationships
between persons operating in the financial sector and two designated
Iranian entities, one of which was the claimant. The legislation also
permitted licences to be issued exempting specified acts from the
legislation. On October 30, 2009 such a licence was issued but the
defendant took the view that this licence meant that it was no longer
permitted to provide insurance cover to the claimant. As a consequence the defendant terminated the insurance cover with effect
from midnight GMT on October 30 on the ground that the contract had
been discharged by reason of frustration or supervening illegality as a
result of legislation passed by the UK government. On October 31, 2009
one of the claimant's ships became stranded in the territorial waters of
the People's Republic of China causing bunker oil pollution and ren-
dering the ship a total loss.

Held ....

❖ (HC) The effect of the licence was to permit the defendant to continue to
provide the claimant with insurance, but only in respect of the risks to be
insured by virtue of the provisions in the Bunkers Convention. The defendants remained liable to meet claims under this part of the contract which
remained lawful and was not dependent on other parts of the insurance
cover, the performance of which had been prohibited by the legislation since
October 30, 2009 and was no longer lawful. [2010] EWHC 2661 (Comm).

LIMITATIONS

Key Principle
Foreseen or foreseeable circumstances which interfere with the performance of the contract will not amount to frustration.

> **DAVIS CONTRACTORS LTD V FAREHAM URBAN DISTRICT COUNCIL 1956**
> P claimed that the contract was frustrated because of the long delay in building the houses. (See above for fuller facts).

Held
❖ (HL) The contract was not frustrated. The shortage of skilled labour and building materials was not unforeseeable. [1956] 3 W.L.R. 37.

Commentary
(1) P should have included in the contract a term which provided for additional costs to be paid in the event of delay.

(2) See also *Amalgamated Investment and Property Co Ltd v John Walker & Sons Ltd* (1976) (see Ch.10) where the court rejected the claim that the contract was frustrated, on the ground that the parties were aware that there was a risk that the building might be listed.

(3) If the contract makes provision for frustrating events, e.g. through a force majeure clause, or a hardship clause then the doctrine does not apply.

Key Principle
Circumstances must be actually foreseen or there must be a high degree of foreseeability for the doctrine of frustration not to apply.

> **WJ TATEM LTD V GAMBOA 1938**
> During the Spanish Civil War, D chartered a ship for 30 days for the purpose of evacuating the civilian population from northern Spain. Fourteen days into the charter the Nationalists seized the ship, which was not returned to P for more than eight weeks.

Held
❖ (KBD) The parties had not provided for this eventuality in the contract, even though they had foreseen the possibility of seizure. The foundation of the contract was destroyed and so the contract was frustrated. [1938] 3 All E.R. 135.

Key Principle

The test of comparing the probable length of the delay with the unexpired duration of the charter is only the starting point for deciding whether a contract has been frustrated.

> EDWINTON COMMERCIAL CORPORATION AND OTHERS V TSAVLIRIS RUSS (WORLDWIDE SALVAGE & TOWAGE) LTD (THE "SEA ANGEL") 2007
> A ship, the *Sea Angel*, was chartered by TR from ECC for 20 days to assist with a salvage operation near the port of Karachi. Three days before the end of the charter the port authorities illegally detained the ship for approximately three months. TR argued that the charter was frustrated when there was a temporary breakdown in negotiations because the length of the detention was much greater than the period of the charter.

Held

❖ (CA) the contract was not frustrated. Unlike the position in *Tatem v Gamboa* (see above), the detention could be rectified. A solution to the dispute was possible through co-operation with other interested parties, negotiation with the port authority and litigation. The supervening event came at the very end of the charter, with only redelivery of the ship being outstanding. TR had agreed to be liable for delay generally. The risk of detention was foreseeable. It would not be just to relieve TR of the consequences of their bargain. [2007] 1 CLC 876.

Key Principle

Self-induced frustration will not discharge the contract.

> J LAURITZEN A.S. V WIJSMULLER BV, THE "SUPER SERVANT TWO" 1990
> D contracted to transport P's oil rig from Japan to Holland using either the "Super Servant One" or the "Super Servant Two" transportation unit. D intended to use the Super Servant Two but it sank. Meanwhile D had allocated the "Super Servant One" to other contracts.

Held

❖ (CA) Where a contract provides for alternative methods of performance, it will not be frustrated if one of them becomes impossible. The contract was not brought to an end automatically by the sinking of the unit but by the decision of D not to use the Super Servant One. [1990] 1 Lloyd's L.R. 1.

Self-induced frustration would also occur where the transportation unit had been sunk deliberately by D or as a result of D's negligence.

Key Principle

The burden of proving that the frustration is self-induced is on the party claiming it.

> JOSEPH CONSTANTINE STEAMSHIP LINE LTD V IMPERIAL SMELTING
> CORPORATION LTD 1941
> P chartered D's steamship. Before a cargo could be loaded a massive
> explosion occurred which, it was accepted, frustrated the charter party.
> If the explosion was the fault of D then the frustration would have been
> self-induced, and P would be able to recover damages for breach of the
> charter party.

Held

❖ (JCPC) D, as the party pleading the defence of frustration, did not have to prove that it was not self-induced. The onus of proof was on P. [1941] 2 All E.R. 165.

THE EFFECT OF FRUSTRATION ON THE CONTRACT

Key Principle

At common law rights accrued under the contract before the frustrating event were enforceable.

> CHANDLER V WEBSTER 1904
> P hired a room for one day in order to see Edward VII's coronation
> procession. The hire charge of £141.75 was payable immediately. P paid
> £100. The coronation was postponed because of the King's illness.

Held

❖ (CA) The contract was frustrated. P was unable to recover the £100 and was liable to pay the remaining £41.75 to D. [1904] 1 K.B. 493.

Commentary

(1) Frustration releases the parties from further performance after the frustrating event.

(2) The House of Lords in the *Fibrosa* case (see above) distinguished this case stating that the principle does not apply where there is total failure of consideration.

(3) The **Law Reform (Frustrated Contracts) Act 1943**, s.1(2) now provides that all sums paid or payable before the frustrating event cease to be payable. Most contracts fall within the statute, but some, for example charterparties, are still governed by the common law rules: s.2(5).

Key Principle

The court has a broad discretion under the proviso in **Law Reform (Frustrated Contracts) Act 1943**, s.1(2) in deciding whether to recompense a party who has incurred expenses before the frustrating event.

> GAMERCO S.A. V ICM/FAIR WARNING (AGENCY) LTD 1995
> P, Spanish pop concert promoters, entered into a contract with D, whereby the group Guns n' Roses would perform at a stadium in Madrid on July 4, 1992. On June 30 engineers found structural defects in the stadium. On July 1 the Spanish authorities banned the use of the stadium and revoked the permit to hold the event. P had paid D $412,500 on account. Both P and D had incurred expenses in preparation for the event. P sued under s.1(2) to recover the advance payment.

Held

❖ (QBD) The contract was frustrated because the stadium was unsafe and its use banned. P was entitled to recover the advance payment. Bearing in mind the extent of P's loss no deduction would be made to cover the expenses incurred by D before the frustrating event. [1995] 1 W.L.R. 1226.

Commentary

In exercising the discretion under the proviso the judge rejected total retention of expenses by D or equal division of the expenses between the parties. This was the first case to consider the exercise of the discretion.

Key Principle

At common law money payable under the contract after the frustrating event need not be paid.

APPLEBY V MYERS 1867

P agreed to install machinery on D's premises at a cost of £459. When most of the work had been done, an accidental fire destroyed the premises and the machinery. P sued to recover £419 for the work done and materials provided.

Held

Both parties were excused from further performance, which meant that D was not obliged to pay P anything. (1867) L.R. 2 C.P. 651.

Commentary

The **Law Reform (Frustrated Contracts) Act 1943**, s.1(3) now provides that where one party has received a valuable benefit (other than money) before the frustrating event, the court has a discretion to award a just sum not exceeding the "benefit" received by the other party.

Key Principle

The "valuable benefit" in **Law Reform (Frustrated Contracts) Act 1943**, s.1(3) should be valued after the frustrating event.

BP EXPLORATION CO (LIBYA) LTD V HUNT (NO.2) 1979

D owned an oil concession in Libya, half of which he transferred to BP in return for oil, cash and a share of the revenues if oil was found and exploited. BP was to fund all the development costs, but D would reimburse BP their costs from his share of any revenues. D found a large oilfield, but five years after it came on stream the Libyan government expropriated BP's interest which frustrated the contract between D and BP. BP claimed a "just sum" under s.1(3).

Held

❖ (QBD) BP could recover $35 million as the just sum, being the costs which had not been reimbursed by D at the date of the expropriation. [1979] 1 W.L.R. 783.

Commentary

(1) The valuable benefit which D received was about $85 million, being the development of the concession by BP together with the oil and cash he received.

(2) This is the only case on s.1(3).

THINK POINT

When is consideration (satisfaction) not required for a contract to be discharged by agreement?

An owner of land and a building developer entered into an agreement for a residential development to be built on the owner's land. Twelve months later, the property market crashes and the developer does not wish to proceed with the project, stating that it is not possible to do so because either:

(a) there is a severe shortage of skilled bricklayers; or
(b) there has been repeated severe flooding of the land attributable to climate change.

What effect would each of these events have on the rights and obligations of the parties to the contract?

Discharge by Performance and by Breach

....

14

INTRODUCTION

This chapter sets out the main principles applicable to the third and fourth ways in which a contract may be discharged, that is terminated.

Discharge by performance

Once the parties have performed their side of the bargain their rights and obligations come to an end. The law is strict in deciding what amounts to "performance", although the strictness is alleviated by exceptions and by application of the *quantum meruit* principle, which enables the party in breach to be paid a reasonable price for the work done (see Ch.1).

Discharge by breach

Not every breach of contract will bring the contract to an end. Minor breaches will only enable the innocent party to claim damages; the contract will continue; and both parties will be required to perform their contractual obligations.

However, a repudiatory breach of contract will normally give the innocent party the option of either treating the contract as discharged or affirming the continued existence of the contract.

The courts have adopted a number of tests in order to decide whether or not a repudiatory breach has occurred. These include:
(1) is the term broken a condition rather than a warranty;
(2) is the term an innominate term rather than a condition or a warranty; and
(3) does breach of the term amount to substantial failure of performance.

The traditional distinction between conditions and warranties focuses on the intention of the parties at the time they entered into the contract; whereas the alternative approaches focus on the effect of the breach.

The right to treat the contract as discharged by a repudiatory breach provides the innocent party with an immediate remedy because it is not necessary to go to court to obtain an order that the contract has been discharged. The main problem that might arise in adopting this course is that the party in breach may not accept that it is a repudiatory breach.

While there is a right to treat the contract as discharged once there has been a repudiatory breach, the innocent party does not have an absolute right to affirm the contract.

Most breaches occur during the performance of the contract, but it is possible for a party to do something before the date of performance which makes it clear that it will not be possible for the contract to be performed. This is known as anticipatory breach.

BY PERFORMANCE

Key Principle

A contract is only discharged by exact performance.

> BOLTON V MAHADEVA 1972
> P contracted to install a central heating and hot water system in D's house for £560. He installed the system but it did not heat the house properly and gave out noxious fumes. The cost of remedying the defects was estimated at £174. D refused to pay the agreed price.

Held

❖ (CA) P could recover nothing. The contract was not substantially performed. [1972] 1 W.L.R. 1009.

Commentary

(1) The remedy for failure to perform puts the parties to the contract in the position they would have been in if the contract had not been made. (See also *Appleby v Myers* (1867)) (see Ch.13).

(2) P had refused to remedy the defects; if he had then he could have recovered the agreed price.

(3) This was an "entire" contract, that is payment was only made when P completed the work. P should have made it a term of the contract that a deposit and/or stage payments were made by D. If such payments had been made D would not have been able to recover them because there would not have been a total failure of consideration.

Key Principle

Where there has been substantial but not exact performance the other party must still perform their side of the agreement.

> ### HOENIG V ISAACS 1952
>
> P agreed to redecorate and furnish D's flat for £750. D paid P £400 but refused to pay the balance because there were minor defects in the work. These would have cost £55 to remedy.

Held

❖ (CA) There was substantial compliance with the contract. D must pay the contract price subject to a deduction of £55 being made, which was the cost of remedying the defects. [1952] 2 All E.R. 176.

Commentary

(1) D considered that P should claim compensation on a quantum meruit basis. This would amount to a reasonable price for the work done, and may well have been less than the contract price.

(2) P was in breach of contract, but the breach was not sufficiently serious to discharge the contract (see below). It merely enabled D to claim damages.

(3) In most cases failure to perform and breach are two ways of looking at the same circumstances. It is possible for a failure to perform not to amount to a breach.

Key Principle

Where the promisee has the option to and does accept partial performance, they are bound to pay a reasonable price for what they received.

> ### SUMPTER V HEDGES 1898
>
> P agreed to build two houses and stables for D. The work was partially completed when P ran out of money. D completed the work at his own expense. P sued for the work done.

Held

❖ (CA) P could not recover anything for the work done. He had abandoned the contract. D had no option but to accept the partial performance. He could not be expected to leave the buildings half-finished. [1898] 1 Q.B. 673.

Commentary

(1) If D does have a choice, and does accept partial performance, then a new contract arises with the implication that D will pay for the work which had been done on a quantum meruit basis, i.e. pay a reasonable price.

(2) Building contracts are often broken down into "divisible covenants". Instead of a single payment being made when the entire contract is completed, stage payments are made, e.g. when the foundations are laid, the walls built, etc. The obligation is for substantial performance of each covenant.

BY BREACH

Key Principle

Breach of a condition gives the injured party the right to treat the contract as repudiated.

> THE MIHALIS ANGELOS 1970
> In a charterparty P, the shipowner, stated that the ship would be ready to load on about July 1, 1965. D, the charterer, had the option of cancelling the charter if the ship was not ready to load by July 20. D cancelled the charter on July 17 because they did not have a cargo. In fact as was known on July 17 the ship would not have been ready to load on July 20.

Held

❖ (CA) D was entitled to treat the contract as repudiated in July 17. The "expected ready to load" term was a condition for four reasons: certainty in the law; the shipowner would as a result rarely suffer any injustice from this conclusion; in a contract for the sale of goods to be carried at sea such a term was treated as a condition; and this is the view expressed in Scrutton on Charterparties. [1970] 3 W.L.R. 601.

Commentary

(1) A contract can be discharged by breach where the injured party has the right to repudiate or rescind the contract. Rescind in this context is different to the equitable remedy of rescission, e.g. for misrepresentation.

(2) The injured party is not obliged to repudiate, and can usually choose to affirm the contract instead (see below).

Key Principle ....

Whether a term is a condition or not depends upon the intention of the parties.

> BUNGE CORPORATION V TRADAX EXPORT 1981
>
> A contract for the sale of soya bean flour required the buyers to give the sellers at least 15 consecutive days' notice that a ship was ready to load the flour. The sellers then had to nominate a Gulf port. The buyer gave less than 15 days notice. The seller repudiated the contract and claimed damages because the market value of the flour had dropped.

Held ....

❖ (HL) The obligation to give 15 days notice was a condition. The intention of the parties is determined by looking at the contract and the surrounding circumstances. [1981] 1 W.L.R. 711.

Commentary ....

(1) In mercantile contracts usually "time is of the essence" which means that a term as to time is treated as a condition. In other contracts time clauses are normally treated as warranties, unless the parties intend otherwise.

(2) Lord Wilberforce stated that the courts should not be too ready to interpret contract terms as conditions. He commended the more flexible approach adopted in *Hong Kong Fir Shipping Co Ltd v Kawasaki Kisen Kaisha Ltd* (1962), but considered that the courts should first look at the intention of the parties.

Key Principle ....

Using the word "condition" within a particular term of a contract does not automatically make that term a "condition" in the legal sense.

> L. SCHULER A.G. V WICKMAN MACHINE TOOL SALES LTD 1974
>
> Schuler (D) granted P sole selling rights for D's machinery. Clause 7(b) of the agreement stated that it was a "condition of this agreement" that P's representatives should visit the six largest UK motor manufacturers at least once a week to obtain orders. P was in breach of cl.7(b) and D repudiated the contract. P claimed damages for wrongful repudiation.

Held

❖ (HL) D was not entitled to treat the contract as repudiated. Looking at the contract as a whole cl.7(b) was not intended to be a "condition" in the legal sense. [1974] A.C. 235.

Commentary

Note that "condition" has various meanings including "condition precedent". See, e.g. *Total Gas Marketing Ltd v Arco British Ltd*, *The Times*, June 8, 1998, where the HL held that buyers of North Sea gas were entitled to terminate the contract where the sellers failed to comply with such a condition.

Key Principle

In a contract for the sale of goods if some of the goods do not correspond with the contract description then the buyer usually has the right to reject all the goods.

RE MOORE & CO AND LANDAUER & CO 1921

S agreed to sell tinned fruit to B in cases containing 30 tins. The agreed number of tins was supplied but about half the cases contained 24 rather than 30 tins.

Held

❖ (CA) B could reject the whole consignment. [1921] 2 K.B. 519.

Commentary

(1) The court was influenced by the fact that the cases may have been brought for subsequent resale which would have involved repacking to obtain the correct number of tins.

(2) The **Sale of Goods Acts 1893 and 1979** provided that terms in contracts for the sale of goods were either conditions or warranties. A breach of warranty does not allow the injured party to terminate the contract, only to claim damages. This dichotomy is used by the courts in many other types of contracts. However, the innominate term approach can also be used in contracts for the sale of goods (*Cehave v Bremer* (1975) (see below)).

(3) Section 13(1) and s.13(1A) of the **Sale of Goods Act 1979** provide that where there is a contract for the sale of goods there is an implied condition that the goods will correspond with the description. However, s.15A removes the right of a business buyer to reject the goods where the breach is so slight

that it would be unreasonable for the buyer to do so. The buyer will only be able to claim damages for breach of warranty.

Key Principle

If the subject-matter of the contract fails to correspond with its description then the buyer should only have the right to reject if there is also a substantial failure of performance.

REARDON SMITH LINE V HANSEN-TANGEN 1976

P chartered a tanker to D. The ship was to be built by a Japanese company. In the charterparty the ship was identified as Osaka No. 354, but the company sub-contracted the work to the Oshima yard where it was described as Oshima 004. The tanker market collapsed and D wanted to cancel the contract, so they claimed that the tanker did not comply with its contract description.

Held

❖ (HL) D was not entitled to reject the tanker. The breach was technical; it did not amount to substantial failure of performance. [1976] 1 W.L.R. 989.

Commentary

This case reintroduced the need for substantial failure of performance (see below) into the condition/warranty analysis of contract terms, and threw doubt on *Re Moore and Landauer & Co* (1921) (see above). Section 15(A) of the **Sale of Goods Act 1979** reflects this change of approach.

Key Principle

Where a breach of a term amounts to a substantial failure of performance, the injured party has the right to treat the contract as repudiated.

POUSSARD V SPIERS 1876

P, a singer, agreed with D that she would play the leading role in an opera for a three-month period. P became seriously ill five days before the first performance, and it was uncertain how long her illness would last. D found a replacement and refused to take P back when she was better after 11 days.

Held

D was entitled to treat the contract as discharged by P's breach. (1876) 1 Q.B.D. 410.

Commentary

(1) The court accepted that it was not possible for D to find a temporary replacement just to cover the period of P's illness.

(2) The court looked at the effect of P's "failure of performance" on D.

(3) The obligation on P to perform has also been categorised as a "condition" (see above).

Key Principle

Where a breach does not amount to a substantial failure of performance, the injured party does not usually have the right to treat the contract as discharged.

> BETTINI V GYE 1876
>
> P, a singer, agreed with D that he would play tenor roles during the 1875 Covent Garden season, which ran from the end of March to the middle of July. In breach of a contract term that he should be present six days before the first performance for rehearsals, P arrived three days late because of illness. D terminated P's contract.

Held

P could still substantially perform his contract. D was not entitled to treat the contract as discharged by P's late arrival. (1876) 1 Q.B.D. 183.

Commentary

The obligation on P to be present for the rehearsals has also been categorised as a "warranty".

Key Principle

Where a breach of an innominate term deprives an injured party of substantially the whole benefit of the contract that party is entitled to treat the contract as repudiated.

P chartered a ship to D for 24 months. P undertook to supply a sea-worthy ship. However, the engine room staff were inefficient and the engines were old. During the first four months the ship was delayed by repairs for five weeks. Further repairs which would take 15 weeks to complete were then found to be necessary. D repudiated the contract, and P sued for wrongful repudiation.

Held

P's undertaking as to seaworthiness was neither a condition nor a warranty, but an innominate term. D was not entitled to repudiate the contract because P's breach did not deprive D of substantially the whole benefit of the char-terparty. [1962] 2 Q.B. 26.

Commentary

(1) Lord Diplock's view was that many terms cannot be categorised as con-ditions or warranties. Such terms are "innominate". (*Bunge v Tradax* (see above)).

(2) This results in "the wait and see" approach, i.e. the injured party will only know whether breach of a particular term entitles them to repudiate once the effect of the breach is known. Although this approach avoids the rigidity of the condition/warranty dichotomy it can cause uncertainty.

(3) In *Force India Formula One Team Ltd v Etihad Airways PJSC* 2010 (see below) Rix L.J. used a different form of words. He stated in effect that where the breach of contract is practically not remediable the innocent party is entitled to accept the repudiation as putting an end to the contract.

Key Principle

The innominate term approach can be used where there is a contract for the sale of goods.

B purchased from S for £100,000 citrus pulp pellets for making cattle-feed. It was a term of the agreement that the shipment would be made "in good condition". When the pellets were unloaded from the ship it was found that part of the shipment had been damaged by over-heating. B rejected the whole shipment. The Rotterdam court ordered the sale of the pellets which B indirectly bought for £30,000 and used as originally planned.

Held

❖ (CA) The obligation to ship "in good condition" was not a condition. Its breach did not substantially deprive B of substantially the whole benefit of the contract. [1975] 3 All E.R. 739.

Commentary

The pellets were held to be of merchantable quality as defined by s.14 of the **Sale of Goods Act 1893**. The **Sale of Goods Act 1893** dichotomy did not exclude the innominate term or intermediate stipulation approach.

Key Principle

The innominate term approach is applicable to a long-term contract for the provision of services

> RICE (T/A THE GARDEN GUARDIAN) V GREAT YARMOUTH BOROUGH COUNCIL 2000
>
> In February 1996 P entered into a four-year contract to provide leisure management and grounds maintenance services. The contract provided that P should "provide the service in a proper skilful and workmanlike manner to the contract standard and to the entire satisfaction of [D]", and that D could terminate the contract for the breach of any term by P. In August 1996 D terminated the contract because P failed to comply with a number of contractual obligations, for example, complete the summer bedding and renovate certain football pitches by specific dates. P sued D for money due under the contract.

Held

❖ (CA) Where there is a long-running contract to provide public services the question for the court is whether the cumulative effect of the breaches of contract complained of is so serious as to justify the innocent party in bringing the contract to a premature end. On the facts P's claim should succeed because D was not entitled to terminate the contract. *The Times*, July 26, 2000.

Commentary

(1) Hale L.J. stated that this is a classic example of an innominate term: one which can be broken in so many different ways and with such varying consequences that the parties cannot be taken to have intended that any breach should entitle the innocent party to terminate the whole contract.

Key Principle

An injured party may accept a repudiatory breach simply by failing to perform their own contractual obligations.

> **Vitol SA v Norelf Ltd 1996**
>
> P agreed to purchase a cargo of propane from D. The propane was to be loaded on a ship between March 1 and March 7, 1991. On March 8, P sent D a telex repudiating the contract because loading was not going to be completed until March 9. The telex was treated as an anticipatory breach. D completed the loading, informed P that it had done so, the ship sailed away, and D sold the propane to a third party but for less than half the contract price. D claimed the difference between the two prices.

Held

❖ (HL) D, by neither affirming nor performing the contract, accepted P's repudiatory breach and was therefore entitled to recover damages from P. [1996] 3 W.L.R. 105.

Commentary

(1) All that is required for acceptance of a repudiatory breach at common law is for the injured party to communicate unequivocally his intention to treat the contract as discharged.

(2) Lord Steyn stated that whether failure to perform amounted to acceptance of a repudiatory breach depended on the particular circumstances of each case.

(3) Is there a time limit for accepting the repudiatory breach or affirming the contract? In *Stocznia Gdanska SA v Latvian Shipping Co* [2002] 2 Lloyd's Rep 436. Rix L.J. stated: "There is a middle ground between acceptance of a repudiation and affirmation of the contract, and that is the period when the innocent party is making his mind up what to do. If he does nothing for too long, there may come a time when the law will treat him as having affirmed. If he maintains the contract in being for the moment, while reserving his right to treat it as repudiated if his contract partner persists in his repudiation, then he has not yet elected ".

Key principle

Breaches of contract which are repeated, cumulative and continuing may ultimately become repudiatory.

FORCE INDIA FORMULA ONE TEAM LTD V ETIHAD AIRWAYS PJSC 2010

In April 2007 the claimant, who owned and operated Abu Dhabi's national airline, entered into a three year sponsorship agreement with the defendant Formula One team. In September 2007 the defendant F1 team was acquired by an Indian businessman. The new owner imposed a deliberate and clearly defined marketing campaign which involved abandoning the claimant's name and replacing their country's connections with those of India. The breaches of contract started in October 2007 and did not come to the claimant's notice until November 2007. A meeting was held on December 13, 2007 with a follow up meeting on January 14, 2008. On January 27, 2008 in a letter the claimant purported to terminate the contract in accordance with the terms of the contract.

Held

❖ (CA) The breaches of contract by the defendant were irremediable. The claimant had not affirmed the contract; nor had it waived or acquiesced in the defendant's breaches. The right of the claimant to accept the defendant's repudiation survived until January 27, 2008 and the reference in the claimant's letter to termination in accordance with the contract did not prevent the claimant from terminating the contract at common law. [2010] EWCA Civ 1051.

Commentary

(1) Rix L.J. stated that this case concerned "a complex and medium term relationship, which a takeover has destabilised, and where it necessarily and legitimately takes time for the consequences to become clearer and for the innocent party to consider his position" (para.122).

(2) He also stated that this case "did not present the typical case where mere delay may demonstrate a decision to affirm. Such cases typically occur where time is of the essence, for instance, in an extreme case where markets are always in the move such as in a share transaction, or more generally in a sale of goods case where a seller has to know whether or not his buyer is accepting the goods which have been delivered" (para.122).

(3) He concurred with Moore-Bick L.J. in *Stocznia Gdynia SA v Gearbulk Holdings Ltd* 2009 (see above) when stating that "invocation of a contractual

right to terminate the contract does not prevent the innocent party from relying on the common law right to accept a repudiatory breach" (para.116).

Key principle
The right to terminate in accordance with the terms of the contract is not different in substance from the right to treat the contract as discharged by reason of repudiation at common law.

> STOCZNIA GDYNIA SA v GEARBULK HOLDINGS LTD 2009
> The appellant purchaser of a ship exercised its contractual right to terminate the contract when the vessel was not delivered and to recover the first instalment of the purchase price which had been paid. The purchaser argued that it was also entitled to damages from the seller for the loss of its bargain. The judge, on appeal from the arbitrator, held that by terminating the contract and recovering the first instalment in accordance with the terms of the contract, the purchaser had affirmed the contract, lost its right to treat the contract as repudiated, and could not claim damages at common law for the breach.

Held
❖ (CA) the purchaser intended to discharge the contract with the same consequences as if it had been discharged by repudiation in accordance with the common law principles, and was entitled to damages. [2009] 3 W.L.R. 677.

Commentary
(1) Moore-Bick L.J. stressed that the court must always consider the intention of the parties when deciding whether or not the contractual remedies are alternatives to, overlap with or correspond to a right under the general law.

(2) The repayment of the first instalment of the purchase price is based on restitution because there was a total failure of consideration, whereas damages for loss of a bargain are compensatory (see Ch.15).

Key Principle
The right of an injured party to affirm the contract after a repudiatory breach is not absolute.

WHITE & CARTER (COUNCILS) LTD V MCGREGOR 1962

P entered into a three-year contract with D to make litter bins advertising D's business, but D cancelled the contract the same day. P refused to accept the wrongful repudiation by D and made the bins as agreed. P sued D for all the money due under the contract. D claimed that P was only entitled to damages for breach of contract.

Held

❖ (HL) P was entitled to affirm the contract even though affirmation did not benefit them particularly, and caused D greater loss than a claim for damages would have done. [1962] 2 W.L.R. 17.

Commentary

The decision was by a 3:2 majority. Lord Reid, who was one of the majority, considered that the right to affirm was subject to some limitation. His approach was adopted in the following case.

Key Principle

Where a person has no legitimate interest, financial or otherwise, in performing the contract rather than claiming damages, he ought not to be allowed to affirm it.

CLEA SHIPPING CORPORATION V BULK OIL INTERNATIONAL LTD 1984

P shipowners chartered a ship to D for 24 months. The hire charge was paid in advance. After nearly a year there was a major engine failure and D refused to continue with the charter. Nevertheless P repaired the ship at a cost of £800,000. Nine months of the charter were then left. D refused to use the ship, but P did not accept their repudiation and held the ship ready to sail with a full crew until the charter expired. P claimed that they were entitled to keep the hire charge paid for the last nine months. D claimed P was only entitled to damages.

Held

❖ (QBD) D's argument prevailed. P could not recover the hire charge because they had no legitimate interest in doing so. [1984] 1 All E.R. 129.

Commentary

In *Alfred McAlpine Construction Ltd v Panatown Ltd* 2001, HL Lord Goff stressed the importance of protecting the interest of the innocent party in having the contract performed (see Ch.5).

ANTICIPATORY BREACH

Key Principle
Where there is an anticipatory breach the injured party can accept the breach and immediately claim damages.

> ### HOCHSTER V DE LA TOUR 1853
> In April 1852, D employed P to work for him as a courier in Europe from June 1. On May 11, D terminated the arrangement. On May 22, P brought his action against D who claimed that there was no breach until June 1.

Held
P had the right to have the contract kept open until June 1. D was in breach of P's right on May 22. P could claim damages immediately. [1843–1860] All E.R. Rep. 12.

Commentary
(1) Alternatively P could have kept the contract alive until June 1 and then claimed damages.

(2) See also *Vitol SA v Norelf Ltd* 1996 (above).

(3) In *PT Berlian Laju Tanker v Nuse Shipping Ltd (The Aktor)* [2008] EWHC 1330 (Comm) the court held that the seller was entitled to treat the payment in Singapore, rather than Greece, of the final 10 per cent of the purchase price of a ship as an anticipatory repudiatory breach of condition. The seller was entitled to treat itself as discharged from the contract.

Key Principle
If the injured party does not accept the anticipatory breach then damages will be assessed at the date due for performance.

> ### AVERY V BOWDEN 1856
> D chartered P's ship to carry a cargo from Odessa. The ship berthed at Odessa, but D told the ship's captain that no cargo was available and that the ship should depart. The ship remained in Odessa because the captain hoped that a cargo would be found. The Crimean War broke out before the date due for performance and frustrated the contract.

Held
P's action for damages failed. (1856) 5 W.R. 45.

Commentary

If the captain had accepted the breach, damages would have been recoverable.

Key Principle

An injured party who does not accept an anticipatory breach must continue to perform their own obligations.

> FERCOMETAL SARL v MEDITERRANEAN SHIPPING CO SA, THE SIMONA 1988
>
> D, shipowners, chartered a ship to P, who subsequently cancelled the charterparty. The cancellation was an anticipatory breach, which was not accepted by D. However, D failed to ensure that the vessel was ready to load on the date agreed in the charterparty, and P then cancelled on this basis.

Held

❖ (HL) P was entitled to treat the charterparty as repudiated by D's breach and claim damages. [1988] 3 W.L.R. 200.

Commentary

The injured party will only be treated as affirming the contract where they have made a clear and unequivocal decision which has been communicated to the other party.

THINK POINT

In *Bolton v Mahadeva* 1972 what difference would it have made to the central heating contractor if:
(a) the contract had stated that he must be paid in instalments; or
(b) if the cost of remedying the defects had been £40?

Advise a home owner on the remedies available to her were the facts of *Bolton v Mahadeva* 1972 to arise now, with the difference that the home owner had paid 25 per cent of the cost of installing the hot water and central heating system, and wanted to change contractors because the work was defective.

Remedies for Breach of Contract

15

INTRODUCTION

Damages are the usual judicial remedy available to an innocent party. Where there has been a repudiatory breach of contract the innocent party may claim damages in addition to treating the contract as discharged. Where the breach does not lead to the contract being discharged either because the innocent party has affirmed the contract or because the breach was minor, damages can still be awarded.

Normally the aim of damages in contract is to put the innocent party in the position they would have been had the contract been performed. For example, A agrees to buy 40 tons of sugar from B at £5000 per ton for resale to C, but B does not deliver it on time. As a consequence A has to buy the same quantity from D at a price of £6000 per ton because the market price has increased. A will be able to recover damages from B to cover the difference in price per ton.

In certain circumstances damages will instead be calculated with reference to the injured party's wasted expenditure (reliance loss) or will be restitutionary.

Normally damages are not recoverable for anxiety or distress caused by the breach but there are important exceptions.

In order for the innocent party to recover damages the breach of contract must:

(1) have caused the loss, and
(2) not be too remote.

There are rules setting out how the amount of damages should be calculated (measure of damages). The innocent party is under a duty to mitigate their loss, and may have their damages reduced where they have been guilty of contributory negligence.

Where the court calculates the amount of damages to be awarded, they are known as "unliquidated" damages. Sometimes the terms of the contract fix the amount of damages that should be paid in the event of a breach. They are referred to as "liquidated" damages. Such terms will be upheld by the courts unless they amount to a "penalty clause".

In addition to the common law remedy of damages, certain equitable remedies are available to the innocent party. However, unlike damages these are discretionary. The equitable remedies most likely to be claimed where there has been a breach of contract are specific performance and an injunction.

A claim for damages must normally be brought within six years from the date of the breach. There are no specific time limits for claiming an equitable remedy but the longer the delay the less likely the court is to exercise its discretion in the claimant's favour.

DAMAGES

Types of Damages Recoverable

Key Principle

The aim of damages in contract is to put the parties in as good a position as they would have been in if the contract had been performed.

> ROBINSON V HARMAN 1848
> D agreed to grant P a lease of a house at a rent of £110 a year. The premises were worth considerably more. D did not have title to the house. P sued D for breach of contract.

Held

P could recover damages for the loss of his bargain as well as for his expenses. [1843–1860] All E.R. Rep. 383.

Commentary

This principle is a key characteristic of a contract claim, and should be contrasted with the aim of damages in tort. It enables P to recover damages for loss of profit, and for loss of a bargain. It protects the expectation interest.

Key principle

Damages for breach of contract are normally assessed as at the date of the breach, but in some contexts the courts may take into account later events

> GOLDEN STRAIT CORPORATION V NIPPON YUSEN KUBISHKA KAISHA 2007
> On July 10, 1998 GSC, shipowners, chartered an oil tanker, *The Golden Victory*, to NYKK until December 6, 2005. Either party could cancel the charterparty if war broke out between certain countries including the

USA, UK, and Iraq. On December 14, 2001 the charterers repudiated the charter, and the owners accepted the repudiation. Arbitration between the parties commenced in 2002 but was only concluded after the Iraq war broke out on March 20, 2003. It was agreed first that NYKK would have terminated the charter on the outbreak of hostilities and second, that at the time NYKK repudiated the contract there was a possibility but not a probability that hostilities would break out.

Held

❖ (HL) (3–2) Where a contract for performance over a period has come to an end by reason of a repudiatory breach, and it is certain that the contract could subsequently have been terminated early on the occurrence of a particular event, that must be taken into account when assessing damages payable for breach. The claimant is not entitled to the benefit of more valuable contractual rights than those he lost. The arguments of the owners offended the compensatory principle of damages. The owners were not entitled to damages after March 2003. [2007] UKHL 12; [2007] 2 W.L.R. 691.

Commentary

(1) The majority of their Lordships also considered that a court should consider whether early termination was a real possibility when assessing damages. This approach is similar to where damages are claimed for loss of a chance. Lord Scott commented that the aim of damages in contract is to compensate the innocent party for the loss that they would have actually suffered. This principle is more important than certainty even in the context of commercial contracts.

(2) In a strong dissenting judgment Lord Bingham, with whom Lord Walker agreed, considered that the damages awarded to the ship owner should be assessed as at the date of the breach of contract in December 2001. Such damages should include any loss suffered by the ship owners up to December 6, 2005, subject to normal principles of mitigation. Lord Bingham considered that the majority decision "undermines the quality of certainty which is a traditional strength and major selling point of English commercial law, and involves an unfortunate departure from principle".

Key Principle

Where the claimant has not suffered any financial loss, a reasonable sum in damages for breach of contract may be measured by the benefit the defendant has gained from the breach.

EXPERIENCE HENDRIX LLC V PPX ENTERPRISES INC 2003

In 1967, Jimi Hendrix was sued by PPX for breach of a 1965 recording agreement. Under a settlement agreement, which was reached in 1973, PPX agreed to deliver up to Jimi Hendrix's estate 19 master recordings which were to be destroyed. PPX owned the copyright to these recordings and did not hand over all the masters. Between 1973 and 1983, and 1995 and 1999 PPX, in breach of the 1973 agreement, commercially exploited these master recordings. The judge granted an injunction against PPX but dismissed the claim for damages in relation to the profits made by PPX.

Held

❖ (CA) PPX should make reasonable payment for its use of the masters in breach of the settlement agreement. It would be anomalous and unjust if PPX could by simply breaching the agreement avoid paying royalties to the claimant. [2003]1 All E.R. (Comm) 830.

Commentary

(1) CA applied *Wrotham Park Estate Co v Parkside Homes Ltd* [1974] 2 All E.R. 321, and referred to *AG v Blake (Jonathan Cape Ltd, third party)* [2000] 2 All E.R. (Comm) which the court considered "marks a new start in this area of law".

(2) The claimant conceded that it had no evidence to show that it had suffered any financial loss as a consequence of PPX's breach.

(3) In *WWF–World Wide Fund for Nature v World Wrestling Federation Entertainment Inc* [2007] EWCA Civ 286, the Court of Appeal stated that in this type of case reasonable damages should be assessed on the basis of what one party would have paid the other for the hypothetical release from the restrictive term of the agreement at a date immediately before the party was first in breach of the term. The court also considered that an alternative remedy in such a situation would be for a claimant to ask the court for an order for an account of profits.

Key Principle

An injured party can claim damages for reliance loss instead of expectation loss in certain circumstances.

Anglia TV v Reed 1972

D, an actor, entered into a contract with P to play the leading role in a television play. At the last moment D withdrew and P could not find a substitute, so P abandoned the play.

Held

❖ (CA) P were entitled to recover the expenditure they had incurred in mounting the production, both before and after they entered into the contract with D. [1972] 1 Q.B. 60.

Commentary

Presumably it was easier for P to calculate their wasted expenditure than their loss of profit. Normally a plaintiff can choose whether to claim reliance loss or expectation loss.

Key Principle

An injured party can claim restitutionary damages where there is a total failure of consideration.

D.O. Ferguson & Associates v Sohl 1992

P, a building contractor, entered into a contract with D for building work. The contract price was £32,194. P completed part of the work, and D had paid P £26,738, but the value of the work done was £22,065. D had the work completed by another builder for less money than the contract price. P sued D for damages and D counterclaimed for the overpayment of £4,673.

Held

❖ (CA) D could recover the overpayment. The work had never been done by P. There was a total failure of consideration for that part of the contract. *The Times*, December 24, 1992.

Key Principle

As a general rule damages are not recoverable for injury to feelings, mental distress or damage to reputation caused by the breach of contract.

Addis v Gramophone Co Ltd 1909

P was employed by D as a manager. He received a salary and earned commission. He was given six months' notice in accordance with his contract but was immediately replaced and was unable to work out his notice as manager. P was awarded damages. D appealed against that part of the award which was to compensate P for the harsh and humiliating way in which he had been dismissed.

Held

❖ (HL) P could not recover damages for such loss. The court is not concerned with the motive or the conduct of D. Damages in contract are compensatory, not punitive or exemplary. [1909] A.C. 488.

Commentary

(1) In *Malik v BCCI (in liquidation)* (1997) 3 W.L.R. 95, HL distinguished Addis. In principle an employee may be able to recover damages for financial loss, arising out of loss of reputation, caused by the employer's breach of the implied duty of mutual trust and confidence in contracts of employment.

(2) In *Johnson v Unisys 2001 Ltd* [2001] 2 W.L.R. 1076 (HL) an employee claimed damages for psychiatric injury. The majority of their Lordships considered that the implied duty of trust and confidence did not require the power of dismissal to be exercised fairly and in good faith.

Key Principle

Where the purpose of the contract is to provide entertainment and enjoyment, damages are recoverable for disappointment, distress, upset and frustration caused by the breach.

JARVIS V SWAN'S TOURS 1972

P booked a two-week "houseparty" holiday with D in a hotel in Switzerland. The brochure stated that visitors would have "a great time". During the first week there were only 13 other guests, but there were none during the second week, and the hotel proprietor did not speak English.

Held

❖ (CA) P was entitled to be compensated for his loss of enjoyment. [1973] 1 Q.B. 233.

Commentary

See also *Jackson v Horizon Holidays* (1975) (see Ch.5). Damages are not normally recoverable for anguish and vexation caused by breach of an ordinary commercial contract.

Key Principle

Where the purpose of the contract is to provide relief from mental distress, damages are recoverable.

> HEYWOOD V WELLERS 1976
>
> P employed D solicitors to obtain and enforce an injunction to prevent a man molesting her. The solicitors were negligent, and as a result she was molested on three or four occasions.

Held

❖ (CA) P was entitled to damages for mental distress. [1976] Q.B. 446.

Commentary

See also *Hamilton-Jones v David & Snape* [2003] EWHC 3147 (Ch) where the High Court held that the claimant was entitled to damages of £20,000 for mental distress caused by her solicitor's failure to re-register the claimant's three children with the Passport Agency. This enabled her ex-husband to take two of the children to Tunisia in breach of a court order. The solicitors were instructed by the claimant in order to retain custody of her children for her own pleasure and peace of mind.

Key Principle

Where a major or important object of the contract is to give pleasure, relaxation or peace of mind, damages are recoverable for loss of amenity.

> FARLEY V SKINNER 2001
>
> P was considering buying a country house about 15 miles from Gatwick International Airport. He wanted to be reasonably sure that the property was not seriously affected by aircraft noise, and asked D, a surveyor, to inspect the house and in particular to investigate whether the property would be affected by aircraft noise. He told the surveyor that he did not want a property on a flight path. The surveyor stated that it was unlikely that the property suffered greatly from aircraft noise. In fact the house was close to a navigation beacon and was markedly affected by aircraft noise. P sought damages from D because his use and enjoyment of the property was impaired by the aircraft noise.

Held

❖ (HL) D was in breach of his contractual obligation to provide P with accurate information about the aircraft noise. D was entitled to damages for being deprived of the chance of making an informed choice whether or not to buy the property which resulted in mental distress and disappointment. The award of £10,000 by the judge for loss of amenity was confirmed, although it was considered by their Lordships to be on the high side. [2001] 3 W.L.R. 899.

Commentary

(1) Their Lordships applied *Ruxley Electronics v Forsyth* (see below) in holding held that P was entitled to damages for loss of amenity (an example of non-pecuniary damages).

(2) Their Lordships considered that P could alternatively have recovered damages under the principle in *Watts v Morrow* (see below).

Key Principle

Where the mental distress is caused by the physical consequences of the breach, damages are recoverable.

WATTS V MORROW 1991

D, a building surveyor, negligently surveyed a house for P, who had indicated to D that they wanted to buy a trouble-free holiday home. P purchased the house for £177,500. P soon discovered that major internal and external repairs needed to be undertaken promptly. The repairs took approximately six months to complete.

Held

❖ (CA) P was entitled to a modest sum of £750 as compensation for the discomfort suffered from having to live in a house undergoing major repairs. [1991] 1 W.L.R. 1421.

Commentary

(1) In *Farley v Skinner* (above) Lord Scott considered that "physical" in the context of physical inconvenience and discomfort means "sensory (sight, touch, hearing, smell, etc.) experience".

(2) See also measure of damages below.

CAUSATION

Key Principle
The breach of contract must be the effective cause of the injured party's loss.

COSSEY V LONNKVIST 2000
D agreed to buy a butcher's shop from P. An accountant X agreed to assist D obtain finance from a bank for the purchase. The bank asked X for details of the trading activity for the year up to the end of June 1991. X provided details, but relied on out of date information that covered the period up to December 1990, and did not check the 1991 figures. D obtained the finance and purchased the shop, but it ran at a loss. P sued D for the balance of the purchase price. Part of D's defence was that X owed them a duty of care in the preparation projections of the shop's likely profitability.

Held
❖ (CA) X was in breach of the contractual duty owed to D to exercise due care in providing accurate information to the bank. D suffered loss because they purchased a business which subsequently failed, which they might not have purchased had they known of downturn in trading in 1991. X did not owe D a duty to alert them to such a downturn. Therefore, X's breach did not cause D's loss. [2000] Lloyd's Rep. PN 885.

Commentary
(1) Sir Anthony Evans (dissenting) held that the chain of causation was not broken because X's breach deprived D of the opportunity for reconsideration and not proceeding to buy the shop.

(2) Compare *Stovold v Barlows* (1995) (see below).

REMOTENESS OF DAMAGE

Key Principle
Damages are recoverable for loss or damage which arises naturally from the breach in the ordinary course of things, or which were in the contemplation of the parties at the time they entered into the contract.

HADLEY V BAXENDALE 1854
P's mill in Gloucester was brought to a standstill by a broken crank-shaft. P engaged D a carrier to take the crankshaft to London where it

was to be used as a pattern for a new one. D, in breach of contract, delayed delivery by five days. Unknown to D, P only had one crankshaft and so the mill was out of action for longer than need be. P claimed damages for loss of profit caused by this delay.

Held

P could not recover such loss, because it could not fairly and reasonably be considered to arise naturally from the breach. [1843–1860] All E.R. Rep. 461.

Commentary

(1) If P had told D at the time of entering the contract that this was the mill's only crankshaft, P could have recovered under the second limb of the principle.

(2) Although this principle has been refined in later cases, it remains an accurate statement of the law.

Key Principle

The test of remoteness is whether the loss is reasonably foreseeable as liable to result from the breach, bearing in mind the knowledge, imputed or actual, of the party in breach.

VICTORIA LAUNDRY (WINDSOR) LTD V NEWMAN INDUSTRIES LTD 1949
D sold a large boiler to P who were launderers and dyers. D knew that P wanted the boiler for immediate use in their business. The boiler was delivered five months late. P sued D for the loss of profits during that period.

Held

(CA) P could recover for loss of profits on the ordinary laundry business. They could not recover damages for the loss of profits that they would have made on lucrative dyeing contracts, because D did not know of these contracts at the time they entered into the contract with P. [1949] 1 All E.R. 997.

Commentary

(1) Imputed and actual knowledge correspond to the two limbs of the principle in *Hadley v Baxendale* (1854) (see above).

(2) Asquith L.J. used the phrase "reasonable foreseeability" as opposed to "reasonable contemplation".

The question is whether a reasonable man in D's position would realise that P's loss was sufficiently likely to result from the breach.

> **KOUFOS V C. CZARNIKOW LTD, THE HERON II 1967**
> P chartered D's ship to carry a cargo of sugar to Basrah. In breach of the charterparty the ship deviated from its route which delayed its arrival by nine days. The market price of sugar had fallen during that period.

Held

(HL) P could recover the difference between the price for which the sugar was sold and the price at which it would have been sold if there had been no delay. [1967] 3 W.L.R. 1491.

Commentary

(1) Lord Reid used the phrase "not unlikely" rather than "sufficiently likely".

(2) The phrase "reasonable foreseeability" does not mean the same as "reasonable foreseeability" in the test for remoteness in the tort of negligence. In contract there should be a serious possibility that the particular consequences would occur whereas in tort it would be enough if there was a slight possibility.

Key Principle

The test of remoteness should result in the same amount of damages being recoverable whether a plaintiff brings an action in contract or in tort.

> **PARSONS (LIVESTOCK) LTD V UTTLEY INGHAM & CO LTD 1977**
> D supplied and installed a bulk food storage hopper for P, who were pig farmers. D forgot to unseal the ventilator and the pignuts stored in the hopper went mouldy. As a result of being fed the nuts, 254 pigs died. P claimed damages for breach of contract, including a claim for loss of sales and turnover. D claimed that damages for loss of sales and turnover were too remote.

Held

❖ (CA) D was liable for the loss of the pigs that died, but not for loss of profit on future sales. [1977] 3 W.L.R. 990.

Commentary

(1) Lord Denning considered that the test of remoteness should depend not upon whether the claim was brought in contract or in tort, but upon whether the claim was for physical damage or for loss of profit.

(2) Lord Scarman suggested that there is no substantive difference between reasonable foreseeability in tort and reasonable contemplation in contract.

Key Principle

A single principle underlies both limbs of the rule in *Hadley v Baxendale*, which is that damages should be awarded on the basis of what the parties knew or must be taken to have known, so as to bring the loss within the reasonable contemplation of the parties at the time they made their contract.

JACKSON AND ANOTHER V ROYAL BANK OF SCOTLAND 2005

In 1990 the claimants, trading as Sansom (S), entered into an agreement with Economy Bag (EB) whereby S imported dog chews from a supplier in Thailand (P) which they sold on to EB. By coincidence RBS was the banker for both S and EB. The bank administered the payment arrangements. In February 1993 S asked RBS to pay P. In March 2003 RBS inadvertently provided EB with details of a recent transaction which showed how much S were paying P. This revealed to EB the extent of the mark-up being charged by S. As a consequence EB terminated the relationship with S. EB was S's main customer and they ceased trading. S sued RBS for loss of profits on future business arising from the bank's disclosure of this confidential information. RBS argued that such loss was too remote because it was not foreseeable that EB would terminate the relationship with S as a result of the bank's disclosure.

Held

❖ (HL) The loss of repeat orders was not too remote. RBS's liability under the terms of the contract with S was open-ended. Their Lordships restored the award made by the trial judge which was for loss of profits for a period of four years on a reducing basis. [2005] UKHL 3; [2005] 1 W.L.R. 377.

Commentary

Students may be reassured to know that the HL considered that the CA had misunderstood the effect of the rules in *Hadley v Baxendale* (1854). This was because the CA had considered what was in the reasonable contemplation of the parties at the time of the breach instead of at the time S entered into the contract with RBS. The CA limited the bank's liability to one year.

Key principle

The context, surrounding circumstances or general understanding in the relevant market may show that a party would not reasonably have been regarded as assuming responsibility for the losses that occurred.

TRANSFIELD SHIPPING INC V MERCATOR SHIPPING INC (THE ACHILLEAS) 2008

In September 2003 the respondent owners of a ship, *The Achilleas*, chartered it to the appellant charterers, who were required to return the ship by May 2, 2004. They were not able to do so until May 11. In April 2004 market rates for such a charter had doubled and the owners chartered the ship to different charterers from May 8, 2004. The first charterers were unaware that the owners had entered into the second contract. By May 5 the owners realised that the ship would not be redelivered by May 8 and significantly reduced the rates charged to the second charterers in return for their agreement to extend the start date of the charter. The owners claimed that they were entitled to damages from the first charterers based on the $8,000 loss per day ($1.37m approx in total) that they suffered over the 191 day duration of the follow-on charter because of the reduced rates charged. The charterers claimed that the owners were only entitled to damages ($0.16m approx) amounting to the difference between the market rate and the charter rates of hire for the overrun period of nine days; and that they were not entitled to loss of profits on the subsequent fixture because it had not expressly been brought to the charterers' attention when the contract was made.

Held

❖ (HL) The charterers were not liable for the owner's loss of profit on the subsequent fixture. This was because the amount of profit lost was a result of volatile market conditions which amounted to an unusual occurrence outside the parties' contemplation. The charterers were liable for the difference between the charter rate and any higher market rate during the period of overrun [2009] 1 A.C. 61.

Commentary

(1) Three of their Lordships (Hoffman, Hope and Walker) adopted a new "broader approach" to remoteness based on an "assumption of responsibility".

(2) Lord Hoffman recognised that the orthodox approach will continue to be applicable in the great majority of cases

(3) Lord Rodgers adopted the orthodox approach and held that the owner's loss of profits from a nine day overrun could not have been contemplated in the ordinary course of things.

(4) Baroness Hale highlighted the differences between the orthodox approach derived from *Hadley v Baxendale* and *The Heron*, and the broader approach adopted by at least two of their Lordships. She allowed the appeal on the same ground as Lord Rodgers.

(5) Lord Walker stated that he also agreed with the reasons given by Lord Rodgers.

(6) In *Sylvia Shipping Co Ltd v Progress Bulk Carriers Ltd* [2010] EWHC 542 (Comm) Hamblen J. distinguished on the facts the case before him from *The Achilleas*. The owners of a ship were liable to pay damages to the charterers for their loss of profits on a sub-charter which was cancelled because the owners in breach of their contractual obligations failed to ensure that the ship was ready to load a cargo. He stated that the orthodox approach "remains the 'standard rule' and it is in only in relatively unusual cases, such as *The Achilleas* itself, where a consideration of assumption of responsibility may be required". In his view: "Usually the fact that the type of loss arises in the ordinary course of things or out of special known circumstances will carry with it the necessary assumption of responsibility".

Key principle

The "assumption of responsibility" approach may result in a loss not being too remote even if it would not have occurred in ordinary circumstances

SUPERSHIELD LIMITED V SIEMENS BUILDING TECHNOLOGIES FE LIMITED
2010
The respondent was responsible for supplying and installing a sprinkler system into a new office building for solicitors, Slaughter and May, in the City of London. The appellant sub-contractor installed the sprinkler system. A nut and bolt connection on a float valve failed and water from a storage tank overflowed into the basement of the building. Drains in

the tank room floor were partially blocked and the Building Management System displays were not being monitored at the time of the incident. Extensive damage was caused by the water to electrical equipment. The respondent settled the claim against it and sought to recover 20 per cent of the settlement costs from the appellant. The appellant argued that the sum for which the respondent settled was not reasonable bearing in mind the strength of the defences available to it. In particular the escape of water was too remote a consequence for the respondent to be liable for the damage in accordance with the rule in *Hadley v Baxendale*.

Held

❖ (CA) The loss resulting from the flood was not too remote. The respondent assumed a contractual responsibility to prevent the escape of water. Even if the escape of water from the sprinkler tank was unlikely it was within the scope of the respondent's contractual duty. [2010] EWCA Civ 7.

Commentary

(1) Toulson L.J. stated that *The Achilleas* is authority that "there may be cases where the court, on examining the contract and the commercial background, decides that the standard approach would not reflect the expectation or intention reasonably to be imputed to the parties".

(2) He also noted that in that case the effect was exclusionary, that is "the contract breaker was not held liable for the loss that resulted from its breach even though some loss of the kind was not unlikely". Whereas in this case the effect is inclusionary.

MEASURE OF DAMAGES

Key Principle

In a contract for the sale of goods damages are normally assessed using the difference in value between the market price and the contract price.

WERTHEIM V CHICOUTIMI PULP CO 1911

P agreed to buy wood pulp from D. It was delivered seven months late by which time the market price had fallen from £3.50 per ton to £2.12 per ton. P's loss was £1.38 per ton. However, P had resold the wood pulp at £3.00 per ton.

Held

❖ (JCPC) Because of the resale D was only liable to pay damages to P of 50p per ton. [1911] A.C. 301.

Commentary

(1) This principle is to be found is s.50(3) (remedy for the seller) and s.51(3) (remedy for the buyer) of the **Sale of Goods Act 1979**. Where the goods sold have a latent defect the buyer may recover the actual loss suffered rather than the difference in value: *Bence Graphics International Ltd v Fasson UK Ltd* [1997] 1 All E.R. 979.

(2) The difference in value test is used in the majority of contract cases where there is a claim for expectation loss.

Key Principle

Where there is no available market the seller can still recover damages for loss of profit.

> WL THOMPSON LTD V R. ROBINSON (GUNMAKERS) LTD 1955
>
> D refused to accept delivery of a new car from P, car dealers. There was no demand for the car, so P mitigated their loss by persuading the manufacturers to take back the car.

Held

❖ (Ch D) P was entitled to recover damages for the lost profit. [1955] 2 W.L.R. 185.

Commentary

If P could have sold the car to another customer at the same or a higher price then P would only be able to recover nominal damages: *Charter v Sullivan* [1957] 2 W.L.R. 528.

Key Principle

If a party to a contract fails to provide the standard of service agreed the other party can claim damages for the difference in value between the standard agreed and that received.

> WHITE ARROW EXPRESS LTD V LAMEY'S DISTRIBUTION LTD 1995
>
> P operated a mail order business and entered into a contract with D, who agreed to deliver and collect goods sold to customers. P claimed

damages for D's failure to provide the enhanced level of service for which they had paid.

Held
* (CA) P had not submitted specific evidence of the difference in value between what they contracted for and what they received. Therefore, they were only entitled to nominal damages. *The Times*, July 21, 1995.

Commentary
(1) The difficulty P faced was in quantifying what damage/loss they had suffered as a result of the breach. The Court of Appeal considered that if A hired and paid in advance for a four-door saloon at £200 a day and received delivery of a two-door saloon available for £100 a day, he suffered loss; the measure of damages being the difference between the price paid and the market value of what was obtained.

(2) *Durham Tees Valley Airport Limited v BMIBaby Ltd* [2010] EWCA Civ 485 illustrates the uncertainty which can arise on how to quantify the loss where there is a single contractual obligation but the party has a wide discretion how to perform it. The CA held that it was not possible to specify a minimum number of flights which the airline would be bound to operate throughout the duration of the contract. If the contract required the airline to maintain a two aircraft based operation at the airport, it may be difficult for a court to assess how the airline would have been likely to have fulfilled that obligation, but the court should conduct a factual inquiry as to how the contract would have been performed had it not been repudiated.

Key Principle
In building work the cost of reinstatement is the normal measure of damages.

EAST HAM CORPORATION V BERNARD SUNLEY & SONS LTD 1966
D, a building contractor, defectively attached cast stone panels to the external walls of a school owned by P. The panels fell off.

Held
* (HL) P could recover as damages the cost of reinstating the panels, rather than the difference or diminution in value of the property. It was reasonable for P to insist upon reinstatement. [1966] A.C. 406.

Commentary
This test for measure of damages is often described as the "cost of cure".

Key Principle

The cost of reinstatement can be recovered so long as it represents the loss suffered.

TITO V WADDELL (NO.2) 1977

In 1913 an agreement was made with the landowners of Ocean Island to mine for phosphate. It was a term of the agreement that the mining company would return all the worked out land to the owners and would replant the land with food-bearing trees. Most of the island had been mined and islanders no longer lived on the island. P, an islander, brought an action for damages against D because no replanting had occurred. Should the measure of damages be the cost of replanting or the difference in value between the replanted island and the island as it was?

Held

❖ (Ch D) P was entitled to damages for the difference in value. It was unreasonable to treat as a loss the cost of replanting which was unlikely to be done. P owned small scattered plots of land, other islanders might not replant, and P was now settled elsewhere on a larger island unaffected by mining. [1977] 2 W.L.R. 496.

Key Principle

In deciding whether to award the cost of reinstatement the court should take into account whether P intends to reinstate and whether that intention is reasonable.

RADFORD V DE FROBERVILLE 1977

P sold part of his land to D who agreed to build a brick boundary wall on her land. D failed to do so and sold her property. P sued D for the cost of building such a wall on his side of the boundary.

Held

❖ (Ch D) P could recover the cost because he intended to build the wall and it was reasonable for him to do so. [1977] 1 W.L.R. 1262.

Commentary

In *Ruxley Electronics Ltd v Forsyth* (1995) (see below) the House of Lords placed more emphasis on the requirement of reasonableness. P's intention should only be relevant in so far as it affects reasonableness.

Key Principle

The diminution in value rule is almost always appropriate where property is acquired following negligent advice by surveyors.

> ### WATTS V MORROW 1991
>
> P instructed D, a building surveyor, to survey a house. D negligently carried out the survey. P then purchased the house for £177,500. P discovered that major internal and external repairs were needed. P claimed £33,961 as damages, being the cost of the repairs.

Held

❖ (CA) P was entitled to damages of £15,000 being the difference between the value of the property as represented by D and its true value. [1991] 1 W.L.R. 1421.

Commentary

P is compensated for the loss caused by D's negligent breach of contract, e.g. paying more for a house than it was worth. D did not promise that no repairs other than those noted in the survey, were needed. See also *Banque Bruxelles Lambert SA v Eagle Star Insurance Co Ltd* [1996] 3 W.L.R. 87, HL in respect of negligent valuations for commercial purchasers.

Key Principle

Where the cost of reinstatement is out of proportion to the benefit obtained by P then damages should be assessed by reference to the diminution in value of the property.

> ### RUXLEY ELECTRONICS AND CONSTRUCTIONS LTD V FORSYTH 1995
>
> P sued D for the balance due on a contract to build a swimming pool in D's garden. D claimed that P were in breach of contract by building the pool six feet deep when it was agreed that the pool should be built to a depth of seven feet six inches deep. The county court judge found as a matter of fact that the shallower pool did not affect the value of D's

property. D counter-claimed damages of £21,560 being the cost of rebuilding the pool to the correct depth.

Held

❖ (HL) P could not recover damages for the cost of reinstatement. Their Lordships agreed that there was no diminution in the value of P's property but awarded P £2,500 for loss of amenity. [1995] 3 W.L.R. 118.

Commentary

(1) Their Lordships placed considerable emphasis on the requirement that it should be reasonable to incur the cost of reinstatement. On the facts of this case it was unreasonable to incur the cost of demolishing the existing pool and building a newer and deeper one.

(2) See also *Farley v Skinner* (see above) on damages for loss of amenity.

DAMAGES FOR LOSS OF A CHANCE

Key Principle

The loss of a right to belong to a limited class of competitors is of pecuniary value for which damages can be awarded.

CHAPLIN V HICKS 1911

D advertised in a national newspaper inviting applications from female readers for work in the theatre. There were 12 positions which would last three years. 10 applicants were to be shortlisted in each of five areas by readers of the newspaper. D would then select 12 from the shortlist of 50. P came top of her area, but was not given a reasonable opportunity of presenting herself for the final selection by D.

Held

❖ (CA) P was awarded damages because she lost the advantage of being in the final selection. [1911] 2 K.B. 786.

Key Principle

The court should evaluate the loss of P's chance rather than consider on a balance of probabilities whether the breach caused P's loss.

STOVOLD V BARLOWS 1995

P received an offer of £505,000 for his house from X. D solicitors were instructed to carry out the necessary legal formalities. Five days after D agreed to send the title deeds and a draft contract, X's solicitors had still not received them. X then decided to purchase another property. P's house was subsequently sold at a lower price and P claimed damages of £96,312.

Held

❖ (CA) The chance of the purchase going ahead was 50 per cent and so the plaintiff was entitled to 50 per cent of the damages claimed. *The Times*, October 30, 1995.

Commentary

The judge at first instance considered that there was an issue of causation. P had shown on a balance of probabilities that if the documents had arrived on time then X would have bought P's property. Therefore P could recover his full loss. CA disagreed with the judge's approach and considered that even if the documents had arrived on time X might still have decided to buy the other house.

MITIGATION

Key Principle

The injured party is under a duty to take all reasonable steps to mitigate any loss consequent on the breach.

BRITISH WESTINGHOUSE ELECTRIC AND MANUFACTURING CO V UNDERGROUND ELECTRIC RAILWAYS CO OF LONDON LTD 1912

P agreed to supply D with turbines, but the turbines supplied did not meet the contract specification. D used the turbines for several years, but then replaced them. The replacement turbines were more efficient. P claimed the unpaid balance of the contract price. D counterclaimed and recovered the increased cost of operating D's machines, but also claimed the cost of replacing them.

Held

❖ (HL) D could not recover the cost of the new turbines. D was not under a duty to mitigate by buying new turbines. The cost of operating them was less than the cost of operating D's turbines. Those savings had to be set off against the cost of buying them. [1911–1913] All E.R. Rep. 63.

Commentary

If the injured party does not take reasonable steps to mitigate their loss then they are not able to obtain damages for that loss.

Key Principle

In commercial contracts the duty to mitigate will often require the injured party to enter into a new contract with the contract-breaker.

> ### PAYZU V SAUNDERS 1919
>
> D agreed to sell goods to P over a period of nine months. Payment was to be made within one month of delivery. P failed to pay the first instalment in time. D refused to continue to deliver on these terms, but offered to continue to supply P if P agreed to pay cash with each order. P refused and as a result sustained considerable losses.

Held

❖ (CA) P should have accepted D's offer. As a result of not doing so they sustained a large measure of loss which they ought to have avoided. [1918–1919] All E.R. Rep. 219.

Key Principle

The injured party has to give credit for benefits arising directly from the consequences of the breach.

> ### HUSSEY V EELS 1990
>
> P purchased a bungalow from D for £53,250 in reliance on a misrepresentation that the property had not been subject to subsidence. The true value of the bungalow was £36,250. P could not afford to stabilise the foundations. After two years of living in the house P applied for and eventually obtained planning permission to demolish their bungalow and build two new bungalows on the land. P then sold the land with planning permission for £78,500. The county court judge rejected P's claim for £17,000 on the ground that their gain on the re-sale wiped out their initial loss.

Held

❖ (CA) P was entitled to damages of £17,000. The profit on the resale was not a direct consequence of D's breach. P bought the house to live in, not for its development potential. [1990] 2 Q.B. 227.

The key principle was also applied in the *British Westinghouse* case (see above). A recent case involving the application of this principle is *R & M Stansfield Enterprises Ltd v Axa Insurance UK plc* [2006] EWCA Civ 881.

CONTRIBUTORY NEGLIGENCE

Key Principle
Where D is in breach of a contractual duty of care and a duty of care in tort, the defence of contributory negligence is available to D.

FORSIKRINGSAKTIESELSKAPET VESTA V BUTCHER 1988
P, a large Norwegian insurance company were liable under an insurance policy for damage caused to a fish farm on the coast of Norway by a severe gale. P had reinsured with Lloyds of London. D was an insurance broker. P sued D both for breach of contract and the tort of negligence when D refused to pay under the reinsurance contract.

Held
❖ (CA) The defence of contributory negligence was available to D, who was only 25 per cent to blame for P's loss. [1988] 3 W.L.R. 565.

Commentary
(1) In Q.B.D., Hobhouse J. identified three types of situations:
 (i)   where D is in breach of a strict contractual duty;
 (ii) where D is in breach of a contractual but not a tortious duty of care; and
 (iii) as in this case.

(2) The case went to the House of Lords but not on this point.

Key Principle
Where D is in breach of a strict contractual provision which does not depend upon a failure to take reasonable care the defence of contributory negligence is not available to D.

BARCLAYS BANK PLC V FAIRCLOUGH BUILDING LTD 1994
D agreed with P to clean and treat the asbestos roofs of two buildings used by P for the storage of documents. In breach of the contract D did not use specialist contractors and did not use workmanship that was "the best of its kind". As a result the buildings were contaminated by

asbestos dust, which would cost £4 million to remove. D argued that P was at fault in failing to ensure that D fulfilled its obligations under the contract.

Held

❖ (CA) P's claim should not be reduced. The defence of contributory negligence was not available to D. In any event, P was not under a duty to prevent D from committing breaches of the contract. [1994] 3 W.L.R. 1057.

Commentary

This decision corresponds with the recommendations of the Law Commission in 1993 in its report, Contributory Negligence as a Defence in Contract (Report No.219).

PENALTY CLAUSES

Key Principle

A penalty clause is aimed at punishing the party in breach and is invalid.

> DUNLOP PNEUMATIC TYRE CO LTD v NEW GARAGE & MOTOR CO LTD 1915
> P, tyre manufacturers, supplied tyres to D, who agreed not to sell the tyres to retailers at a price below the manufacturer's list price. If D did sell or offer to sell the tyres below this price then D had to pay P £5 by way of liquidated damages.

Held

❖ (HL) The obligation to pay £5 was not a penalty clause, and so was enforceable by P. [1915] A.C. 79.

Commentary

(1) A liquidated damages clause is a genuine pre-estimate of the damage likely to be caused by the breach. A penalty clause, according to Lord Dunedin in *Dunlop*, is "extravagant and unconscionable".

(2) In *Philips Hong Kong Ltd v A-G of Hong Kong*, *The Times*, February 15, 1993 the JCPC held that the status of the clause had to be objectively judged at the time the contract was made.

(3) In *Jeancharm Ltd (t/a Beaver International) v Barnet Football Club Ltd* [2003] EWCA 58, the CA held a clause which required interest to be paid at five per cent a week (260 per cent per annum) for late payment of an invoice was a penalty clause. The CA stated that the classic statement of the law is to

be found in the Dunlop case; that there was nothing in *Philips Hong Kong Ltd v A-G of Hong Kong* which departed from that case; and that the courts should be careful before deciding whether or not a clause is a penalty when the parties are of equal bargaining power.

Key Principle

The court should adopt a broad approach in deciding whether a particular clause is 'extravagant and unconscionable'

MURRAY V LEISUREPLAY PLC 2005

The case concerned the validity of a 'golden parachute' clause which provided for the payment of a year's gross salary on the termination of a company director's employment. The company argued that it was a penalty clause.

Held

❖ (CA) The court found that it was not a penalty clause. Although the terms were generous they were not unconscionable. The company was unable to demonstrate that the terms were extravagant [2005] EWCA Civ 963; [2005] I.R.L.R. 946.

Commentary

(1) Arden L.J. considered that the question was whether the sums which the parties agreed to be paid on breach differ substantially from the sums that would be recoverable at common law and whether there is shown to be no justification for that.

(2) Clarke and Buxton L.J.J. disagreed with her. They considered that this introduced a rigid and inflexible approach into what should be a broad and general question. Their view was that the court should consider as a guide whether the clause was agreed in order to *deter* a party from breaking the contract or to *compensate* the innocent party for the breach. In commercial contracts great caution should be exercised before striking down a clause as penal.

(3) The burden of proving that a clause is 'extravagant and unconscionable' rests on the party arguing that it is invalid.

EQUITABLE REMEDIES

Key Principle

Specific performance is an exceptional discretionary remedy.

> COOPERATIVE INSURANCE SOCIETY LTD V ARGYLL STORES (HOLDINGS LTD) 1997
>
> D leased their supermarket premises from P. The supermarket was operating at a loss. It comprised 30 per cent of the letting area of the Hillsborough Shopping Centre. D decided to sell it and on not finding a buyer had closed and stripped out the supermarket despite a "keep open" covenant. It would cost £1 million to reinstate the supermarket. P applied for an order of specific performance.

Held

❖ (HL) Such a covenant was not normally specifically enforceable because precise formulation of the order would be difficult; and, if the order was not complied with, the punishment of contempt was heavy-handed and unsuitable. [1997] 3 All E.R. 297.

Commentary

In *Highland and Universal Properties Ltd v Safeway Properties Ltd*, *The Times*, March 22, 2000, the Inner House of the Court of Session (Scotland) was prepared to grant an order requiring the tenant of retail premises to keep them open for trading. The Lord President stated that Scottish experience did not bear out the House of Lords' fears.

Key Principle

An order for specific performance may be made where damages would be nominal only.

> BESWICK V BESWICK 1968
>
> (See Ch.5 for facts).

Held

❖ (HL) P suing as administrator would only be entitled to nominal damages because her deceased husband's estate had not suffered any loss. Specific performance was granted. [1968] A.C. 58.

An order for specific performance is unlikely to be made where it would cause severe hardship to D.

> PATEL V ALI 1984
>
> D sold her house to P. There was a four-year delay before P sought an order of specific performance.

Held

The order was not granted because of D's disabling illness, which made her dependent on her neighbours, and her husband's bankruptcy. Both of these events occurred after the sale. [1984] 1 All E.R. 978.

Commentary

Examples of cases where an application for specific performance was refused, although not on the grounds of hardship to D, are: *Gibson v Manchester City Council* (no agreement); *Redgrave v Hurd* (contract rescinded for misrepresentation); *Shell UK Ltd v Lostock Garages Ltd* (P acted unfairly).

Key Principle

Where the grant of an injunction would be oppressive, damages in lieu would be appropriate.

> JAGGARD V SAWYER 1995
>
> P purchased a house in a housing development on a private road. Each house was conveyed subject to a restrictive covenant: not to use any unbuilt land other than as a garden. In 1987 D bought a house on the development. They then bought a piece of land with no right of access to the road and obtained planning permission to build a house. P objected but only applied for an injunction once the house was almost built.

Held

❖ (CA) The injunction was not granted. [1995] 1 W.L.R. 269.

Commentary

If P had applied for an interlocutory injunction before the house was built the court considered that it would have been granted.

REMEDIES FOR BREACH OF CONTRACT

Key Principle

Where there is a contract for personal services the court will not generally grant an injunction where that would compel the performance of the contract.

PAGE ONE RECORDS V BRITTON 1968

P, the manager of D (The Troggs pop group), claimed that he had been dismissed and sought an injunction to prevent them from employing another manager.

Held

❖ (Ch D) P's application was refused because D could not work without a manager and the effect of an injunction would be to force D to continue to employ P. [1968] 1 W.L.R. 157.

Commentary

(1) An order of specific performance will not be issued for the same reason.

(2) Prohibitory injunctions are often the main remedy where there is a breach of a valid contract in restraint of trade.

LIMITATION PERIODS

Key Principle

In an action for relief from the consequences of a mistake the requirement that "reasonable diligence" be used to discover the mistake, means doing what an ordinary prudent person would do in the circumstances.

PECO ARTS INC. V HAZLITT GALLERY LTD 1983

P purchased a drawing from D for $18,000 relying on the recommendation of an expert. It was a term of the contract that the drawing was by Ingres. In fact it was a copy. P discovered the mistake 11 years after the purchase when it was revalued for the second time. D admitted liability to return the price paid, but argued that the claim was statute-barred.

Held

❖ (QBD) P obtained rescission and recovery of the purchase price. P had been reasonably diligent having relied on an expert, and the reputation of D, as well as the fact that the first revaluation did not reveal that the drawing was a copy. [1983] 1 W.L.R. 1315.

Commentary

(1) The **Limitation Act 1980**, s.32(1)(c) provides that the period of limitation runs from when P could with reasonable diligence have discovered the mistake.

(2) See common mistake (see Ch.10).

(3) Presumably P did not sue for breach of contract because such a claim would have been statute-barred (**Limitation Act 1980**, s.5: six years).

(4) *Leaf v International Galleries* (1950) was distinguished.

Key Principle

Equitable remedies such as rescission are subject to the equitable principle that delay defeats equity.

> ### LEAF V INTERNATIONAL GALLERIES 1950
> (For facts see Ch.9).

Held

❖ (CA) P could not, five years after the purchase, choose to repudiate the contract because of D's breach. P had accepted the picture. If P claimed rescission for misrepresentation that too was defeated by P's delay.

Key principle

The six year limitation period in s.5 of the **Limitation Act 1980** does not apply by analogy to claims for specific performance because no comparable remedy is available at common law

> ### P & O NEDLLOYD B.V. V ARAB METALS CO 2006
> In May 1998, the claimant agreed with the first defendant (D1) to ship scrap metal in containers from Egypt and deliver it to the third defendant's (D3) premises in Hamilton, Scotland. On arrival at the premises it was found that radioactive materials were present in the containers and D3 refused to accept delivery of them. The claimant stored the containers at its Coatbridge depot. Unsuccessful attempts were made to return the containers to Egypt. In March 2004, the claimant applied for an order for specific performance of the contract of carriage in an attempt to force the defendants to take delivery of the containers. In July 2004, the claimant claimed damages and a declaration. These

claims were held to be statute barred. In 2005 a decision was made to sell the Coatbridge depot.

Held

❖ (CA) the claimant's claim for specific performance was not time-barred. At trial it would be subject to the equitable doctrine of laches. [2006] EWCA Civ 1717; [2007] 1 W.L.R. 2288.

Commentary

(1) The **Limitation Act 1980** s.36(1) provides that the time limit under s.5 shall not apply to a claim for specific performance unless before the **Limitation Act 1939** a court of equity would have applied by analogy the six year statutory limitation period to a claim for specific performance of a simple contract. No previous case provided a definitive answer.

(2) The doctrine of laches enables the court to refuse relief when delay on the claimant's part would make it inequitable to grant it. Moore-Bick L.J. considered that in principle unjustified delay coupled with an adverse effect on D or a third party could provide a defence even before the expiration of the limitation period.

THINK POINT

What is the aim of damages in contract? How does it differ from the aim of damages in tort or in restitution?

What is the test of remoteness of damage in contract in the light of the House of Lords' decision in *Transfield Shipping Inc v Mercator Shipping Inc (The Achilleas)* 2008?

Index

This index has been prepared using Sweet and Maxwell's Legal Taxonomy. Main index entries conform to keywords provided by the Legal Taxonomy except where references to specific documents or non-standard terms (denoted by quotation marks) have been included. These keywords provide a means of identifying similar concepts in other Sweet & Maxwell publications and online services to which keywords from the Legal Taxonomy have been applied. Readers may find some minor differences between terms used in the text and those which appear in the index.
Suggestions to **taxonomy@sweetandmaxwell.co.uk**.